"My Laſt Shift Betwixt Uſ & Death"

The Ephraim Blaine Letterbook 1777-1778

—⁓⁓⁓—

Joseph Lee Boyle

—⁓⁓⁓—

HERITAGE BOOKS
2016

HERITAGE BOOKS
AN IMPRINT OF HERITAGE BOOKS, INC.

Books, CDs, and more—Worldwide

For our listing of thousands of titles see our website at
www.HeritageBooks.com

Published 2016 by
HERITAGE BOOKS, INC.
Publishing Division
5810 Ruatan Street
Berwyn Heights, Md. 20740

Copyright © 2001 Joseph Lee Boyle

All rights reserved. No part of this book may be reproduced or transmitted in any form or by any means, electronic or mechanical, including photocopying, recording or by any information storage and retrieval system without written permission from the author, except for the inclusion of brief quotations in a review.

International Standard Book Numbers
Paperbound: 978-0-7884-1776-4
Clothbound: 978-0-7884-6333-4

CONTENTS

Preface v

Introduction vii

Editorial Procedure xv

The Documents 1

Document Chronology 206

Index 215

PREFACE

To paraphrase Nathanael Greene, "Whoever heard of a Commissary?" Among the many forgotten heroes of the American Revolution are the commissaries, the hundreds of men who worked to supply the fighting men with arms, clothing and food. In that, and every conflict, the fortunes of war are vastly affected by unspectacular activities such as the purchase and delivery of flour and meat.

One of the most persevering commissaries in feeding the Continental Army, was Ephraim Blaine of Carlisle, Pennsylvania. Though he complained repeatedly, and threatened to resign in twice in 1778 alone, he remained in an official post until November 1781, and then remained active in supplying the army under the new contract system, serving for seven consecutive years of the war.

The intent of this work is to present the Letterbook of Ephraim Blaine for the period from August 20, 1777 through May 30, 1778. The original contains 315 documents, all of which appear here. The manuscript letterbook can be found in The Peter Force Collection, Mss. 17,137, Series 8D, No. 12, Container 6, Ephraim Blaine Letterbook, at the Library of Congress. Though this is called the Ephraim Blaine Letterbook, it would be more proper to call it the Commissary of Purchases Letterbook. While Blaine wrote many of the letters, more than half were actually written by John Chaloner, the Assistant Commissary of Purchases assigned to Washington's Army, who worked directly for Blaine.

In the year 2001, it is common to pick up a telephone or turn on a computer and order innumerable objects from across the world, which can be shipped to you overnight. The choice of food products in supermarkets is ever expanding, and restaurants of all types and prices prepare ethnic foods never heard of in 1777. Consider the difficulties in supplying an army of more than 17,000 men at Valley Forge, Pennsylvania and Wilmington, Delaware in December 1777. Communication was by horseback; if you needed to get meat from Connecticut, you sent a letter by an express rider, asking your assistant to buy barrels of pork or beef, or cattle and have them sent to you. Of course most rivers of any size had no bridges, so crossing was by ferry. A wagon with a load of supplies would be doing well to make fifteen miles a day on good roads. On roads of mud from rain or snow melt, progress was reduced considerably, and there are many references in contemporary documents to roads being totally impassable, particularly during the winter months. There were so many interdependent aspects in the transport system alone, that failure in any one, often resulted in food not arriving on time.

In the course of three months, December 1777 and January and February 1778, more than 2,225,000 pounds of beef, 2,297,000 pounds of flour, and 500,000 gills of rum and whiskey, were consumed at Valley Forge. While much of this came from Pennsylvania and adjacent states, vast quantities came from Virginia and Connecticut and the rum was brought through the British blockade from the Caribbean.

Consider that even the containers for transporting good were handmade and expensive. Food that was not on the hoof was transported in barrels of various sizes. Obtaining and keeping barrels for transport and storage was a continual problem. Hoops were usually made of wood, not iron, and they were relatively fragile. They were difficult to store properly when empty, and if stored near an army encampment, were soon used for firewood. Another item now taken for granted is salt. As refrigeration and canning did not exist, salt was absolutely vital as a preservative for food. At the outbreak of the war, salt was being imported, but the British fleet interdicted supplies, which led to chronic shortages and even salt riots. The early part of the letterbook shows plans to ship flour by wagon from Pennsylvania, in exchange for salt from Massachusetts.

The commissaries also struggled with congressional inefficiency, poor wages, lack of cooperation from state and local authorities, disdain from Continental Army officers, and desperate financial problems. One historian commented that the chronic food shortages were "a great phenomenon of the Revolution—an almost starving army in a country of abundant food resources." Despite suffering much criticism and frustration, the commissaries were an absolutely vital link in winning the war. Their patriotism and espirit de corps, as well as concerns for honor and reputation, were every bit as strong as the men in "the fighting line."

Introduction

In June 1775, the Continental Congress faced the problem of supplying the newly created Continental Army. The army around Boston was a spontaneous affair of the New England colonies, and the troops were supplied by their home towns. This method was immediately successful, but all were aware a more permanent method would be needed to pursue a successful war.

On July 19, Joseph Trumbull of Connecticut was appointed Commissary General of Stores and Provisions. Though Congress created a Commissary, it waited two more years to create a regulatory system for the department. Trumbull developed and implemented his own system to purchase and issue food. Though there were some lapses, overall Washington's men were well supplied with provisions.

Unfortunately a series of problems led to Trumbull's resignation in 1777. These were caused in part by intersectional jealousies, Trumbull's desire for cash commissions for his purchases, and inconsistent direction of the department by Congress. The single biggest problem was Congressional concern for frugality. Many thought that the existing system was too expensive, and should be replaced with a purchase by contract system.

The situation came to a head in early 1777. Trumbull had left a man named Carpenter Wharton to supply Washington's army in New Jersey while he returned to Hartford, Connecticut. Wharton was inadequate to the job, and the army had suffered during the Trenton-Princeton Campaign. Investigation led to a report by the Board of War in February 1777, which suggested separating the purchasing and issuing functions into two departments. Washington agreed with this concept, as he thought the job was too big for one man.

In March 1777, Congress appointed a committee to inquire into the conduct of the commissaries in the "Middle Department." Their report found evidence of fraudulent raising of prices as well as lack of integrity or capacity in some of the employees. Trumbull responded well to the charges and fired Carpenter Wharton. However he was immediately in opposition to some of the new Congressional proposals to organize and regulate his department.

Trumbull was completely against the continuance of a fixed salary for himself, and suggested, as he had several times before, that he receive a commission on the money that passed through his hands. Though he was willing to see the department split into separate purchasing and issuing departments, he was disappointed by the lack of consultation he had expected from Congress in the planned reorganization. Meanwhile his absence from the army, while detained by Congress, had allowed a shortage of provisions to occur in the army. When he did rejoin the army, Trumbull found his staff in disarray and wrote on June 15, 1777, that "An Angel from Heaven could not go on long in my Situation."

On June 10, Congress approved detailed new regulations. These divided the Commissary into separate departments of Purchases and Issues, but established such detailed procedures and record keeping, that administration of the system was inevitably ineffectual. Fixed pay and rations for the staffs were continued, which was not well accepted in a time of rising inflation.

On June 18, Trumbull was elected as Commissary General of Purchases, with Charles Stewart of New Jersey established as Commissary General of Issues. The new organization led to a large number of resignations by various members of the staffs of both departments. Frustrated by not being paid a commission, and the fact that Congress would not even let him appoint his own deputies, Trumbull submitted his resignation on July 19, to be effective on August 20.

On August 5, 1777, Congress picked William Buchanan, a Baltimore merchant, to succeed Trumbull. Buchanan lacked experience and assumed his duties during a crisis with a small and incomplete staff. He was being ordered to feed the major American army during four of the most active months of the war, with many vacant staff positions, and new men in some of the key jobs.

The British fleet with Sir William Howe's army on board had sailed out of New York Harbor on July 23, 1777. Washington was kept guessing for a month about Howe's intention, which led him to march his army to Pennsylvania, and then start to move back to New York again. Not until August 22, was Washington certain Howe was coming up the Chesapeake Bay, with the expected intent of invading Pennsylvania.

Fortunately for the Continental Army, Ephraim Blaine of Carlisle, Pennsylvania, had been selected to be Buchanan's deputy in the Middle Department, which included Delaware, Maryland, New Jersey, Pennsylvania, and part of New York. Blaine in turn appointed John Chaloner and James White, Philadelphia merchants, as his assistants. Chaloner was assigned permanently to Washington's army, to respond immediately, whenever Blaine himself was absent.

Blaine was diligent in his work, but was hampered by a variety of factors. One the biggest was the failure of Buchanan and Congress to staff and organize the Eastern Department, which was composed of the New England states. Congress delayed several months in appointing a deputy in that department. Peter Colt of Connecticut received his appointment on August 24, but objected to operating under the new regulations, and the principal cattle buyer in Connecticut, Henry Champion, refused to serve. Congress loosened its regulations, but from August to November, 1777, cattle purchases in the Eastern Department were suspended. Forwarding of other supplies was frustrated by poor communications, transportation difficulties, movements of British forces, and the worsening status of Continental money.

Complicating the delivery of the food supply was the British Army, which captured and destroyed stores at the Head of Elk in August 1777, and Valley Forge in September. Washington was defeated at the Battle of Brandywine on September 11, and the British occupied the American capital of Philadelphia on September 26. Forced evacuation of stores from Philadelphia and Trenton no doubt led to significant losses, and the hungry British foraging parties swept up or destroyed vast amounts of food that otherwise would have supported the Americans.

Meanwhile the Commissary Department had to compete with civilian purchasers, speculators, and other branches of the American military.

For example, each side had to provide food for its prisoners held by the other side. This required Elias Boudinot, the American Commissary General of Prisoners to purchase food and send it under a flag of truce to American prisoners. This was certainly necessary, but food that was eaten by American prisoners in Philadelphia, was not available to feed Americans still under arms.

Another necessary evil was feeding the horses, without which the army had no means of transportation. Blaine writes on April 30, 1778, that "the Forage Masters are Destroying the Wheat all Over the Country in getting it chop'd to feed to Horses." On May 30, there were 1372 horses at the Valley Forge Encampment alone, with hundreds more employed traveling to and from camp. On average twelve pounds of hay and eight pounds of grain were needed each day to feed a horse. In turn numerous teams of horses had to be employed in bringing feed to the horses at camp, not to mention feeding the cattle kept in herds near the camp, for slaughter as needed.

Only a small percentage of Americans in the twenty-first century are engaged in agriculture. But in the eighteenth century these percentages were reversed. William Hooper wrote in 1778 that "a Soldier made is a farmer lost." All the farmers on the firing line, and there were thousands, reduced the production of food, but did not diminish the number of hungry mouths.

In the late summer and fall of 1777, Washington had repeatedly complained of shortcomings in supplying his men. After the army reached Valley Forge he bluntly wrote the change in the Commissary Department was "contrary to my judgement" and that "Since the Month of July, we have had no assistance from the Quarter Master Genl. and to want of assistance from this department, the Commissary Genl. charges great part of his deficiency."

Food supply was so short on that December 22, 1777, when General Howe led most of the British Army out of Philadelphia on a foraging expedition, Washington could do little more than send out harassing parties. Charles Stewart, the Commissary General of Issues wrote that day "I returned to Camp three Days ago, and found not a Barrel of Flour or one fatt Ox or Cow on hand His Excellency amazed and highly offended at this failure collected the General officers who declared their Difficulty to prevent a Mutiny among the Troops for two Days past."

This was the first of two major food crises which befell the Army at Valley Forge. The second in mid-February, 1778, was so dire that Washington wrote "The distress of this Army for want of provisions is perhaps beyond any thing you can conceive; and unless we strain every nerve to procure immediate relief, a general mutiny and dispersion is to be dreaded." Even as the army prepared to leave Valley Forge, another food crisis developed as thousand of new recruits and returning veterans taxed the supply system mightily. On May 30, the exasperated John Chaloner described some poor cattle being brought to camp from Pottsgrove as "my last shift betwixt us & Death."

A significant chronic problem for the Commissaries was the weather. Contrary to popular legend of an exceedingly cold winter with frequent heavy snowfalls, the weather of 1777-1778, was a typical Pennsylvania winter. The temperature never fell below zero, and there were only a few significant accumulations of snow. General James Mitchell Varnum of Rhode Island commented on March 7, that "Here, there is no Distinction of Season. The Weather frequently changes five times in Twenty four Hours: The Coldest I have perceived has been in this month. Snow falls; but falls only to produce Mire and Dirt." The "Mire" created massive problems for the army's creaky transportation network.

Freezing temperatures produced ice in the rivers, but usually only enough to impede and endanger the ferries. One of Washington's aides-de-camp, who had to wait nine days to cross the Susquehanna River, wrote on February 16, "when I did It was not without great difficulty & some danger." The Hudson River was also a problem. General Israel Putnam wrote from West Point, New York that "The Winter has been such, as has Made the Passage on & over the River, exceeding Difficult, nothing can be brought from above or below this Post by Water." A colder winter, which froze the rivers hard enough to transport supplies over the waterways, might have been kinder to the men at Valley Forge.

In addition to the weather problems, Washington's men suffered due to a lack of wagons to transport food to camp. Congress limited the price paid for the hiring of wagons, teams and drivers, to the extent that staff officers were often unable to procure transportation. Contributing to the problem was the resignation of Thomas Mifflin from the post of Quartermaster General on October 10, 1777, and the failure of Congress to replace him until March 2, 1778. This delay was nearly fatal as the Quartermaster Department was in disarray, and Mifflin's deputy, Henry E. Lutterloh, was inadequate to the challenge.

In January 1778, Congress dispatched a committee to camp to evaluate all the problems of supply and organization. This "Committee at Camp" was vital in working with Washington and his staff to reorganize the army and its logistics to sustain a viable force in the field. The full Congress, meeting at York, reached the obvious conclusion, that the purchasing system it had instituted in June 1777, was incapable of supplying the army. The inept Buchanan was on the verge of being fired, but resigned instead on March 20, 1778. Jeremiah Wadsworth of Connecticut was elected in his place on April 9, and accepted the position.

On April 14, 1778, Congress adopted a new plan which instituted most of the recommendations that had been made by Trumbull during the summer of 1777. The Commissary General of Purchases had full control over his staff, and commissions on purchases were allowed to attract the most competent men. Ephraim Blaine, who had proved his effectiveness, continued in the Middle Department.

While the Commissary Department functioned relatively smoothly for the rest of 1778, problems began to multiply and by 1779 many complaints were being registered. These led to Wadsworth's resignation, and the appointment of Ephraim Blaine as Commissary General of Purchases on December 2, 1779, a position he held for nearly two years. Minor changes in 1780 led to another reorganization by Congress in November 1780, and a supply by contract system was eventually instituted. However the troops suffered intermittent food shortages for all the factors mentioned above and others, until the end of the war.

For an overview of the campaign of 1777 in Pennsylvania, suggested readings are: John S. Pancake, *1777: The Year of the Hangman*, University: The University of Alabama Press, 1977 and John F. Reed,

Campaign to Valley Forge; July 1, 1777-December 19, 1777, Philadelphia: University of Pennsylvania Press, 1965.

While much has been written on the Valley Forge Encampment of the Continental Army, it has not yet been the subject of a readily available scholarly history. John W. Jackson's *Valley Forge: Pinnacle of Courage*, Gettysburg, Pa.: Thomas Publications, 1992, is the best currently available. Also see John B. B. Trussell Jr., *Birthplace of an Army: A Study of the Valley Forge Encampment*, Harrisburg: Pennsylvania Historical and Museum Commission, 1977. The three volume "Valley Forge Report" (1980-82), by Wayne Bodle and Jacqueline Thibaut, written for the National Park Service, is recommended, but it received limited distribution.

The operation of the commissariat is well covered by E. Wayne Carp, *To Starve the Army at Pleasure: Continental Army Administration and American Political Culture, 1775-1781*, Chapel Hill: University of North Carolina Press, 1984, Victor Leroy Johnson, "The Administration of the American Commissariat During the Revolutionary War" Ph. D. diss., University of Pennsylvania, 1941, and Erna Risch, *Supplying Washington's Army*, Washington: Government Printing Office, 1981.

Joseph Lee Boyle   Birdsboro, Pennsylvania

EDITORIAL PROCEDURE

For the most part, these letters were originally entered into the letterbook in chronological order. In some cases they were entered out of order, but have been rearranged in this work to appear by date. Undated letters are assumed to have been written between the dates of letters preceding and following.

Letters are introduced by the names of the addresser and addressee. The dateline falls just below the heading, though the original document may have it at the bottom. The complimentary close is brought up flush with the last paragraph and the closing signature has been omitted. A descriptive note at the foot of each entry shows the location of the document presented, and identifies the recipient, where possible, the first time each individual appears.

These documents present a literal transcription with spelling, punctuation and grammar remaining as they are found in the originals. Abbreviations and contractions are also preserved as they are found. As a letterbook was intended to serve as a reference copy for the writer, abbreviations, misspellings, and errors are far more common than in the "fair copy" that would have been sent to the intended recipient. Many of these documents do not conclude their sentences with periods, and use commas, colons, or semicolons instead, if anything at all.

Capital letters follow the text of the originals, although it is often a guess whether a letter is a capital or not. Brackets indicate questionable or illegible letters and words. *Sic* is used very sparingly as it would quickly detract from the text, given the numerous variants of spelling and oddities of expression. Crossed out material has been omitted. Margin notes are shown as postscripts, except where obviously keyed to the body of the document.

The index includes the names of all mentioned persons. Place names are selected, depending on relevance and frequency. Casual references to New York, for example, have been omitted. Mentions of foodstuffs such meat, cattle, pork, beef, and flour occur so frequently in the text that they have not been indexed. Less common food references such as tongue and bacon, have been indexed.

Ephraim Blaine to William Buchanan

D^r. Sir,   Cross Roads 16th. August 1777

I find the Difficulty attending the purchasing Commissarys business, relative to the Slaughtering of Cattle, and delivering it to the Issuing Commissarys, will be very troublesome, and also a great expence to the public; upon the present plan there is a Commissary and three Assistant Clerks to Each Division of the Army, and four Butchers; that number would be very sufficient to answer their Appointments, and Superintend the Slaughtering of Beef, upon the new Regulation; should it not take place there must be a Master Drover, and Butcher, who can be entrusted with the Delivery of the Beef, which will be a great loss of time to those whom I have here for that business; I have been with the Commissary of each Division of the Army, and have made an Estimate as follows: Including the park of Artillery, and those people employ'd in the Staff department Viz—

    General Greens Division 4,200 Rations
    Genl. Stephensons D^o. 3,750 D^o
    Genl. Lincolns   D^o. 3,600 D^o
    Genl. Stirlings   D^o. 3,800 D^o
                                15,350 Total

When the Salt provisions are done, which is near a close there will be Slaughtered about forty five head of Cattle daily, now in Camp about two hundred head; M^r. White must Write Morris, and Hugg, to forward their Cattle immediately, as they will be wanted the first of next Week; The Butchers are some the very worst of Mankind, and have from Seven and Sixpence to ten Shillings p[er]: Day, and two or three Shillings, perquis'd upon each Hide, there is only two of whom I can depend on for Master butchers, that are willing to continue—

His Excellency cannot yet fix the route of his Army, but recommends large Quantitys of provisions to be collected and deposited in Magazines contiguous to the Road easterly and Southerly, so that there may be no risque of the Army being pleintifully supplyed. There is very few Candles, Soap and Spirits; M^r. White must immediately contract with proper persons to furnish large Quantities of Candles and Soap: The preference of some part the public Tallow, might be an Inducement to engage them upon the most reasonable Terms—Colonel Trumbull is just set of Home, wish you had seen him before he went, I have begg'd him to

continue M^r. Champions supplys of Cattle till you go there, which he has partly engag'd to do; The express deliver'd your Letter before he came to me, or I should have detain'd it, he just inform'd me he has answered you fully; if nothing happens too Morrow shall be down with you, and am Dear Sir—Your Most Obed^t. and Very hble Servt.
Frame 1108.

William Buchanan was the Commissary General of Purchases.

Blaine to Mr. Dunham

Sir,   20th. of August 1777

You must be exceeding careful how you proceed in the purchasing of Beef Cattle, the very extraordinary price which has been given last Spring, and this Summer will make it difficult for some time to reduce them to a reasonable and Generous price, as you see Cattle fit for killing, let that be your directions in buying; You must confine your price from three pounds, to four pounds, ten Shillings p[er]: hundred, sinking the Fifth Quarter: Your method of purchasing must be by estimation, or otherwise if you can safely Agree; Estimation is a very dangerous way of taking Cattle without great judgement; therefore you must be very careful when you buy in that way, that no advantage may be taken; all the Cattle which comes from the Eastward, ought to be sorted, forwarding all them which are good beef: But in case larger supplys should come from that Quarter; you are hereby impowered to appraise good pastures, in a safe place, and have the Cattle therein; employing drovers sufficient to take care of them, 'till they are Ordered to the Army. Your Attendance at Head Quarters will be necessary every two Weeks: But for the present have every thing in your district properly regulated before your return. Correspond by every opportunity, with me or my Assistant M^r. Chaloner at Head Quarters, and give information where you may be Wrote to for supplys: When you stand in need of Cash, Apply to M^r. James White in Phil^a. who will advance it you, I am wishing you a good Journey—Your Most Obed^t. and Very Hble Servt
Frame 1108.

This was probably sent to Azariah Dunham, Assistant Commissary of Purchases at Morristown, New Jersey.

Blaine to Mr. Murdock

Sir 20th. August 1777
 Your favor of the fourth Instant to M^r. Buchannan I had the perusal off, and observe the Contents; The County of Frederick is included in M^r. Gasts Districts as purchasing Commissary; However M^r. Buchannan and my self with the Approbation of Congress, have thought it adviseable to employ, Suitable persons at Detach'd posts, when Troops marches through to purchase and Issue: In this Character you'll please to Act; at the Same time beg you may use every means in your power, to reduce the extravagant prices, as much as possible of Provisions: You'll hear a Thousand reports, the prices of Beef at Camp, but be assured not more will be given in Common, than four pounds p[er] Hundred, sinking the Fifth Quarter. Should you meet with any good Cattle in M^r. Gasts absence, and in your power to purchase pray do it, and forward them to Camp, under the direction of some careful person: Inclosed you have your appointment, your pay for Services will be as heretofore, under late Commissary General; until I may have the pleasure of seeing you, unless your business be encreas'd, in that case you will be particularly considered. You must be exceeding careful how you keep your Acc^{ts}, inclos'd you have a Specimen how to enter your Beef Hides, and Tallow; you also must comply with the inclos'd Resolves of Congress, as near as you possibly can, have sent. am Sir Your very hble Servt.—
Frame 1109.

Blaine to William Buchanan

Sir Camp Cross Roads 21st. August 1777
 Please to write by express to M^r. Dunham, to forward One Hundred head of Cattle Immediately to Head Quarters, as they will be wanted by the last of this Week; Also see that Cattle sufficient are laid in at Phil^a., Billingsport, Marcus-hook, and all those posts down the River. A M^r. Ramsay is appointed Issuing Commissary for Billingsport; his supply will come handier from Messrs. Morris & Hugg: Let nothing be wanted on our part, that is necessary to provide for the Army, I am Sir—Your Most Obed^t. and very Hble Servt.
Frame 1109.

Blaine to William Buchanan

D^r. Sir,   Cross Roads 22^d. Augt. 1777
     I have drawn upon you in favour of M^r. Dunham for three thousand pounds, which please advance him, without delay; have ordered him to proceed to Head Quarters, with another drove of Cattle, which I hope he will be expiditious in doing; as I shall want his Assistance in the Jerseys: My hopes are very dubious of much supplys from the Eastward, and indeed my situation on that Acc^t. very disagreeable, as I find every thing wanting here, in the Victualling Department is look'd to me for, which makes my Situation very disagreeable, however shall continue with the Army, 'till I fix upon a regular footing every thing in my power: If the Jerseys don't afford us an immediate supply of Salt, the Army will want in a very short time, as the Salt Provisions are nearly out and so large a Consumption of Fresh beef, beg this matter may not be Neglected—I have given M^r. Dunham his appointment; please get him to take the Necessary Oaths of Office, shall write you in a few Days more fully. I hope M^r. Resburgh will forward all the Stores he can to Corryell's Ferry, and Head Quarters—I am with much Esteem Sir Your Obed^t. Hble Servt.
Frame 1109.

Blaine to Nehemiah Dunham

Sir   Camp Cross Roads 22nd. August 1777
     Upon the Recommendation of Col^o. Stewart, have fixed upon you as a proper person, to go with M^r. Champion to Ulster County, and receive a number of Cattle, purchased under the direction of Col^o. Trumbull, for the use of the United States: I beg you may proceed immediately and receive the same, bringing all thats fit for present use with you, and leaving the residue, under care of M^r. Eph^m. Wells, at Wall Kills, who has already had the charge of them; I also impower you to purchase all the fat Cattle, you can meet with in that County; and upon the most reasonable Terms; as it is the duty of every friend to his Country, to use his utmost endeavors to reduce the present exorbitant price of every necessary article for the use of the Army. Your good Character and Attatchment to the Cause, leave me no doubt of your exerting your utmost endeavours to prosecute so Salutary a purpose: For which you have my Warrant Inclos'd; what Money you may want draw upon me in Phil^a. which shall be honored: Desire you may order the Cattle down to

head Quarters, and that as expitiously as possible. Your pay as an Assistant purchaser shall for Four Dollars p[er] day, and when travelling upon public business, an Allowance of One Dollar and one Third p[er] day—Shall be glad to hear from you p[er] first Opputy. the mean time remain your—Most hble Servt.
Frame 1107.

Nehemiah Dunham was a purchaser of cattle in New Jersey.

Blaine to Zebulon Hollingsworth

Sir, Wilmington 30th. August 1777
You will exert your utmost abilities to fetch off from the Neighbourhood of Elk, and the County Adjacent to the Enemys Encampments: all publick Stores, especially those under the direction of the late Commissary Genl. Your Superior knowledge of their Situation and Quantity, renders instructions needless, other than that the Salt provision must be the first object of your attention, and brought off to a place of safety at all events. Twenty or five and twenty Barrels of which may be left with either of the Issuing Commissarys with our Army, in that Neighbourhood: Taking duplicate Receipts for the Same. This done, You'll then proceed to Secure the Corn with all possible dispatch removing the Same out of danger; Let the flour either publick or private be the next object of your attention, of which bring of all you can, giving the Owners thereof Receipts for the Same, who shall be paid at a Generous price; of this also leave with the Issuing Commissarys as much as they stand in need of, taking Receipts as above. I am Sir Your very hble Servt.
Frame 1110.

Zebulon Hollingsworth was a merchant at the Head of Elk, now Elkton, Maryland.

Blaine to Thomas Richardson

Sir Wilmington 31st. Augt. 1777
Upon the Recommendation of M^r. Buchannan the Commissary General, Col^o. Biddle-and his, further I have appointed you an Assistant purchaser of provisions, for that part of your State, as is mentioned in your Warrant, only leaving a blank for two Countys, which M^r. Buchannan has

agreed to add to your district—as it is pretty large. I agree to allow you an Assistant Occasionally who you shall agree with upon the most reasonable Terms you can—Inclosed you have Instructions for the present, which must be complied with, as far as in your power; The necessary Oaths of Allegiance and Office, you must take before some State Magistrate, which Inclose me by the first safe Opportunity, As also a Bond with Security for your performance, of thirty Thousand Dollars; from your Known good Character would not require this, only the modes recommended by Congress must be comply'd with, and I have made a point of it with every person whom I have appointed, you must not purchase more flour than is Necessary to supply the Troops within your district, from time to time, Inclosed you have Instructions how to purchase; make enquiry what price Salt is in your Neighbourhood, and what Quantity, which inform me off by first safe hand. Congress have taken the supplys of Salt upon themselves, therefore you cannot purchase any, but what is Sufficient to supply the Troops in your district; 'till such time as I have the Approbation of the Committee of Congress for that purpose. The procuring of Pork in the Season for Salting, will be one of your greatest objects, purchase no beef Cattle, but such as are good beef. your purchases must not extend beyond the limits of your district. Inclosed you have a Blank appointment for an Issuing Commissary, beg you may appoint a proper person: Write to me in Phil^a., or in my Absence to M^r. James White, who is my Assistant there. Your Orders from time to time for the Necessary Cash shall be Honoured; will be glad to hear from you by first safe Opportunity, and am in the mean time Sir—Your Most Obed^t. and very hble Servt.—
Frame 1110.

Thomas Richardson was an Assistant Commissary of Purchases at Georgetown, Md.

Blaine to Ludwig Karcher

Sir,   Wilmington 9th Septr 1777
I request upon the Rec^t. of this, you will employ a sufficient number of persons to assist in driving of all the Beef Cattle upon the Island[s] and near the River; first engaging and fixing a reasonable price, think you ought not to exceed four pounds ten Shillings per Hundred—should you meet with Persons who are unreasonable in their prices, give them

Certificates—Pray be Active, as there is danger of the Enemys being in Possession of that Country in a few Days I am Sir Your very Hble Servt.
Frame 1111.

Ludwig Karcher or Karchar was a Pennsylvania merchant.

Blaine to Peter Aston

Sir,   Wilmington 9th Septr. 1777 two OClock in the Morning
     Upon Receipt of this proceed with all possible speed to all the Mills about and in the Neighbourhood of Downingstown. eng, take a particular Acc^t of what Wheat there may age each of them in Grinding flour for our Army be in each Mill, and also the Quantity of fresh Flour; let no time be lost in doing this: Stop sending any further supplies to this place, shall be glad to hear from you as Soon as possible, and am Sir— Your Obed^t. Hble Servt.
Frame 1111.

Peter Aston or Ashton, was an Assistant Commissary of Purchases who acted as a roving purchaser.

Blaine to Ludwig Karcher

Sir   Wilmington 9th Septr 1777
     I request upon the Receipt of this you employ a Sufficient number of persons, to assist you in driving off all the Beef Cattle upon the Islands, and near the River, first agreeing and fixing a reasonable price, think you ought not the exceed four pounds ten Shillings, per hundred—Should you meet with Persons who are unreasonable in their prices pay no Respect to their Demand, give them Certificates specifying Quantity and Quality. Pray be Active, as there is danger of the Enemys being in possession of that tract of Country in a few Days, I am Sir Your Obed^t Hble Servt
Frame 1111.

Blaine to John Patton

Sir   Lancaster 13th Septr 1777
    You'll immediately engage with a number of Coopers at Lancaster, Reading, and Lebanon, for all the beef and pork barrells you can contract for, your price must not exceed fifteen Shillings or twelve and Sixpence, allowing a ration to each barrell: A special charge must be given the Issuing Commissarys at the different posts to be exceeding careful of all the empty Hogsheads, Barrells, and other Vessells, which may be in there Stores; and have them Hoop'd, and Taken care of, an estimate of the number: You'll also, use every Means in your power to reduce the very extravagant price of every Article which lays in our way to purchase for the Army. A return of the Whiskey remains in Store at this place must be Immediately made and the same forwarded to Camp: No Whiskey issued but to those people upon fatigue, as all we can purchase is Scarcely sufficient for those in the field; pray forward all the Flour you possibly can, I am Sir Your Obed^t. and very hble Servt.
NB enquire what Bakers might be engaged to bake hard Bread at Lancaster, Reading, Lebanon & any other place in your district, enquire about Tallow Chandlers, and send them to Contract with the Commissary General; for supplying the Army, with Soap & Candles—
Frame 1111.

John Patton was an Assistant Commissary of Purchases, based in Berks County, Pennsylvania.

Blaine to William Buchanan

Sir   Lancaster 13th September 1777
    I have sent M^r. Graff, over to you, if you think him equal to the business necessary to be done to the Eastward; beg no time may be lost in sending him of. I believe him to be very Active, and at present can think of no other person more Suitable, but such as is otherwise engaged: M^r. Patton and M^r. Shalase, has promised to send such Persons as understand the Tallow Chandling business, over to York, to engage with you; M^r. Patton has received Instructions from me to engage all the Coopers, and has limited him to the price he must give, he will also enquire about persons capable of Baking hard bread, this will also refer to you: Have been Informed great Quantitys of Salt is in Maryland, would request you

would write M^r. Gasts, to procure all he can, depend it will be much wanted; especially what may be necessary, for the Magazines west of Susquehannah: Sundry persons are daily buying up all they can meet with, beg you may have an eye to this Immediately. M^r. Slough has engag'd to rebout all the flour, which is upon the turn, Col^o. Patton will try to furnish a sufficient Quantity of Wheat for that purpose—No news from Camp worth communicating, my Compliments to M^r. Robert and am Dr Sir Your Obed^t and very Hble Servt.
Frame 1112.

Blaine to John Chaloner

Dear Chaloner,   Phil^a. 17th Septr 1777

I have been exceedingly unwell since I parted with you, and my complaint not likely to be removed; had been very Uneasy about you, and the Situation you must be in; if a plentiful supply cannot be laid in for the Army: Nothing but confusion prevails here, I have sent Major Smith, and M^r. Ashton to your Assistance; Beg for Gods sake that nothing may be wanted, that is in our power to procure; Shall be with you as soon as I possibly can ride—let me hear from you by very first opportunity, and am Dr Sir Your Obed^t. Servt
Frame 1112.

John Chaloner to Aaron Levering

Sir   19th. September 1777

His Excellency Genl. Washington has informed me, that there is carried into your Neighbourhood, a drove of Cattle (which was intended for the use of our Camp) by order of General Armstrong. They are wanted for immediate use, you will therefore give Orders to the person, who has the care of them, to drive them on towards this place immediately, avoiding the Roads leading to Sweeds ford, fatland ford, and the Valley-Forge Sir I am Your very hble Servt.
Frame 1112.

Levering was a Colonel in the Maryland Militia.

Blaine to William Buchanan

Dear Sir,   Camp New Hanover 24th. Septr 1777
     Last night I received the inclosed by M^r. M^c.Garmont which has given me great uneasiness, am astonished Mr Gast, did not furnish the necessary supplys before he left General Smallwood, His Excellency has had the Acc^{ts}., and is very much displeas'd, this Morning early sent off M^r. M^c.Garmont with a supply of Rum, Flour, Salt &ca—
     Genl. Wayne and Smallwood, has been much distress'd for the Necessary supplies, for their people, suppose you have heard of their being surpris'd in the night by the Enemy, and a good deal worsted; The Number of our loss not properly ascertained, but Considerable. I have fixed by Chaloner, who will give constant attendance at Head Quarters, and two persons to render the supplys of Flour; Col^o. Hugg, with the Assistance of M^r. Kuher to furnish the Beef—Will leave Camp for ten Days, must go home, and fix proper persons to go up to Fort-pitt, to regulate our department there—and Fetch down a Quantity of Beef Cattle, for the Army: it is full time you would look out for a proper supply of Salt, that Article will be wanted very Shortly, beg no time may be lost, in fixing upon some Method of bringing a Quantity from the Eastward; have purchasd a Quantity of Rum, at Pottsgrove, the Army plentifully supply'd with that Article, have this Day Rec^d. four Hund^d. and odd barrells of Flour; The Waggons I keep loaded for a moving Magazine, some loaded with Biscake and twelve Loaded with Rum: Should the Army keep at one place the supply would be much easier; am quite discouraged about our proceedings, God knows how it may end; They English seems to get the Advantage upon every movement of our people, where the fault lays, am not able to judge—Pray have an Eye to the Army 'till I return, that nothing may be wanted; daily complaints are making to the General, tho' never was Troops better Served with Flour, Beef, and Rum; Several of the Issuing Commissarys, by no means, answers their appointments, the neglect of making applications for proper supplys, and indeed uses great waste in the Issuing: If you have heard any thing of M^r. Pollock, and where he has taken the Beef Cattle, pray inform me. Would be exceeding glad to see you before I leave Camp, and am Dear Sir Your Most Obed^t. and very Hble Servt.—
Frame 1113.

Chaloner to Mr. Swaine

Sir   Head Quarters on Skippack 2nd. Octr 1777
The late reinforcements which have arrived at Camp, requires the supplys of Cattle should increase in proportion. I have been very uneasy least the Troops should suffer for want of Beef, the supply by Capt. Rudolph happily prevented it, for at his arrival, we had not one beast, but what was disposed of to the Issuing Commissaries—
You will immediately on Rec^t. of this dispatch some careful person with all the Cattle you have on hand, provided they do not exceed 500—And then pursue such measures, as will enable you to send to head Quarters the like N^o. in four days at furthest from the time those can arrive here, and if possible send twice a Week 500 Head until further Orders. You will in future be careful to advise me whenever you drive Cattle from any place, they have been Stationed at, where they are sent to, and to whose care, so that if necessity require sending for them, no disappointment may arise— you will also if obliged to move yourself send the like information. Suffer no difficulties whatever to prevent your sending the Cattle on hand with all speed as our Stock at this time does not exceed forty head—Your attention to the above instructions is of great importance and must be strictly adhered to. If M^r. Karchar Falls in your way, show this Letter to him, and desire him to attend to it also—I am Sir Your very hble Servt.
Frame 1113.

Chaloner to Blaine

D^r. Sir   Camp 4 Miles below Skippack 2nd. Octr 1777
I expected to hear from you long e'er this, as also to have rec^d. a quantity of Whiskey—M^r. Jones has wrote to Stewart for Spirits, Soap, Candles, and Salt all of which have been much wanted & are not yet come to hand. I wrote to M^r. White to provide a Substitute for Phil^a. to supply Soap, Candles, &ca As also to procure Salt of the makers in Jersey for the Camp. The tallow in Camp is Spoiling for want of being used—Our Consumption of Cattle is now upwards of 800 head Weekly—I have with great difficulty kept up a supply, owing to want of Information where they are; have wrote to Swain always to give information of their moving. Have not seen Col. Jos Hugg since we parted with him, begin to suspect he is not agreeably housed. M^c. Dormont is gone to Lancaster County, to forward a drove of Sixty head, he has purchased, and from thence to

proceed to the lower Counties, to buy and Forward all that could be produced, have also Wrote to Dunham, on the Same subject, find by a Letter from him, he is Sick, and has done nothing. Picture to yourself my Situation, have not left Camp an hour since I saw you, and from the best information I can procure here, the One that I wanted to go and see, is by accident left in the City. I can bear it no longer, and am determined to see for my self: shall not be absent more than 12 Hours, and shall then see that plenty is on hand, my Compliments to Alex and am with assurance of my utmost endeavors to render your absence, as little inconvenient as possible—Dear Sir Your hble Servt.

P:S: If the department to the Eastward is neglected any longer, we shall soon be ashore—
Frame 1114.

Chaloner to Blaine

Dear Sir   October 2nd. 1777

  Since writing you this Morning, I have Received information from the best authority that Ludwick Karchar has engaged to procure Cattle for General Howe, and he is now useing all his diligence to provide for our Enemys. Jos. Hugg apprehends that he has let the Enemy have 100 head of our Cattle. I dispatch this evening an express to Bethlehem to pay no attention to his Orders—Pray appoint some one speedily in his place, as the demand for Cattle is very great, I am Sir Your very hble Servt.
NB: fetch some assistants to superintend the Butchers.—
Frame 1114.

Chaloner to Blaine

Sir,   Camp 4 Miles below Skippack 3^d. Octr. 1777

  Yours of the 27th. per Col. Patton, came to hand Yesterday am much oblig'd to you for sending the Col^o. to my Assistance, but from experience and good information, am Certain that the Country around here is such that his stay at Camp would only be a Sacrifice of his time. I have therefore advised his return to procure Whiskey and Flour: The Former we are in immediate want of, and the latter after we have

consumed what is at Bristol, and the [St]ate in the Country will be much wanted: Our Reinforcements are so great, as to consume upwards of 800 head of Cattle p. Week—This will soon destroy our little Stock, and I cannot hear from or know where to direct to any of the purchases to warn them of the Demand: Col^o. Patton I hope will also purchase some beef—Salt is an Article we want, and daily consume a large Quantity of, have Wrote James White to purchase of the Makers in Jersey, for the consumption of the Camp, and keep the imported for preserving provisions: As also to procure a supply of Soap and Candles, which is much wanted: depend on my Utmost exertions, and remain with respect Sir Your very hble Servt.—
Frame 1114.

Chaloner to William Buchanan

D^r. Sir,　　　　　　Camp North-Wales Road Octr. 11th. 1777
I have this day been waited on by M^r. Gray, D.C.G. of Issues for the Eastern department, complaining that in that quarter there is no Commissary of purchases as yet appointed, on which account the Troops there have greatly suffered; I have thought it my Duty to give you this early intelligence of their Necessitys, that a remedy may be appointed, before the Calamity is too great. Must request you will stimulate the purchasers of Whiskey to procure and sent to Head Quarters at least Forty Hogsheads Weekly: it is ordered to be delivered and a Sufficiency not sent on, which Occasions much murmuring. I have depended on Lancaster, Reading and Yorktown, for four hundred Barrels Flour Weekly, they are very Slack in their supplies; a line from you may perhaps be of Service, You may assure them their Teams, shall not by any means be detained—if my remonstrating to his Excellency can prevent it. The D.C.G. of Issues, has not five Barrells on hand, an immediate supply of that Article, must be sent forward without delay, or the consequence will be complaint to his Excellency, to avoid which shall exert my utmost endeavours. By a letter from Col. Steward of the 8th October from Trentown, am informed "all the Spirits, Soap, Candles, and Salt is gone" from thence, M^r. Buchannan, and M^r. Blaine should set the people of Lancaster at Work to make Soap, Candles, and Whiskey—I should not have troubled you on occasion, but the uncertainty of a live meeting with M^r. Blaine; will I hope together with

the importance and necessity of providing a Supply, sufficiently apologize for this interruption—I am Sir Your very Hble Servt.
Frame 1115.

Chaloner to Blaine

D^r. Sir,   Camp North wales Road 14th Octr 1777

The Bearer is dispatched on purpose to request your attendance here, I wish it only until such time, as you can regulate the supply to Camp, equal to the Consumption thereof. On your departure from Camp, I expected to have heard from you by the Bearer, of Supplies from your Quarter, my dependance on Whiskey & Flour from thence induced me, agreeable to your advice, to send the Spirits purchased in Pottsgrove into the Neighbourhood of Reading, the Disappointment of Whiskey has obliged me to consume, all the West India Rum, as also to purchase more. It was reasonable to expect the Supplies of Beef Cattle, would have been brought to Camp as usual, but as the purchase of that Article, apprehended there was no necessity during your absence, they have not sent me one Single hoof, consequently the Stock laid in at Wilmington is nearly consumed—Shall send for the last Drove this Day, and then depend on providence for Manna and Quail: I have personally acquainted M^r. Patton, M^r. Dermon, and Hugg, the Demands of the Camp; I have not received any from either. Hugg has been from Camp, Several Days, I hope he will soon return with a Drove: I have also wrote to Dunham at Morristown & have receiv'd for Answer, that he is Sick, incapable of duty and did not apprehend the Scarcity, calling out that the Demands of the Militia there is great. Dunham of Kingwood has been here, he has three hundred head in Ulster County, which have ordered him to drive this way, but fear they have fell a prize to the Enemy, they having storm'd and carried Fort Montgomery. Our Magazine of Flour &ca at Trentown, Dowingstown, and in this Neighbourhood are quite exhausted, Flour and Whiskey, must be sent in large Quantities down to Pottsgrove, where Col^o Steward will send a person to superintend and recieve such Stores as may be sent there; This will be as near Camp as can be with safety; and distant enough to remove the fears of the Farmers, having their Waggons press'd or detain'd. From your quarter must be sent Soap, Candles &c^a, and almost every thing that used to be procured from Philad^a. These hints are given in order that before your Departure, you may appoint some person

to execute that which is necessary, to procure the Supplies mentioned. The Store at Pottsgrove must be supplied with 1,500 Barrells Flour Weekly, less will by no means do, also Sixty Hogsheads Whiskey. Be assured the above is real, and not Imaginary, and your presence at Camp is absolutely necessary, to remedy the impending evil; For Gods sake delay not one Moment, Instruct your Assistants to procure a fresh Supply of Flour, it will be soon wanted. I am in a Situation really disagreeable, the prospect bad, no attention paid to my Letters or directions; Indeed too melancholy to write News—Am Sir Your hble Servt.—
Frame 1115

Blaine to Thomas Huggins

Sir   Camp near Trapp 15th October 1777
 Find you have been in the Neighbourhood of Camp, since my absence, and did not wait upon M^r. Chaloner, who transacts my business there; you have been exceedingly neglectful as a purchaser for the Army, was our Supplys from the others as Slack as yours have been, the Army must have suffered long since: Upon the Receipt of this I desire you may bring forward, all the Beef Cattle you have purchased, without one Moments loss of time; I also desire you may not exceed for any you may hereafter purchase, the Sum of four pounds p[er] Hundred, Sinking the fifth Quarter: There is a Resolve of Congress for that purpose, which must be put in Execution, (let no Cattle Escape) Such persons as are not Satisfied with that price, take their Cattle and give Certificates for the Same; will expect two hundred head of good Beef, by next Monday or Tuesday, Col^o. McGermont will inform you, how much they are wanting, will expect your returns of purchases, up to the last of September Am Sir Your Obed^t. Hble Servt.
Frame 1116.

Thomas Huggins was an Assistant Commissary of Purchases who was based at Elkton, Maryland.

Blaine to Robert McGermont

Sir,
 You are to proceed immediately to your district and procure all the good Beef Cattle you possibly can, if you can't purchase the same

upon reasonable terms, have them carefully estimated Sinking the Fifth Quarter, Mentioning no price, and give Certificates for the W^t. Beef, there is a resolve of Congress for that purpose which must be put in execution, be exceeding carefull that neither yourself nor property be in danger of the Enemy—let no Cattle escape you that may be fit, for Immediate use pastures or good Hay, procured for your Cattle, in the Neighbourhood of Nottingham, provided you think it safe, 'till you can forward them to Head Quarters, which you'll be expeditious in doing. All the Salt you may find at Sinipuxent, Seize in behalf of the Army; provided you can remove the same with safety; give Certificates for the same, mention no price, would advise you to send it over the Bay to M^r. Garts, Assistant purchaser at Baltimore, to be forwarded to Yorktown. You'll please to call upon M^r. Huggins, and let him know I shall expect a large supply of good Beef Cattle, when you return will expect account of your purchases up to the last of $Sept^r$., wish you a good Journey and am Sir Your very hble $Serv^t$ Frame 1116.

Robert McGermont or McGarmont was an Assistant Commissary of Purchases, based at Dover, Delaware.

Blaine to Joseph Hugg

Sir,   Camp 21 Miles from $Phil^a$. 18th. Octr. 1777
     Yours by M^r. Denny I rec^d. last Night, and am Sorry to hear of your Brothers indisposition, hope he will soon be better. I am not a little surprized to think that we can expect but small assistance from you in the Beef way, for God sake where is all the Cattle down upon the Jersey shore, certainly there are a great many, the Consumption can by no means be equal, must undoubtedly expect a great supply from you, and hope you will procure all you possibly can. I approve much of your seeking out the largest Cattle, and adding them to those sent up from Philadelphia, as a reserve, hope they are well provided for—I do request you will apply to the Commanding Officer for a party of Men, and proceed immediately to Egg-harbour, and Seize all the Salt you can find, forwarding the same to Pitts-town or some place of safety, (give Certificates for the same mentioning no price) should the Salt be in Bulk, your best method, will be to send empty barrels, from the Store Houses, in the Waggons which goes down for it; and let one or two Coopers, go with them to pack the Salt Am very Scant of Cash, have sent you 3,250 Dollars, shall have a Supply

in a few Days, pray do not loose a Moment in going to Egg-harbour, as Salt is much wanting, will send M^r. White after you, that you may not be detain'd for long, Am Sir—Your most Obed^t. Hble Servt.
Frame 1117.

Joseph Hugg was an Assistant Commissary of Purchases based in Gloucester County, New Jersey.

Blaine to James White

Sir Burlington 23^d Octr. 1777

You will immediately go to Burdentown & Trenton to pay for the Rum, Flour &c. Bought at those places and then proceed to Egg harbour and Seize all the Salt & French Rum you can find, and forward the Same to some place of Safety, towards Corryells ferry, and near the River Delaware, You will give Certificates to the Owners, for the Quantities Rec^d., whom I shall pay or Refer to Congress, immediately, pay no respect to any person, who has any of them Articles, as they are much wanted for the Army: You must make application to the Q^r. Masters, most Convenient to furnish a sufficient number of Waggons, and Transport such Stores as you may Seize, to the above mentioned place of Safety, and with as much dispatch as possible; it will be Necessary to Collect all the empty Barrels, or Hogsheads, you can from the Issuing Commissary, and send with the Waggons to pack the Salt, as also a Cooper with Tools for that purpose, which must go to Eggharbour is there is none there. The Rum, taken from those persons at Bordentown must be paid for, Good Spirits three pounds per Gallon—West India, fifty two and Six pence, French or Common Rum at forty Shillings, and no more. The extravagant price of this Article is Villanious, and the people must not be suffered to have such prices. The Martial Law will support you in taking any Article wanted for the Support of the Army; and request you may put it in execution: Where persons are obstinate in delivering up such property without Exceptions: Great vigilance will be wanting on your part to Render such Supplys, as I shall expect from you—Am sir—Your Obed^t. Servt

P.S. You'll make application to the Commanding Officer of the Militia for what Assistance may be necessary, whom I request to grant you such Aid, as you stand in need of—
Frame 1117.

James White was an Assistant Commissary of Purchases who does not seem to have had a fixed post.

Blaine to Joseph Hugg

D^r. Sir,   Camp 16 Mile Stone 24th. Octr. 1777
    I wrote you a few Lines this Morning by M^r. Kitts, would have gone down to your House had I heard of your being home, but hope to have the pleasure of seeing you in a few days, at your House, or Philad^a., I hope the latter: I give you great joy upon the defeat of the Hessians at Red Bank, hope you have rec^d. no damage from them; I made a Royal escape at Clements Bridge from those Robbers and assure you was a little alarm'd. I would advise you to forward some active person to Eggharbour, to take charge of the Salt and forward it as you order, would not M^r. Denny answer, have given M^r. Dunham an Order for 400 Bushels, he is to procure Waggons to send for it, for Gods sake procure all the Beef Cattle you can as they will be much wanted, those persons who are not willing to part with their fatt Cattle, beg you may take them giving Certificates for the Same, we have a Resolve of Congress, as well the Martial line to Support us, and I beg you may put it in Execution where necessary. I saw a great Number of Beef Cattle, when through your Country, many in the Neighbourhood of Red Bank, request you may take all that may be in danger, or reach of the Enemy; it is full time some preparation was making to secure pork, engage all the Barrels you can, and upon as reasonable terms as possible, it will lay with yourself, where to lay it in, I would advise where it might be most convenient to procure large Quantitys, and the advantages of Store Houses, also convenient to Water carriage; I hope a few Days will determine the safety of this, we must adopt a price which must be given generally for pork: The Governor and Council for this State has fixed ten Dollars per Hundred, for Beef and Pork and no more. If M^r. Kitts can be of any Assistance in purchasing Cattle, I desire he may stay with you; Lay out your account to procure at least 700 head for the Grand Army, they will take Phil^a in a few days and disperse the fleet: Beg you may procure half a dozen good Oxen for Barbycues, which hope we shall have the pleasure of doing, upon the Common near the City, I return you thanks for your Activity, in Securing Salt, and am D^r. Sir—Your very hble Servt.
Frame 1118.

Blaine to Chaloner and Thomas Jones

Gentlemen,   Northwales Road 28th: Octr. 1777
     Inclos'd I have sent you two Letters I Rec^d. at Head Quarters, last night, upon my way hear, you'll observe M^r. Buchannan means the Waggons should proceed to New England for the Salt, however it will be impossible for them to travel for a Day or two; have sent out M^r. Ashton to procure some Superfine Flour. M^r. Pollock and Conroo are gone for a Drove of Cattle. let me know the want of the Army, I dread that of Whiskey, beg you may put every means in Execution to procure all that may be in the Neighbourhood of Camp, let not one barrel escape, this Weather will require a double allowance to keep life in the Soldiers, the Magazine above Pottsgrove out of reach Perkeyoming too high to Cross, shall remain here to Day, if nothing uncommon happens and am Gentlemen Your Obed^t. Hbl. Servt.
Frame 1118.

Thomas Jones was Deputy Commissary of Issues for the Middle Department, stationed with Washington's Army.

Blaine to John Patton

D^r. Sir,   Camp 28th. Octr. 1777
     Upon the Receipt of this I beg you may Immediately procure Whiskey sufficient to Load two Brigades of Waggons more if in your power, The daily Consumption is beyond Conception: Those persons who has and are not disposed to take a Reasonable price, I request you may Seize the same and give Certificates, the Quantitys and Qualitys; I hope you'll be able to forward me 1,000 head of good Beef Cattle: Can't you collect a large Number County? [sic] those persons who are not disposed to Sell, take them, the Army must not Suffer; will expect to hear from you by every Opportunity: Wish you would engage some good Active Man to Receive all the Whiskey, that comes in to York: The Germans makes great Quantitys, and are very good; Am wishing to Receive two hund^d. Head of Cattle weekly from you. Am Sir—Your hble Servt.
Frame 1119

Blaine to William Buchanan

Sir, Camp 16 Miles North Wales Road 28th Oc^r. 1777
Your favor of the 22^d. I've rec^d. and observe the contents, you seem to think my hint of resigning in my last to you, only a piece of folly, but be assured it is Sincere, and from no other motive than the unhappiness I undergo, from the appearance of want in the Army, which you may be assured of. No Man in the World would I serve with more chearfullness than yourself, and I would with pleasure tender you any service in my Power; you mention your want of information, and the Monthly Returns of the Assistant Purchasers, as well a return of the Stores, belonging to the late Commissary General; the former be assured are not more than the daily consumption, and the latter, except what Flour may be at York and Lancaster, in the Middle Department are quite exhausted: As soon as I can obtain the returns will forward them you. The Cattle you mention which was in Ulster County, was only four hundred some odd, 180 of which, I have Receiv'd, the remainder expect here daily, my Writing to M^r. Colt & Champion, was I of opinion it would answer any good purpose, would with Chearfulness, but their Backwardness on Account of some dissatisfaction would take proposals from me Impertinent, those offers ought to be from you; it would be taking a Liberty which I could not Account for—I have made an Estimate by Enquiry, from all the Assistant purchasers in my Department, and find it will not afford two Months Beef, you can have no Idea of the daily consumption; Inclosed you have an Acc^t. of the Weekly Rations issued at Head Quarters, which is not much above half, large numbers of the Militia call'd out, not the least appearance of any Assistance from any Quarter, my Endeavors to render the Supplies, will prove ineffectual, Reflections will lay against me as the Deputy Commissary General of Purchases, upon the Spot, numbers of those persons I have under my Directions, not equal to my expectation, Disappointments and losses daily, complaints hourly, (Mutinies in the Army, the Scarcity of Beef will follow) my Character lost any Money spent, the very unreasonable and exorbitant prices of every Necessary wanted for the Army; all those Circumstances has induced me to Write the Honorable Congress my Resignation, and beg you may Recommend some Person Immediately, as I am determin'd I will not stay, any Service I can render you by going to New England, or elsewhere will do with Pleasure. Have procured two thousand Bushels Salt at Egg harbour, and expect M^r. M^c.Dermont will secure as much at Senipixin, as I

have sent him there, will forward all the Waggons we can Spare to New England for the Salt there, two Brigades sent to Eggharbour. Request you will hurry the Quarter Master in forwarding the Stores at Lancaster and York, Flour and Whiskey is much wanted, would be glad M^r. Smith could forward two or three Brigades of Waggons loaded with Whiskey—any expectations I had from the Westward of a Supply of Cattle and a great Quantity of Pork, are quite gone, would be reasonable to expect Supplies from a Deputy Commissary of Purchases there, or from good Assistants who had peremptory Orders to render such supplies as were Demanded, I doubt the Garrison of Fort-Pitt and its Neighbourhood will be their only object, not the Continental Army; Should M^r. Morgan decline Accepting would recommend my Brother as Purcher, and M^r. John Irwin Issuer, he is very capable, and a good Clerk, but suppose it has been an object of M^r. Morgans to have it a seperate district And be the purchaser himself and have the Recommending of the others, who are to be employ'd—I have a number of Cattle which is my own private property, beg you would afford my Brother a Special order to bring them down and a liberty of Purchasing all others he can meet with on the Road to Fort Pitt. your granting this favour & an Immediate Recommendation of a Deputy Commissary General to Congress will greatly oblige Sir, Your most obedient & most Hbl Servant

NB I have no trusty Person at Camp which I can spare would request you would send some careful person which might be trusted with 100,000 Dollars or more If you could conveniently send it I want Cash very much Frame 1119.

Blaine to Robert McGermont

Sir,   November 1 1777
    Yours of the 25th came to hand yesterday am much disapointed in the Number of Cattle I expected at least Two Hundred head of Beefs from you ee'r this: You well know that Congress has extented the Martial Law thirty Miles distance from the Enemys Lines and of Consequence would protect you in taking of Cattle within that Limits however for the present Wave every difficulty and forward to head Q^{rs}, in Seven days from this 300 head of Fatt Beefs on the best times you can—At present there is but little Cash at Camp shall send you all I have and on receiving a fresh recruit Shall forward you more—

I have Just now heard of a Snow one of the Enemys transports being blown ashore near to Lewis that her Cargo consisted of Pork Bread & articles essentially wanted for the army—am surprised no person in that neighbourhood had confidence enough in the publick credit and regard for their Country to have purchased the greater part of her Cargo for the use of the troops however of a bad bargain make the best immediately repair (after securing & forwarding the Cattle above) to the shore and purchase on the best terms you can all such pork Beef Bread Soap Candles Salt &^{c} which you may find to be disposed of forwarding the same to a place of better Security on the means of doing this must you govern your purchases—This effected immediately proceed to Sinnepuxent there secure all the Salt you can lay your hands—the Cargo belonging to Wm Pollard C^o. hope you have already transported to Baltimore as also— several others which I hear have arrived there. No difficulty will with respect to M^r. Pollards they having received of me a very considerable Sum on Account thereof—shall do every thing in my power to render the Seizure of these articles as little inconvenient as Possible to the owners; the wants of the army [author's blank] for an Immediate exertion of authority which would be no ways warrantable did not the generals inclination to monopolize fuly Justify the measure Should this Spirit long prevail the wants of the army will force us to pursue the same Conduct in respect to every article necessary for their subsistance—the appearance of which must lament & hope the people will have virtue enough to prevent it by parting with their Stock at reasonable prices & giving that Credit to the Curr: which is their Interest to do—My assistants have had great Success in new Jerseys with respect to salt Hugg has seized at the Egg harbours & other inlets in that neighbourhood near 6000 Bushels—I hope to hear of you exceeding him—indeed I expect you will more than Double This quantity—lay your hands on all that comes and suffer none to escape you, Authorize some person in this Neighbourhood to look out and act for you whilst you are engaged in search of Cattle which must by no means be neglected, Harry Fisher would be a good hand if you could engage him I think his attachment to the Country would intruduce him to accept of a reasonable offer I am persuaded he can serve you much respecting the Snows Cargo—Since you was here have seen M^r. Huggins do not apprehend he will exceed you in the price of Beef however suffer nothing to prevent large supplys coming from you. and you will oblige your Most obedient Most Hb^l[1]. Servant
Frame 1120.

Blaine to Horatio Gates

Honoured Sir   Camp Whippain Township Novem^r. 2th 1777

    I having received Information that the DCG of Purchases appointed by Congress for the Eastern department Has declined to Act in that Capacity—as also that in consequence of your orders M^r. Ephaphoditus Champion has purchased a Quantity of Cattle for the use of the Army under your command—Obliges me to Request as a particular favour, that You would Order Mr Champion to purchase all the Beef Cattle he can possibly procure on the best terms he can agree for and after leaving a sufficient Number of the use of the troops under your Command forward the rest to me at Head Quarters Mr Champion may rest assured that his Accounts shall be discharged with the utmost Punctuality and that I shall by no means consider him as Acting under the late resolves of Congress under which he has declined to Act but as contracting with an individual

    The Necessity and importance of Beef being Procured for the Army in proper time will I hope sufficiently apologise for this Freedom—any person forwarding Cattle in Consequence of your orders their Draughts on me shall be Duly honord I have the Honor to be Sir your Most Obedient Humble servant

Frame 1121.

Major General Horatio Gates commanded the Continental Army in New York, and had been victorious at Saratoga the previous month.

Blaine to John Patton

Sir,   Camp Whissahicking Novr. 3 1777

    I wrote you the 28th Instant in the most pressing terms for Whiskey and flour I should have thought your own Reason destitute of the advices you have from time to time rec^d. from me and my Assistant here that we where in great want of Whiskey and flour there is not one barrel of Flour in Camp nor any Whiskey but what was Seized from the Suttlers in Camp When I wrote you last I was in the greatest distress For want of both of those articles which never could have happened had timely attention been paid to my advices I must now once for all tell you that you Must send me weakly [sic] at least 60 hhds of Whiskey and 200 blls of Flour all the Suttlers in Camp have had their Liquors seized from them and

are henceforward forbid to suttle so that of Course there will be no other demand for Whiskey but through your Channel you will therfore of Course have it in your power to reduce the price which must be an essential point with your taking care not to prevent a sufficient supply Those persons who are not satisfied with a reasonable price you have full power to seize the same which I request may be done The army Depending intirely on us for Liquor will greatly murmur if not punctually supplied with their daily allowance and of Course complaints will be daily presented to the General I must therefore request in future that If you have any regard for my peace and Interest with the General that you will by no means disappoint my expectation as above I wish to remove every difficulty in the way of bringing supplies to the Camp therefore in order to remove the Difficulty & plea of Waggoners being detained at Camp they purpose to Establish a store at the trapp for the reception of all Stores necessary for the Camp from whence we may daily bring supplys. what you may now send must come to Head Quarters and a large Quantity must be forwarded to the Trapp immediately, advice us of its coming that we may send a person to receive it I shall be glad of a line from you by every opportunity. I remain yours &^{c}
Frame 1121.

Blaine to Mr. Gartes

Sir Head Quarters 3th Novr. 1777
I have long since expected you at Camp with a very large supply of Beef Cattle, you must Certainly know so large an Army as are to be provided for will consume a great Quantity of Beef—and its an article beginning to get scarce—from the bounds of your district hope by this you have procured at least 1200 head of good Beef Cattle, which forward to Camp by droves with all dispatch and Continue to purchase every Ox in your power as all we possibly can procure will be wanting—I hope you have purchased largely of Salt and are making great preparations for falling Pork have you a number of Barrels in view for that purpose fix proper persons at such places opinion will answer to take in Pork & let no time be lost in preparing for that Business pray forward us a few droves of Cattle without Loss or time, let me hear from you every opportunity and am Sir Your most Obedient Hble Servant

NB. Should you stand in need of Cash apply to Col°. Buchannan at York Town who will afford it you To M^r. Gartes Virginia p M^r. Vanhorn Frame 1122.

Blaine to William Buchanan

Sir,   Camp 3th November 1777
In my last I mentioned to you my respecting of the Cattle coming from Ulster County which M^r. Dunham brought the next Day out of the 1000 you had Information of being here I have received Two hundred and Ninety head, the residue except some poor ones all used at Fish Kills, this may alarm you, there will be a Scarcity of Beef, General Gates on his way with 5000 men the Jersey Militia all calld out a Large Number call'd from this state maryland & virginia. And no other Assistance from any other District, be Assured the purchasers to the Eastward have Declined Buying, two men was with me Yesterday who Informs me the were bringing the last Drove of Cattle which General Putnam took from them at the north River, and that M^r. Colts was Determined not to Accept of his Appointment, this I believe you may Depend, on given information to his Excellency and therefore I expect to be free from blame I have wrote down every thing in my power, but have not the least Expectation from it, Much—Lament your not fixing some Alternitive upon M^r. Colts resignation, Indeed can think of none but your presence there, Mr Trumbills Conections will make it absolutely Necessary, those men Informs me there is Great numbers of Beef Cattle—pray what Mr Garts about, you know the Man I have not received a single Hoof or line from him he Certainly has it in his power to procure a great number of Cattle for god sake write him also, to make Great Preperations for procuring & salting Pork, I have wrote him on that subject, I hope you have sent me two or three Hundred thousand Dollars we are greatly in want of Cash— has borrowed while my Credit held Good in Camp I set of to Morrow for red bank in order to receive the Supplys sent into the garrison Including the Jersey Militia there is about three thousand men to provide for shall expect to hear from you I heartly and am Sir—
Through of my representation to his Excellency the Suttlers are forbid to Come to Camp—in Consequence of which Whiskey must fall—It therefore behoves us to see that plentiful supplies are brought in, and that

the men be punctually served with their allowance If this be not complied with we shall have great complaints, and remain your most Obedient Humble servant
Frame 1123.

Blaine to Unidentified

Dear Sir, Head Quarters 3th November 1777
I daily forsee the approaching Scarcity of Beef am Exceedingly unhappy on that Accompt doubting a proper remedy for relief being by M^r. Buchanan, my expectations from you are very great, both for supplys of Beef Cattle and Whiskey, I know great numbers are both in York & Cumberland Countys, do Collect & Seize every Hooff except a sufficiency for Familys Use, and such as are making preparations for stall feeding Get some Active persons to Assist you a few Days on whom you can depend Mr Polloch will be one and give a week Assistance I hope eer this reaches you there is one or two Large Droves on their way to Camp youl'l all those which are their in flesh and them properly taken care off the [sutlers] are stopped in retailing Whiskey in Camp which will reduce the price of that unreasonable Article hope you will have it your power to Afford us a large Quantity and upon every reasonable terms, as the daily Consumption is very great Compliments to all friends & am you most Obedient Humble servant
Frame 1123.

Chaloner to Mr. Buff

Sir Camp Whissiakicking Nov 5 1777
I expected before you left this you would have rendered me your Accompts of purchases & voucheres—since your departure several persons has presented me your receipts for Cattle without ever estimating the weight &^{c} must request that you will settle those Accompts as speedily as possible transmitting the same with your vouchers of delivery on the Comissary General Your compliance will much oblige your very Humble Servant
Frame 1122.

Chaloner to Mr. G.

Sir   November th5 1777

Before this I expected to have heard from you respecting the Beef which myself and Colonel Blaine requested you to make enquiry of said to be disposed at old Mr Johnstons as also to have received eer this a very considerable number of Beef Cattle, I hope they are on Their way to Head Quarters being much wanted—I flatter myself they will not consist of less than 800 head—you must examine the flour purchased by you at Blackles mill and if fitt for use forward it to Head Quarters with all speed unless you have a prospect of consuming it before it spoils, Pray suffer no delay in forwarding the Cattle let them exceed the Number mentioned if Possible—I am Sir your most Humble servant
Frame 1122.

Chaloner to Jacob Shallus and George Echleberger

Sir,   Camp Wissahickin November 5th 1777

The neglect of supplies from your quarter is somewhat extrodinary That the Army is now suffering for want of Flour owing to the neglect of the Issuing Comissaries at Lancaster & York Town is a truth and you may be Assured will be represented—from those two Magazines has the Chief disappointment for the articles of Flour & Whiskey been placed—of the former you have in abundance and must be accountable for Its not coming forward, I am informed by Colonel Buchanan C G of Purchases that there is a large Number of Waggons coming forward from Lancaster to head Quarters with flour & afterwards to proceed to New England for salt—as they will be immediately ordered on their Journey you must put no dependance on their return, but provide yourself with Teams sufficient to send to Head Quarters Weekly 1000 Barrels untill further order By the resolves of Congress on the Sixth of October you have authority to impress Waggons for this purpose consequently if this order be not Complied with you must be accountable for the Consequence
To Geo^e.Echleberger York town you must send us Weekly 60 Hhds Whiskey
Frame 1123.

Shallus was an Assistant Commissary of Issues at Lancaster. Echleberger held the same post at York, Pa.

Chaloner to William Buchanan

Sir,   November th5 1777

The Bearer waiting on you on particular business gives me an Opportunity of Informing you that Colonel Blain is gone into Jersey not as he inform'd you to red Bank but by the Express order of his Excellency to Morristown in order to lay in a large Store of Provisions—at his Departure I was left without a barrel of Flour depending only on the mills around here with whom I am obliged to fix a guard to keep at Work & cannot make them produce more then 8 barrels p[er] Day—continue yet in the same situation complaints have been made to his Excellency—and our excuse have been that the fresh's have prevented the teams of Crossing the Creeks—this is now subsided & should supplies not come to hand this night, I fear the Consequences—Colonel Patton has been [ex]ceedingly backward with respect to the supplies of Whiskey—all Sutling being forbid in Camp he must be punctual in procuring the necessary to Comply with General orders, I cannot exist here If supplies do not come forward more punctual—The General recommends either at potts grove or the trap at one of which places we must keep on hand at least 10 days provision of flour and Whiskey, this will effectually remove the fears of the Waggoners being detailed or impressed at Camp—The wants of Cash has induced he to Draw several orders on you Colonel Blaine & myself are in great arrears here I hope you will send the needfull which he has requested to Discharge him, I am Sir yours &
Frame 1124

Chaloner to Joseph Hugg

Dear Hugg,   Camp Wissahickin November th5 1777

Yours of Yesterday 4 OClock in the morning was handed me this Afternoon at three, observe the Contents and wish it had arrived in time to have met with Colonel Blaine, who is gone to Jersey, and will no Doubt call on you before his return I am glad to hear of your success at Eggharbour doubt not but you will continue in well doing, and procure of the different articles   as much as will be wanted—with respect to your dispute with Colonel Bradford do not undertake to determine, but would observe that no Officer in the army has a right to expect us to supply them

with wine, Youll therefore procure pay for what you have delivered, in the best manner You can—this I mean as advise only—What authority Colonel Bradford derives from his being one of the Navy Board to purchase I know not, nor can I say whether there is any distinction between the army and Navy with respect to purchases—I can only tell you that the president of this state in a Letter to Colonel Blaine says At his (Colonel Buchanans) request to Comisary of the naval Armament in Delaware, will be immediately directed to Conform to such regulations, as you may publish, in his purchases. You certainly where right is [sic] seizing such as was wanted for & customary for the Army—I am greatly afraid red bank is not the only post where the publick suffers by the loss of hides, shall make known your bargain to Mr Ewing who directs that Department and doubt not but he will approve your Conduct—As you cannot half say what you have to say by Letter, hope youll come here if possible in a day or two, you know it is highly necessary—I thank you for your care & attention to Garrisons exert yourself for us also, or we shall soon be in a pitiful situation, have frequently a prospect of a famine—Our Army will soon greatly encrease, pray be vigilant in forwarding Cattle we have received none from you a great while, suppose you have detained a large fine drove to tantalize the New England Men with when they arrive, for this purpose they must be very good or else the Credit of Jersey must suffer I am for Colonel Blaine Yours &^{c} &^{c}
Frame 1124.

Chaloner to William Buchanan

Sir,   November th7 1777
      Yours of the Third to Ephraime Blaine DCG of Purchases was handed to me Yesterday together with 25 quire of Paper counting 81-250 Dollars which have examined found right, and Inclosed you my receipt for the same—M^r. Blaine being absent, I have taken upon me to set you right respecting the scarcity of Beef and the cause of his resignation—It is not I apprehend, as you seem to Imagine from a belief that there is not more than two months beef to be procured for the Army, (in this Assertion he was confined solely to his own Department because there was not sufficient care taken to procure & forward supplys for the Eastards & south Departments, there could be no dependance placed on more than what was procured under his immediate direction, The Stock purchased

by the late Comissary General is now Exhausted for the use of the army at the Eastward as Col°. Blain has informed you; and his suspicions of the neglect of purchasing to the Eastward to cofirmed by the testimony of all comes from thence by letter from Major General Heath of the state of Massachusetts to his Excellency on that subject, abstract of which you have here p[er] Colonel steward so that his resignation is owing to the neglect of purchasing to the Eastward yours on the subject of limiting the prices of Beef & Pork &c the method for procuring Flour with Advertisements from Mr Graff of Lancaster is received and believe Col°. Blain as well as most of his Assistants with whom he has conversed with on the subject, is of opinion that so sudden a fall in the price and the great Demand of every article evident to every one, would prevent the necessary supplies being procured A matter equally deserving your attention as well as the sale [sic] of the present exhorbitant prices, demanded for every necessary for the Army. Where I to give my opinion on this subject, Should, first recommend a supply to be procured sufficient to Justify us or at least to Deceive the publick in saying there is enough for present use, before we adopt too great a Deduction on the present prices—This I know to be Colonel Blaines sentiments respecting Whiskey.—provided 2 Months Consumption of that article was laid in, so as to send it here at 18 or 20/ we could then rest on our oars & the demand not being pressing would induce the propiertors to part with it on more reasonable terms— To effect this by force, must certainly be a dangerous experiment, and I fear totally impracticable. for how should we thrash Wheat enough for the Army where the Inhabitants disposed not to do it for us, to seize it in the Sheaf would be no means Answer the purpose for making flour or Whiskey—I wrote you the fifth Instant p[er] Mr Pollard respecting the supplies of Flour and Whiskey not coming forward least Mr Pollards should be detained and it not arrive in time, suffer me to say that, the supplys by no means equal to the Consumption of Camp: I find the Issuing Comissarys (provided they have supplies) depend on the teams employ'd at Camp to bring them forward and I believe this is the Cause of our being put to such difficulties on our part a Magazine is thought of in the neighbourhood of Pottsgrove or the trapp—to supply which must be the business of those Issuing Comissary stationed at the Magazines of Lancaster and Yorktown, Many difficulties occur which prevents us sending teams from Camp to put dependance on them is rather to precarious teams must be impress'd from the Country for this purpose I have engaged all I can procure of threashed Wheat in this neighbourhood

and am gitting it made into Flour this with the trifling supplies received has not been sufficient to prevent Complaints. tho has saved us from much suffering this relief of Thrased Wheat will be done in a day or two, and I dread the Consequence if supplies do not come on more punctual & regular—we are now feeding the troops from day to day with short allowance, looking for the Morrow to provide for itself, in this situation should a Fresh overtake us God knows what we shall do—I hope some speedy step be taken to prevent the threating evil. I am Yours
Frame 1125.

Chaloner to John Patton

Sir, November th9 1777
Our necessity for flour and Whiskey is such that I have dispatched the Bearer in hopes that he will meet with their Teams on their way to Camp. you have had due notice of the Demand of the Camp and must be accountable for the want of such articles as are to be had within your district, And of which you have had due notice. I expect moimentiy to be call'd on by his Excellency to answer for the wants of flour & Whiskey—I have nothing to say but that of Colonel Blaine & myself have given sufficient warning, whether the fault lays with you for not Providing or the Issuing Comissary for not forwarding it must appear when enquir'd into and depend on it should not a supply arrive in Twelve Hours from this a court of enquiry will be ordered the Saddle will then be fixt on the right horse, for Gods sake do your utmost to forward on Whiskey and flour, Of the first 60 Hhds. pr Week of the latter as much as you can forward untill we say enough—One Your Assistants Stansbury has been at Camp boasting of the Quantity flour he could send had he orders for so doing If I see him shall not want for them in the most pressing terms I am sir, Your very Humble Servant
Frame 1128

Blaine to Robert McGermont

Sir, Camp 11th November 1777
Am exceeding sorry to find so few virtious in that Quarter of the World where your lott is cast, and people so unfriendly to the General Cause, I do insist that you will use every Means in your Power to prevent

those Monopolises and fore [writer's blank] from procuring one single Bushel its Owing to those persons the very extravagant prices of Salt and Rum upon Receipt of this if no Other Method will do, send this by express cross the bay to baltimore to Mr Garts Purchasing Comissary who I make no doubt can have the governors special orders to seize all the salt in that Quarter for the Army as its so much wanted, I request you may exert every measure and dont suffer a bushel to Miss you Otherwise we Shall be ruined continue buying all the good Beef you possibly can and forward the same by droves to Head Quarters with all Dispatch we are greatly in want of beef—have hopes you will have it in your power to forward Six or Seven Hundred head at least, I hope you will be able to Procure a great Quantity of salt, let me hear from you every Opportunity am Sir. Your Obedient Servant
Frame 1125.

Blaine to William Buchanan

Sir, Camp 12th November 1777
I have sent the Bearer Mr Sproul express for Cash & Inclosed you have my order & Eighteen thousand seven hundred and fifty dollars which please pay and give him a great Charge to come on with great care, should he not have room in my portmeantue for all the Cash you will forward the residue by some safe Opportunity I hope you will repair Immediately to Head Quarters on your way to New England am, very certain never was your presence more necessary on many Accounts at any place than there,—Colonel Morgan arrived with his regiment of Riffle Men last night, a large part of Genl. Gates Army on their March hear, Our Army daily increasing no supplys from any Quarter—Even Lancaster and York where our Magazines of Flour and Whiskey are—am sure there can be no Difficulty in procuring Waggons, for god sake where are all the Waggons intented to be sent to New England for the salt very few of them have made their Appearance at camp, what is the Comissarys and Quarter Masters about, our Supplys from those places are not one Seventh equal to the Consumption—the want of proper Attention and regular supplys from the purchasing Comissaries, makes me the most distress'd wretch living—here is the Season Advanced for salting Beef and Pork was there plenty, what Method do you propose to secure salt, for that purpose, the triffling Quantity which may be in the power of my Assistants purchasers

to seize will by no means be equal to half the Quantity of Pork which they can purchase, those persons who Colonel Hugg has seized salt from at Egg harbour are very impatient, and much Disatisfied with the price I have ordered him to give, which is Four pounds p[er] bushell as the are Importers would request you to lay it before Congress and wish they would fix a price, should they Decline, let me have it in writing from you what they ought to be Allow'd—press M^r. Garts to secure all the salt he possibly can am Inform'd there is great Quantitys upon the shore—have not time at present to answer yours of the Third Instant but shall make a few remarks thereon, my settlement with You will be the first Object which I shall put in execution and hope to Accomplish, shou'd Congress take no Advantage or Accompt of [writer's blank] which am sure the will not, you must expect that any person who has a regard for his own reputation, and has been in publick trust will study to give that satisfaction, which Every honest man ought to do (that is settling his Accompts) this I hope will be in my power, though my Resignation was Expected of—my having it in my power to Quit the service with more honour than at present I see but little Appearance of, you are well inform'd and cannot but know the Difficulty I have Daily to render the supplies for the present, my Idea does not extend to laying up Magazines nor will it ever be in my power till you Regulate Matters in some other way for Assistance from the Other States you mention your expectations from the Eastward are very great for the supplys of Cattle so it ought from thence you must expect all the winter beef for the Army, you also well know what method has been putt into execution to have those supplys, do assure you I shal not be Disappointed shou'd the continue to render such Assistance as the have done this two Months past the reducing the price of provisions for the Army so Rapidly as you mean to do is beyond my capacity to put in execution and I dread the Consequences—being under the Necessity of seizing all the Provisions Necessary to support an Army who Draws above forty thousand Rations p[er] Day leave you to Judge; why dont Congress or the Legislative Authority of each State, but [sic] this propos'd plan into Execution (not a Deputy Comisary of Purchases) the Scarcity of salt I cannot remedy, had I not Acted contrary to your Opinion the Army wou'd have suffered longer this. we are now quite out—I have taken a very Active part in seizing and reducing the price of Whiskey and having the Sutlers deprived the priviledge of sutling in Camp this may be the means of reducing the price in the Country wou'd be glad how soon, but shall not undertake to seize upon your terms, as it will be the Means of keeping

back regular Supplys from coming forward this also ought to be fixed Governor & Assembly—am now oblig'd to seize all the Wheat and Flour in the neighbourhood of camp and Keep Guards upon the Mills who are grinding for the Army—I allow 25/p[er] Hundred for Common Flour, thus you may Dread the immediate reduction of the unreasonable high price of Provisions—I make no Doubt you have fixed upon some place of having the Pork Purchased in the back parts of Virginia and Pennsylvania, and brought Down to Carlile and Yorktown or any other place you might think proper to fix a Magazine this will be matter of great Advantage to the publick, there must be very great Quantity of Pork in the Back Country, Colonel Stewart is very uneasy, your not being down and fixing with him, some Method of regulating the Eastern Department am Sir— Your Most Humble Servant
Frames 1126-27.

Blaine to Joseph Hugg

Dear Sir,   Camp 12th November 1777
    I received Yours of the Eight Instant by Mr Semple and has had some Conversation with him about the price of salt which he seems much disatisfied with I have wrote to Comisary General and requested him to lay it before congress—and shou'd the think the price you Offered not sufficient for Imported salt for him to signify to me what ought to be Allowed, Mr Semple reflects your not granting him the same priviledge you have done to others in sparing a few Bushels to Assist him in procuring Flour to load out his vesel—could it be spared wou'd have no Objections but leave you to Judge of those matters, which I make not the least doubt you will without Partiality—I have heard of a sloop with a large Quantity of salt up Thoms river This I doubt has Miss'd your Notice the farmers geting such a Quantity of salt will be a injury to our Business, beg you may secure all in your power, I hope your Brother and Mr Morris will have it in their power to procure largely of Pork, for god sake let no time be lost in begining to this Business, enclos'd you have the resolves of our Governor and council for the better regulating the price of Provisions for the Army, this I think cannot be a rule for you to buy without the Assistance of your legislative Authority which I make no Doubt they will do in proper time—however for the present allow you to fix the price at Four pounds p[er] C^t & no more I will give the same Directions to the

Other purchases in your state I beg youll forward all the beef Cattle you possibly can colect, your Attention Must not be wholy taken up with supplying the Troops in the Neighbourhood of Red bank I beg you may not suffer a fat ox or any other of the kind to escape you as we shall want them all, I need not mention to you how great our Demand is for beef, do Assure you I am distressed to Know how the Army will be supported with that article pray be industrious in getting beef enough salted up and sent into the forts, Request you will Immediately make out your Monthly Returns of purchases to the first of this present Month, and Request Mr Morris & your Brother to do the same, which forward me by first safe Opportunity as also, your bonds payable to the president of the Congress for five thousand Dollars as a Security for your performances—you will also forward to me the Necessary Oaths of Office and Fidelity taken before the Most convenient Magistrate those papers with your Monthly return I am to send the Comisary General by the very firs Opportunity—I send you by the Bearer M^r. Whittle twenty thousand dollars which must serve you for the present, I am with much regard Sir Your Most Obedient & Very Humble Servant
Frame 1127-28.

Blaine to Mr. Dunham

Dear Sir   Camp 14th November 1777
    I now send you pr. Your Son Aron Dunham six Thousand Five Hundred dollars, would have sent you more but he has no conveniency of carrying it, He informs me that there is a large drove of Cattle coming from Ulster County by Your orders, we much want them, wish you could so manage matters as to forward us 500 head about a fortnight hence When Gates's Army Joins us, you must exert yourself to procure Beef or we shall be greatly distress'd, this province and the West part of New Jersey have chiefly supported us through the summer do not expect much from them now, it is not in their power to give it and on you is the Chief of our dependance. Colonel Blaine being absent I send you the regulations of the Council of safety for this state to suppress the extravagant prices of grain Beef Whiskey & Colonel Blaine is of opinion that it must be not guide for you unless Adopted by your legislative Authority, at present you are allow'd to give [writer's blank] p[er] Cw^t. for meal and no more. Colonel Blaine is desirous that all the Pork that can possibly be procured

be engaged, I doubt not but he expects from you a large Quantity I am Sir Your very Humble servant
Frame 1129.

Blaine to William Crispin

Sir,
  Will Acknowledge it a particular favor should the Commissary of Issues for Red bank & fort Mifflin Stand in Need of any species of Provisions for the Troops that you possibly can Spare from the Fleet you Affording him such supplies. Should the Communication be Cut off will make you proper Restitution and am Sir Y^r. Obedient Servant
Frame 1154.

Blaine to John Jennings

Sir, Camp November 16th. 1777
  Colonel John Patton Assistant Purchasing Comissary for the Counties of Berks Lancaster & Northampton having Informed me that he has appointed you his Assistant for the County of Northampton occasions my now writing to you on the subject of the Purchases for the Army—
Youll therefore be exceedingly careful to supply the several garrisons within your District with such provisions as may be wanted—let it be in quality of the best, and convince those whom you supply of your Superior merits to your Predecessor—a careful attendance to their wants—Colonel Patton Assures Colonel Blaine D C G of Purchases that in this thro you he will not be Disappointed—
The plentiful extent of Country in the District to which you are appointed forbids even a suspicion that your purchases should be confin'd to supply the different posts therein, from you we expect large supplys for the grand Army—You must therefore foreward to Head Quarters all the flour and Beef Cattle you can collect; for the former 25/ p[er] Cwt & the Latter £4 sinking the Hide and tallow to the Continent for that which is extrodinary £4-10 p[er] Cwt Inform whether or not a supply of Pork may be procured & for what price, All persons who may purchase of the above articles with a view of monopoly or enhancing the Value thereof you must seize the same and give receipt for the Quantity and quality leaving the prices to be settled by the legislative Authority of the State. Youll not exceed 8/6 p[er]

bushel for any wheat you may purchase, and treat monopolizers of this Article as directed above in regard to flour—I am Informed of a certain Jacob [S]houd in your County near Fort Mercer having a large Stock of Cattle & a quantity of flour & wheat which he refuses to part with for Continental currency youll enquire into this Matter and If he refuses to sell seize all he has leaving only sufficient for his family consumption. In this be liberal, If necessary apply to the Lieutenant of the County for a Guard to execute this Business I shall expect to receive from you in 8 or 10 days a Quantity of Beef and flour in mean time Sir Yours & Frame 1129.

Jennings was an Assistant Commissary of Purchases based at Allentown, Pa.

Blaine to Thomas Huggins

Sir, Camp November 18th 1777
I received your favour by M^r. Campbell with four hundred and fifty head Beef Cattle, I wish they had been twelve Hundred and much Better Beef, am much surprised you would write me respecting salt when you had my special Orders to seize all within the limits of your district, especially from those persons who are known to be forestallers and Monopolizers, I again request you may not left one Bushell escape you, and inform me by the first Opportunity your success, expect that you will have it in your power to salt up one Thousand Barrels of Beef and pork, very little beef must be salted as we shall have none to spare from present Consumption. therefore must keep a sharp look out for pork, the highest price is four pounds p Hundred Secure all the good barrels you can and upon the most Reasonable terms, was out of Cash, could not send you more than 3250 Dollars, shall have plenty by the return of M^r. Campbell, with whom shall expect to receive four hundred good Beef Cattle in twelve days from this date, Let me know if you might have it in your power to purchase a quantity of Wheat & what price the people ask for Common Merchant flour, You [with] use your utmost endeavours to forward all the salt provisions, have some thoughts of fixing a Magazine some where near the great Valley; this would be very Convenient to You, write M^r. Garts to take more care in packing the Hard Bread which he is forwarding from Baltimore. I remain Sir Yours
Frame 1129.

Blaine to Peter Colt

Sir,   Camp 18th November 1777
   Yours of the 10th November have received p[er] express & am exceeding Glad to find you have Accepted of the appointment of Comissary of purchases for the Eastern Department. from you I hope to enjoy great ease of body & mind by receiving Weekly Assistance from you for supporting the Army—which be Assured is much wanted the Enemy having possession of Philadelphia and the river Delaware, and the Communication from Virginia from whence we had a very Considerable supply of barrelld Pork & bacon & the great Consumption of beef Cattle this two Years past in this state and Jerseys had Rendered that Article Very Scarce, Shall fix Matters with Mazeniah Dunham who is my Assistant Purchaser at Morris Town, to Receive the Cattle from your drovers, and will fix with a proper person at Camp to Superintend the Slaughtering. shall want a great Number of Cattle therefore woud Recommend to you to purchase all the good beef you Possibly can, and fix it so as to forward four hundred head Weekly, make not the least doubt but you will regulate Matters with your Assistant Purchases, so as to have their first droves upon the way in a very few days, our supplys of beef from this State begins to come in very slowly and our Army increasing daily which makes the above one hundred p[er] day—the procuring largely of Pork and salting the same ought to be one of our first Objects hope you will be able to do something very handsome in that way shall use every Means in my power to procure largely of that Articles. but am great in want of salt to effect the Comissary General has ordered sundry Brigades of Waggons to the North River to Load from hear with Flour and have it so fixed that waggons from Hartford with salt will be there to Exchange Loading the Comissary General of Issues will write Mr Gray upon that Subject,
   Am sorry to find the infection which Prevails here has reached Your State, it is a Callamity which I doubt prevails over the Continent, the legislative Authority of this State have Regulated and fixed the following prices Viz—
   Good Beef Whiskey 8/6 p Gallon Wheat 8/6 rye 8/6 Indian corn 6/6 p Bushell Beef sinking the fifth Quarter ten Dollars p hundred, Pork seven Dollars—presume Jerseys will follow the same Example—our Army are encamped twelve Miles from Philadelphia, and Generally in good Health am not able to Inform you when we shall have another Brush

with the Enemy hope in a few days and that I shall have it in my power to give you a good Account of General Howe before Christmas please favour me with a line by every Opportunity and what success your Assistance Purchasers, have am Sir Your Most Obedient & Very Humble servant
NB Inclosed I have sent you resolves of Congress which I received since I wrote Your Letter as also a Copy of a leter which I received the Other day from his Excellency General Washington to which please to Attend to in which You and M^r. Gray will Act in conjuction, and use every Means to forward the salt and spirits
Frame 1130.

Peter Colt was the Deputy Commissary General of Purchases for the Eastern Department,

Blaine to Anthony Broderick

Sir, Camp 20th November 1777
I received Yours p[er] M^r. Finn and am greatly Oliged to You for being so Industrious as you have in forwarding beef Cattle, hope You will have it in Your power to procure a great Number More which request you will forward by every Opportunity, you mention your Purchasing Stall fed Cattle but will be Obliged to give a higher price, you have my Approbation to advance a little more, buy none in Common but such as is good passable beef—I hope will have it in your power to salt up a great Quantity of Pork, you must not exceed four pounds p hundred and as much under as you can possibly purchase, from 12/6 to fifteen Shillings for good Pork barrells, this is the price generally fixed with the Coopers,—I am not a Judge at so great a Distance what you ought to give for good Hay The Customary price by the Quantity in Your Neighbourhood and Your own Judgement must Direct you in this Matter I have given M^r. Finn directions where you are to apply for salt, when you are prepared to salt Pork, great care must be taken not to Waste the salt at the same time You must run no Riskue in curing Properly. allow half a bushell of the strong Coarse will be quite sufficient, and have Stinted my Assistant Purchasers to that Quantity, will use every Method in my power to procure a Quantity of salt sufficient to lay up pork equal to the Demand we may have next summer—have sent [writer's blank] thousand Dollars which must do with for the present, let me hear from Your by every Opportunity

shall expect a drove of Cattle Weekly from you. am sir Your Most Humble servant
Frame 1131.

Anthony Broderick was an Assistant Commissary of Purchases, based at Sussex, New Jersey.

Blaine to Joseph Hugg

Dear Sir,   Camp 20th November 1777
You cannot be two Active in Securing salt upon every Occasion as we Shall fall far short of a Quantity sufficient to supply our Magazines—The Unreasonable demands of the importers have Obliged me to write Congress and the Comissary General to fix a price, the express had not yet returned as soon as I receive advice from them shall Inform you the news from your side the Water this Evening if it shou'd be confirmd is very Disagreeable, but I have hope its not so (I mean the Evacuation of Fort Mercer—
I make no doubt you will have a great deal of trouble, but hope with the Assistance of Mr Morris & your brother you will be able to surmount all Difficulty and put it out of the power of our Enemys to reap any advantage from our labours,—I hope the Majority of the good People in your Neighbourhood will freely Assist in driving off all their fatt Cattle Hoggs and Sheep, and dispose of the same with Chearfulness to you, shou'd they fail in this the approbation of your legislative Authority with your own power, and some good Active Man to put in execution, will enable you to procure a large Quantity of Pork, god knows where will be proper places to erect Magazines, must leave that to your own—General Green with his whole Division & Colonel Morgan with the regiment of riffle Men are Marched this Morning to your Assistance youl please delay sending any more Cattle, as I am of opinion you will want them there, let me hear from you by every Opportunity & am D^r. Sir your $\&^c$ $\&^c$

John Chaloner to Casper Graff

Sir,   November 22 1777
The Bearer M^r. John Magee is appointed to succeed Mr Jacob Shallus as Issuing Comissary for the Magazine at Lancaster. The cause

of his being Superceded is want of attention to his business and neglect of Advising the D C G of the state of his Magazine—Those deficiencies I hope and believe will be amply removed by the Assiduity of M^r. Magee—I have only to request that You will use your utmost endeavours to assist M^r. Magee in forwarding the necessary supplies for Camp, advise M^r. Blaine D C G of Purchases at head Quarters or myself of your transactions, do your Utmost to procure flour and Whiskey, and by no means let the Issuing Comissary want either of those Articles to forward to Camp resting assured that through the Joint endeavours and Assiduity of Mr Magee & yourself we shall have more constant and regular supplies from your District I remain sir
Yours &
Frame 1132.

This was probably Sebastian Graff, an Assistant Commissary of Purchases at Lancaster, Pennsylvania.

John Chaloner to William Buchanan

Sir Camp November 24th. 1777
Yours p[er] M^r. Sprowl to M^r. Blaine was handed to me this day at noon, I must now inform you that three of Colonel Blaines Assistant Purchasers Azariah Nehemiah Dunham & Anthony Broderick was obliged to return home without Cash after waiting a full Weeke. They declare it is out of their power to continue purchasing and give but little expectation of doing the Services they are appointed to without punctual and regular payments I hope You will enable Colonel Blaine or myself to send the needfull to them in a few days—I have this moment received a pressing Letter from Joseph Hugg late of Gloucester on the same subject, he is with our Army now at Mount Holly. Colonel Blaine is Gone into the Jerseys where he expected a large sum of money to be forwarded to him, but am now without 40 Dollars I enclose You a Letter from M^r. Colt of New haven received by Colonel Blaine a few days past, he himself was favoured with one from that Gentleman advising his acceptance & too which he has fuly answered p[er] Return of Express—No supplies from him as yet—Great part of the Northern Army has Joined us—Our supplies of flour & Whiskey are by no means equal to our Consumption—The Brigades of which you inclosed a List of are all come to hand except two which where Loaded the 17th Instant—On which must observe that the

supplies the army as follows—Flour 5 1/2 days Whiskey 6 days this before the conjunction—All Resources here are now fully exhausted—and our sole Dependance Lancaster & York. The Issuing Comissary at the former is superceded for his neglect of duty; & hope for the future to receive some Assistance from thence, which has hitherto render'd very little—I am sorry to trouble you on a subject that I know does not belong to your department but I hope the Complaints that have been made to his Excellency already & the prospect of their increasing will plead my excuse when I beg it as a favour that you urge the Issuing Comissary to be more Industrious and vigilant. The Teams proceed for the Eastward are now mostly on their way there If with their Assistance we fail of supplies how shall we Shift when deprived of them If Colonel Stewart is also gone to the Eastward

PS Yours of the 6th Ins^t came to hand this moment Shall present it to Colonel Blaine on his return here the Scarcity of flour and the extravagant prices the people of this province demand for it, will assuredly render it necessary as well as prudent to forward all the Bread & flour that can be brought to Elk by water Carriage—In the Jersey they demand 35/ for flour and in this State 80/—The fixing of the ration is a matter well worthy the attention of Congress the Nothern troops has been accustomed to receive 1 1/4 lb flour 1 1/4 Beef & still look for it some others 1 lb flour 1/2 beef & others again 1 lb each this Creates uneasiness and difficulty
Frame 1132

Chaloner to Unidentified

Sir,   November 28th 1777
       The Bearer has deliver'd the Cattle sent by him shall be glad you would purchase and forward all You can procure; those sent are rather small and thin could wish them better.—No news worth communicating am Sir Your very Hble Servt
Frame 1133.

Blaine to Mr. Forman

Sir,   Trenton 29th November 1777
       You must obtain Monthly returns of the Rations Issued by the Quarter Masters then have them Certified by the Commanding Officer of

the Militia before Your Acc^{ts}. will pass, make no doubts You have furnished those persons with the provisions You have Charg'd, You will also allow those persons ought to render an Acc^t how they have disposed of them. General Forman has no Authority to appoint a Comissary of Purchases, nor have you any Right to continue your purchases without an appointment from Colonel Joseph Hugg of West Jerseys or Azariah Dunham Esqr of Morris Town who are regularly Appointed purchasers of live Stock
Frame 1133.

Forman was at Shrewsbury, N.J.

Chaloner to Blaine

Sir, November 30 1777
I now send p[er] the Bearer M^r. Sprowl 91,000 Dollars a part of 124,000 received Yesterday from M^r. Buchanan—I have distributed it as you Ordered in proportion to the sums Received each mans part as follows—
    Anthony Broderick   5 Quire 16250
    Az^{im}. Dunham   8 Quire 26000
    E Blaine   15 D^o. <u>48750</u>
        91,000
The Residue I have kept for our use at home only to Add. that M^r. Buchanan is here impatiently wait^g. Your Return, and that the residue of Your order will come on as soon as Congress has it in their power to forward it—I am Sir Yours & &
Frame 1133.

Chaloner to James Paxton

Sir, November 30th 1777
    The Bearer is sent to meet M^r. Blaine as also to carry to him a Sum of Money he expected to be with You about this time. Should he be absent shall take it as a particular favor you will receive the Money from him and return it for his Order—I should not have troubled You in this Occasion but the uncertainty of Meeting with Mr White will I hope sufficiently apologize—I am Sir Yours & &
Frame 1133.

James Paxton was the Assistant Commissary of Issues at Trenton, New Jersey.

Chaloner to Anthony Broderick

Sir,   November 30th 1777
 I have dispatched the bearer with 16,250 Dollars this is only part of the sum intented for you, but as Congress could not conveniently comply with Colonel Blaines order hope this will arrive in time to enable You to proceed without injury to forward supplies, By the person who Conducts the next drove of Cattle from you shall send a further sum if you think proper to ordert it I am Sir Yours & &
Frame 1134.

Chaloner to Unidentified

Sir,   December 1st 1777
 Colonel Buchanan Comissary General have seen your note to me of this day—In answer thereto he desires me to inform you that from the date of the Acc^t.—he conceives General Sullivans division to have been at that time within the reach of the magazine at Camp—consequently could not be under the necessity of employing a person extrodinary to Collect provision he can pay no person for services in purchasing but those regularly appointed under him agreable to the Resolves of Congress, he further Observes that from the Acc^t presented by M^r. Wright A C of Issues, It does not appear what services Mr Moore has done nor does Mr Wright acknowledge the Rec^t. of or make himself accountable for any provision Rec^d. from Mr Moore which prevents him from making a settlement agreeable to the Resolves of Congress I am Sir Your hble Servt
Frame 1134.

Blaine to Anthony Broderick

Sir   Camp 2nd. December 1777
 You will try to procure a brigade of Waggons which load with flour to be sent to New Windsor There to Exchange their loading for salt, which the Comissary at that place will deliver to Your Order, such

quantitys as you want for salting pork Keep for that purpose, you must exert yourself in Procuring all the Pork you possibly can which have collected in the most Convenient places near the Magazine for salting up—a sufficient number of coopers must be engaged to make Pork barrels, loose no time in forwarding beef cattle, I am Sir Your Hble Servant
Frame 1134.

Chaloner to Joseph Hugg

Dear Hugg December 3th 1777
Business being so exceedingly throng at present owing to the arrival of a Little money that neither Colonel Blaine nor myself can possibly meet you as he promised in order that you may share of our fatigues Colonel Blaine has sent you p[er] the Bearer 18,000 Dollars— which please to receive and acknowledge the Same—The bearer of this has charge of a Number of Waggons destined for Egg harbour 15 to be loaded with Country made Salt for the present use of the Army in order to save the foreign, for preserving meat, Youll give the necessary instructions for facilitating this business to render the rout as agreeable as possible to the bearer who has Charge of the Teams for that purpose I am Sir Your.
Frame 1135.

Unidentified to Unidentified

Gentleman Camp December 4th 1777
Being desirous to exert the duties to which we are severally appointed agreeable to the Resolves of Congress for the Regulating the Comissaries department and anxious to discharge to trust reposed in us without injuring Private Persons or their property induces us to lay before You the following difficulties that have order'd—
Light Dragoons and Scouting parties being frequently detach'd from the grand Army for several are sometimes from inconveniently owing to the distance of their Journeys from Camp the time of their absence and at other times from the neglect of duty in which obliges the proper Officers without provision & the Soldiers from necessity to beg of the Inhabitants. The Officers commanding such detachments have been Accustomed to

give the persons supplying the troops with Provisions, Certificates, setting forth the Number of Men supplied with Breakfast, others Dinner & Suppers, as the case may be The Inhabitants expecting and [Rest Missing]
Frame 1135.

Chaloner to Blaine

D^r. Sir

Yours p[er] M^r. Hackett came to hand at one OClock have detained him for M^r. Jones's return from head Q^{rs}. where he went in consequence of a summons he recd from Capt. Gibbs to attend that instant—he is now return'd and the summons was in Consequence of his Excellency not being supplied with good flour, I heartily wish Aston may be successfull in his searches after that article—I have read the diff^t. Letters & resolve of shall say nothing thereon untill I see you—The prospect of supplies is by no means equal to the Consumption especially Whiskey; this morning there was only 4 Hhds in Store—and several of the Major Gen^{ls}. ordered a double allowance in consequence of the Storm; we must no longer provide from day to day but lay up a Store convenient to the Army against a rainy day—I would advise a messenger to York Town for Cash—as also to reprimand the assistant purchases for there neglect of providing & the Issuers for their neglect of forwarding Such supplies as already procured Impress all the Whiskey in the province, and destroy the Sutlers (whom all allow to be a nuisance) otherwise the Genl. Orders for Issuing a Jill of Liquor p[er] Day cannot be complied with—The Issuing Commissaries of every Brigade making application for Whiskey this day have been refused & order'd to seize the Sutlers to supply their wants—I have heard nothing of their Success, much fear assiduity will not be equal to the Sutlers Cunning every nerve that be exerted here, but this is NOT the place to depend on—Your authority Must extend further than the limits of the Camp or we are ruin'd we shall soon starve for want of Beef flour & advice Yours Sincerely.
PS Cook has not called agreeable to promise
Only 50 lbls. flour in Camp
Frame 1135.

Blaine to Unidentified

That nothing but the most pressing want of Salt in the departm^t. Assigned to your Memorialist (in which the grand American army has been long employ'd) prompted your memorialists to Order his Assistant Purchasers to seize all salt within their district—Your memorialists flatters himself he has a proper Idea of the risk of the importer and the encouragement necessary to be given. Merchants who adventure with patriotick views, on this principle he expected that a generous price form the publick would be satisfactory to the owners especially as the article taken was solely for the publick use. Your memorialist hopes for the legislative Authority of the state of Delaware to enable them to Secure and send forward to his Excellency Genl. Washingtons camp, The aforesaid salt as also all Fatt Cattle belonging to persons refusing to sell when Offer'd an addequate price.—Without your speedy aid and assistance in the premises, your memorialist is certain the Army will be greatley distress'd for the want of those articles, which is not in his power otherwise to procure—Your memorialist begs leave to subscribe himself—The Publick and your honors most Obedient Servant
Frame 1136.

Blaine to John Wilson

Sir,	Camp 8 December 1777
Am exceeding sorry to find Col^o. Hooper has thrown some difficulties in your way respecting the purchasing of Wheat and Flour indeed that mighty General Lissimo has taken the great man upon him in many instances—however request you may go on in your business, paying no regard to Col^o Hooper or his directions, taking all the Wheat and Flour you can meet with in your district agreeable to my directions without exceptions (only such as Col^o Hooper has taken and paid for) inclosed you have a Copy of his Excellencys orders to me for that purpose, shou'd you stand in need of Assistance make application to the most Convenient Commanding Officer of the Militia—engage as many Waggons as is necessary to remove Wheat from where you take it, to such Mills as undertake to grind for you, will it not be in your power to oblige the people you purchase from to carry their Wheat to the Mills, request you may without loss of time secure all you can, as there is a great Number of Waggons now upon there way to North River which you will have to load

(say 250,) I have sent you all the money I have for the present which is two thousand dollars upon my return from Yorke Town will assist you with more; the inclosed letter for Major Shenk Assistant Purchaser at Fish Kill or New Windsor you must forward by express, should you meet with no safe hand for Camp news, refer you to the Bearer, favour me with a line by every opportunity, and what progress you have made and am Sir Your Most Obd^t & Very Hble Servant
Frame 1136.

Wilson was a purchaser in Sussex County, New Jersey.

Blaine to Henry Schenk

Sir,   Camp Decem^r. 8 1777
      Inclosd youl receive a Letter from M^r. Buchanan Com^y General respecting the purchasing of Flour in Ulster & Orange Counties, to forward to the Eastward, you will please to make enquiry & Secure all you possibly can, of which youl answer the Com^y Gen^{ls}. letter & mine by the Return of the Express, a large number of Waggons are on their way to the North River for Salt, which Congress have ordered to be Loaded with Flour, Sundry Disappointments & so large an Army as I have to Feed puts it out of my power to Load above One Third of them from this quarter, therefore the Com^y Genl requests You will use your influence to the residue, should you not be able to accomplish it, please to Correspond with Mr Willson my Assi^t. Purchaser at Hackets Town who has instructions from me to forward, the residue of the Flour you cant make up to Compleat the Loading of the returning Waggons which has brought forward the Salt from the Eastward try you near the North River shall be glad to hear from you & am Sir Your hum^l Servt.
Frame 1137.

Henry Schenk or Shenk was an Assistant Commissary of Purchases at Fishkill, N.Y.

Blaine to Unidentified

Sir,   Camp 9th December 1777
      If M^r. Pollock comes in a few Days, you can fix it so that he will have Charge of all the Continental cattle, would advise him as soon as he

can Settle his Accom[ts]. with M[r]. Swain to discharge him, you will fix Matters so as employ George Kitts, & Conrad Huff to Secure all the midling Beef Cattle & Pork they can meet with, such persons as are well Dispos'd, agree with them at a certain price to be paid either in Cash or Pork again, they must make no Exception where such may be in the power of the Enemy except persons are moving off from the Enemy, Write pressingly to the Assis[ts]. purchasers for Regular Supplies of Beef Cattle, which I hope they will pay due attention to, be assured I shall use every Measure to forward Flour, Whiskey & Beef Cattle from Lancaster, York, & Carlisle, upon my arrival there Write me by every opportunity & how you are for Supplys, I hope M[r]. Ashton will have it in his power to forward you large Supplys of Flour, the Salt which is coming from Egg Harbour must be disposd of at Such places as Magazines are fix'd, only a Sufficientcy for three weeks or a month for Camp Consumption for Col Jones. part must be sent to Easton. I am Sir Your hum[l] Serv[t].
Frame 1137.

Blaine to Unidentified

Sir,

The Season is now arrived for the procuring of Pork for the army, the demand for which is and will be so great, that you cannot procure to much, You must by no means suffer a single fatt Hogg to escape you— The Scarcity of Beef will Require your utmost exertions in prosec[g]. this business—and I flatter myself at the end of the season You will have safely cured 2,000 Barrels. If possible to obtain more do it—You must govern yourself as to price at Ten Dollars p[er] Cwt it being so fixed by the Comissary Gen[l] of Purchases unless the legislative authority of your State Should order otherwise. provided you find the people disposed to Keep their Hoggs rather than part with them at the price above, and the Season likely to pass over without obtaining any, in that case you will advance to four pounds p[er] Cwt—I am convinced that a great part of your time will be taken up in executing this important and necessary business. Never the Less you must by no means neglect or suffer to be neglected the purchasing of Beef within your District. forward to Head Quarters all you can possibly procure.—I shall expect from you in a very short time a drove—In order to render the taking in of Pork more easy to yourself and convenient to the inhabitants of your district you will employ persons as

are necessary fixing them to such places as you may Judge they will be most wanted, in this you must have a view to the Security & safety from the enemy, as well as the plenty of Swine. procure all the Pork barrels you possibly can get at 12 or 15/ each. if more is to be had than what you will want for your district, secure them & advise me that I may dispose of them in season. You inform me that you can purchase a quantity of Peas & Beans—If they are to be had reasonable you may purchase all that offers advising me of your progress.
Frame 1137.

Blaine to Unidentified

Gentleman
    You will immediately proceed from hence to the Neck of Land now between the lines of the Enemys and our troops and there collect all the Beef and pork in and adjacent to that Country. In executing this business you must be exceedingly carefull not to leave any Cattle or Hoggs behind you, more than what will be necessary for the support of the families who possess them. And in order to prevent their falling into the Hands of the Enemys all milch Cows Heffers Steers &^{c} &^{c} &^{c} that are fit for Meat must be brought off, and sent to the Army for immediate use. Hoggs must be sent to the Trapp where you must fix somebody to receive and salt them for winters Consumption. after taking of the Hoggs and Stock in the Country above described you will extend your views as high up as Trenton ferry and across the Country to potts grove, keeping on a line from Philadelphia at or about the distance of 30 or 40 Miles. You'll pay for the same to the owners thereof as follows: 75/ p[er] Cwt and pork 52/6 p[er] Cwt. any person unwilling to receive pay for any thing you may take from them, in that case You'll give them Receipts spacifying the Qu^y. and Qua^y. directing them to the Commissary Genl. for paym^t. In all things you are to Conduct yourself agreeable to the Resolve of the General Assembly of this State: Copy of which you have annex'd for your better Gover^t. I shall add nothing further, but rely in your Industry hope soon to see every temptation to draw the enemy out after provision Removed. and this Resolve of Assembly faithfully executed
Frame 1138.

Blaine to Azariah Dunham

Dear Sir,   Camp 10th December 1777
The daily consumptions of beef is so great must Request every exertion in your power to procure that necessary Article so much wanted for the support of the Army, I have great Hope from the Weekly purchasers you will make and a drove which is to come from the Eastward, that we Shall have large Weekly supplies from you, I set out from Camp to Morrow Morning and shall be absent some time, on Which Acc^t beg you may send all Assistance you possibly can—You may send for a supplie of Cash about the 20th Instant as I shall forward a large sum from York Town, and give directions to M^r. Chaloner howe to distribute it;—My dear Friend I need not Inform you how large our Magazines ought to be with salt pork and every other species of Provisions this Winter for the supplies of the Army the ensuing Year, be Assured without flattery I have great expectations from you as one of my principle purchases, therefore shall drop that subject.
General Howe with his Whole Army lay in view of us three Days, its said he come out with a Determination to fight Genl. Washington and drive him from the Heights of Wight Marsh, however he has thought prudent to Return without making the Attempt, there has been a Considerable skrimishing on both sides our principle loss of Officers is Genl. Irvin wounded and taken prison^r. and Major Morris of Col^o. Morgans Riffle Reg^t. Dangerously wounded, but not prisoner; and several other Subaltern Officers—Shall be glad to hear from you by Every Opportunity and am Dear Sir Yours & & &
Frame 1138.

Blaine to Joseph Hugg or Israel Morris

Dear Sir   Camp 10th Decr. 1777
The Numorouse Army are daily fed upon beef makes the demand of that article very great—upon receipt of this request you may forward by droves to camp all the beef Cattle you possibly can, we have not more than Six days provisions on hand, therefore beg you to be expeditious in forwarding and pray dont neglect purchasing every of the Horned Kine fit for present use, as we shall be in great want of them—and if you and the Assistant purchases do not Exert yourself the army must suffer as I Shall be absent from Camp some time, entreat you to use double Diligence in

forwarding all cattle you can—you may expect a supply of cash about the 20th Instant as my Intentions is to forward a large sum by express from York Towne, upon my arrival there—M[r]. Chaloner will give you early advices of his Necessities for Provisions—am well informed great Numbers of beef Cattle still Remain unsold in your State, pray favour me with a line by the first safe Opportunity and am Gentleman Your & & Frame 1139.

Ephraim Blaine to Unidentified

Dear Sir   Pawlings Neck 11th at Night 1777

M[r]. Campbell and Burner informs me great quantities of old Wheat is in their Neighbourhood, wish some method cou'd be immediately to collect it, information will be given the persons name, Col[o]. Nixon also informs one of his Neighbours has several hundreds of which he will inform, in case M[rss]. Byard shou'd move from where she now lives, She has a Quantity of Wheat and Pork which take and pay her the Customary price, shall write you from great Valley and Lancaster, and forward you every supply in my power, my respects to Col[o]. Jones and family and am Sir. Your Obed[t]. Hbl. Serv[t]
Frame 1139.

Ephraim Blaine to Unidentified

Sir,   Camp 12th Dec[r].

You must immediately proceed through your District and Secure all the Wheat and Flour you possibly can, engage with proper Millers at such distances as the may not interfer with each Others purchases allowing them to pay Eight Shillings and Sixpence p[er] bushell for Sixty pounds Weight, you are to agree With them in the Following Manner, for good Flour twenty two Shillings and Sixpence, pence, per Midlings Eighteen, and Ship Stuff twelve, an exemption of coopers from Military duty sufficient to make Flour and Pork barrells will be all[d] of, for which purpose you have the Resolves of the Assembly with this you will Receive advertisements which have distributed at the Mills in your District, requesting all those who have any Wheat to Spare to thrash without delay to answer the immediate demands of the Army, and which will be the

means of saving us the trouble of using military force—employ proper persons at the most suitable places to receive pork and beef, giving for Pork 52/6 p[er] Cwt, and beef ten dollars p[er] Cwt W^t you will also Observe that you have by the Resolves of Assembly which must be your direction upon every Occasion you will Receive a proportion of the salt coming from Egg harbour in a few days which Distribute among those Persons you Employ allowing half a Bushell of Salt to every barrell of Pork, the persons, you engage to purchase Salt Pork ought to be Men Active & well dispos'd whose pay shall be Commissions at two & a half p[er] Cent & a small allowance of expence when Oblig'd to travel thro his District, those persons to have instructions to stop all Forestallers and Seize all pork & Beef by them purchased, you have the Authority of Congress to impress Waggons when the Service requires it, Your Flour must be forwarded to Head Quarters or such places as Col Jones or Chaloner may instruct you from time to time—You will purchase all the Merchantable Whiskey you can giving 8/6 pr $Gall^n$ for the same, all those who are not Willing to sell seize the same as it is much wanted for the Army. I wish you great Success & am Sir Your very hum^l $Serv^t$.
Frames 1140.

Chaloner to Unidentified

Sir,
    Yours to M^r. Blaine was Deliver'd to me this morning by M^r. Campbell, who has been detain'd here longer than I expected; or could have wish'd for owing to the Movement of the two Armies; he brings you an order for Thirty Thousand Dollars—as M^r. Blaine will be at Carlisle the Messenger who goes to York may easily procure an order for more if wanted.—
    The Waggons you mention, Loaded with Bread, Beef, & Spirits are not as yet arriv'd, they are articles much wanted, & should be glad you will do your utmost Endeavours to forward all you can; especialy of Bread & Beef. You may purchase any Quantity of Wheat you can procure at 8/6 p[er] bushell $weigh^g$. 60. get the same ground. The flour forward to camp, the Shebstuf baked into bread, and the Bran & Shorts dispose of on the best terms you can: giving the Q^r. Master and Forage M^r. the prefference: or if the Millers will purchase the Wheat & deliver the Flour at 22/6 it would be more preferable. I remember at Wilmington Capt Black call'd on

me to Remove a large Q^{ty}. of flour purchas'd by you, hear since the enemy has not destroyed it. If it be not spoil'd pray forward it as expeditiously as possible, I will expect from you 200 barrels flour by this day week and that Q^{ty}. or more Weekly: You cannot send to much Write to the Q^r. Master for Waggons who must by no means disappoint you. If he should, you have Authority to impress them yourself must request you will forward all the Beef you can possibly obtain. for news refer you to the bearer and remain Sir. Your very hble. Servt
Frame 1140.

Blaine to John Chaloner

My Dear Friend M^r. Cheneys 13th Decr. 1777
      Last night I fell in with two Brigades of Waggons above this loaded with Flour which have hurried off this Morning the Moment they onload order them back to this place to be loaded with Flour, with what Captain Weed has will have sufficient to load twenty Waggons—I have appointed Col^o. W^m. Evans Assistant Commissary of Purchases he appears a Stanch Whig, have given him such instructions if put in execution, as will render you esential Service, hope he will have it in his power to send you a great Quantity of Flour,—though I have been so long Absent from a Dear and Affectionate Wife and every temptation to induce me to be there, a House which afford peace & plenty and tur lauley loys, [sic] yet be Assured for my own Reputation and your peace will sacrifice those enjoyments a few days to forward you every aid in my power, you will hear of me doing great things in the Neighbourhood of Paveaslin, mean to take in a person capable of the Mineese Party who has great influence and will have it in his po[wer] to procure large Quantities of Wheat, as also Whiskey, which I hope the soldiers will be so surfeited with it as will make it as Disagreeable as the Stinking fish.
      I hope you left our Host and his Dear and affect^e. Wife well suppose there was many tender Night in parting With You more especially on Acc^t the pretty little Major, I feel for the poor Woman—Shall write you from Lancaster more particular and am Gentleman Your Most & very Hble. Servt
Frame 1141.

Blaine to Sebastian Graff

Sir,   Lancaster 15th Decr. 1777

    Without loss of time you will please to proceed through District and procure all the Beef Cattle Pork and Whiskey you Possibly can giving the Following prices for the present Viz for good Beef sinking the Fifth Quarter four pounds p[er] Ct weight Pork four pounds p[er] Ct, and Whiskey Eight Shillings and six per Gallon or what ever price the President Council or Assembly may fix hereafter, wou'd Recommend you to fix some persons near the lower part of this County—Adjoining Cicil to purchase Pork Am inform'd Considerable Quantities, is in that Neighbourhood, whose pay shall be Commissions on what he may procure let the person you Appoint be a prudent Active Man who you can intrust with Money for that purpose, as I mean to fix a Magazine at Middleton and appoint some person to Superintend it, to take in all the Pork which can be purchas'd up Susquehanah and Juniata River you will be saved the trouble of sending or going up in that Country to purchase what Beef you can procure in two [ ] Weeks must be immediately salted down, using great care not to Waste but a little of the salt, you must use the Country Made salt for that purpose, as we shall want all the imported for Pork, I wish you great Success in Your Purchases & am Sir. Your Very Hble Servt
Frame 1141.

Blaine to Unidentified

Sir   Lancaster 15th. Decr. 1777

    Without loss of Time you will Please to engage with proper Millers at such Distances as may not interfer with each other purchases—for wheat 8/6 p[er] bushell allowing sixty pounds weight, or such other price as may be fixed by the president Council or Assem^y. and in proportion for Flour, the Millers be paid forty shillings p[er] ton for grinding & packing—the Ship Stuff Bran &^{c} to be delivered to the Q^r. Masters taking his Rec^t. for such Quantities as may be delivered from time to time, an exemption of coopers from Military duty sufficient to make Flour and Pork Barrels will be Allowed of—with this you will receive advertisements which have been distributed, at the Mills in your district, requesting all those who have any Wheat to spare, to thrash without delay to answer the immediate demand of the Army, and which will be the

means of saving me the trouble of applying for and using Military Force, such persons as willingly bring in what Quantities of Wheat they have to spare, to such Mills as the purchasing Commissary shall order, may be Assured General Washingtons protection for the Residue
Frame 1141.

John Chaloner to Unidentified

Dear Sir   Decr 16 1778 [sic]
    No doubt M^r. Buchanan in his way home ward you of our distress for the want of flour we have been fed from hand to mouth for several days past and the demand are now got a head of us at present we are without one barrell of flour & have been 10 or 20 hours hope to receive some aid from you to day If we cannot procure supplies of flour so as to establish magazines at or near the Camp it is impossible but the army must suffer and the Reputation of all concern'd in the Vict^g. department will fall a sacrifice to the indolence and indulgence of some individuals. I thank you for your late supplies & hope you'll continue to send us greater plenty—I am in the utmost distress for want of Provisions for the Army Dr Sir Your very Hble Servant
Frame 1142.

John Chaloner to Peter Aston

D^r. Uston   Camp Gulp Decr. 17th 1777
    Yours of the 15th & 16th was handed to me Yeste^y. observe what you say with Respect to taking of Pork. I would advise You strictly to Adhere to the instructions giving advising timely of the difficulties; and by no means vary untill you are ordered so to do: I expect the cry of the people When they see that the publick are determined not to advance their price and monopolizers are discourag'd by the legislative Authority. As to Magazines, and the No. of them you must be the best Judge, and in which your Authority is discretional. after thanking you for your services and your timely supply of flour I must call on you to continue your diligence and increase the q^{ty} four fold—if possible do more and by no means Slacken untill you are told from us it is enough, Sett two or three Brigades of Teams in the Service and keep them Constantly driving to head

Quarters—Could wish you would employ some other person to aid for Wheat and not hinder the Waggon M^r &^{c} &^{c} with his Teams must return with flour immediately, at his arrival we had not one bll of flour. I have done the Needfull for Mr Funks cooper should he not be return'd shall call the Officer to Acc^t. You mention that you have procured a place for my Horse but neglect to inform the terms and with whom. shall be glad to know this before I send him. Receive my thanks for your attention to my Affairs but more so for your steady perseverance in behalf of the publick. I am Dr Aston Yours &c &c.

NB Direct the teams to cross Shulkill at the flatland or Pawlings ford as we move this day for the Valley Forge—
Frame 1142.

Blaine to Chaloner

Dear Sir, Cave 20th Decr. 1777
    I came home the 18th. much Fatigued & used every method in my power to Forward provisions hope by this you have a plentiful supply of Flour as the Quarter Master at Lancaster assured me he wou'd Forward all the waggons in his power,—the Assistant purchasers have not been able to procure One Gallon Whiskey at the limited price, I have made application to M^r. Buchanan to adopt some Method to procure Whiskey as the army will much want it this Severe Season, which hope with the Assistance of Congress he will do, nor can my Assistants purchase one barrell of Pork at the limitation, therefore Tom Will and Hary must be served before the army and we shall never have a plentiful supply till the purchasers for the Army have the regulating of the Market which have but little hopes as yet under present appearances, While the spirit of exortion prevails so much with the farmers, the Commissary Genl. studying to reduce their unreasonable and very extravagant Demands the purchasers restricted in their prices the supplys coming in very slow those Circumstances will bring the army to want. I have wrote M^r. Buchanan to Forward you immediately One hundred and fifty thousand Dollars inclos'd you have a list how to pay it, or rather leave you to Judge the payments agreeable to them rendering you supplys and the Demand, do not stop at Ninety Shilling[s] p[er] hundred for good beef and Pork when in your offer, favour me with a line informing where and what place you are

Quartered in and if our army means to pass the winter there my Kind respects to Friend Jones and the family believe me Dear Sir Yours & &
Frame 1147.

Chaloner to Peter Colt

Sir, $\qquad$ Decr 21th. 1777

Col^o. Blaines absence from Head Quarters for some time past and not expecting his return for some days lays me under the necessity of writing you on the subject of supplies from your quarter

On your accepting the appointment of D.C.G. of Purchases for the Eastern department Col^o Buchanan flatter'd himself that you would have been able to send to Head Q^{rs} several hundred head of Cattle p[er] Week—but in this your Assistants have been far Short, I must inform you, that the Consumption of Beef Cattle in this department exceeds 200 head p[er] day that there is little or no Beef to be purchas'd it being already used by the army, consequently our dependance in future will be entirely on you for that article, should your supplies not increase three fold very speedily; we must break on the little quantity of salted Pork we have been able to collect here; the consequence of which will be fatal—Col^o. Blaine expected to have Rec^d. several droves from you weekly of 100 each instead of which they are brought on by 40 and sometimes less. this is certainly adding to the expence & the retard^g. the supplies as the difference between bringing on 40 and 100—is little more than that of foddering The procuring of fodder will I hope be more easily obtain'd in future as I understand Magazines of forage are establish^d at Pitts Town, Sussex Court house and New Winsor.

My troubling you with this letter solelye arises from my anxiety in Col^o. Blaines absence, and want stareing us in the face which I hope will induce you, not only to excuse this free^m. but to throw in an immediate supply I am Sir Yours & &
Frame 1143.

Chaloner to Henry Miller

Sir,
  You being appointed to the Command of the Detachment ordered out this day. I take the liberty of informing you the rout of the Country in which you are to proceed. From hence you will go to Downingstown and extend your people as low as Concord Road including the forks of Brandywine and as far South and East as may be thought prudent, the situation of the Enemy must govern you in this respect. The instructions you will receive from the Adj^t. General on this subject is so full and particular that I have little or nothing to ad Col^o. Evans of Chester County Ass^t. Comm^y of Purc^s. will accompany you and as he is acquainted with the Country will be capable of advising you in this business. he will inform what mills are to be employ'd and where the grain when thrash'd to be hall'd to be manufactor'd into Flour he will have with him proper persons for collecting cattle and hogs to whom also you will please to give necessary aid and Assistance if wanted—I heartily wish you may be able to compleat this business so as to answer the purposes of the army with satisfaction to yourself and all concerned—Shall be glad to hear from you p[er] every oppo and remain Sir. Yours & &
Frame 1143.

Miller was Major of the First Pennsylvania Regiment.

Chaloner to Unidentified

Sir
  The want of flour has been so great and distressing in Camp to induce his Excellency to Issue orders for several detachments to go in the Country to compell the unwilling to thrash their grain that it may be manufactred into flour for the immediate use of the Camp, Copy of the Genl orders as far as it related to your district you have herewith
  I must request of you to accompany Major Miller who is appointed to the command of the several Detachments within your District you will point out to him in the Country that will best afford an immediate supply of grain and inform him what Mills you think most proper to set to work for us, you will at the same time do all in your power to prevail on the farmers within your district to thrash their Wheat Show them the Gen^{ls}. order respecting this Matter—assure them the Genl. is seriously

concernd that he is reduced to the necessity of compelling, but the army must not suffer it will not suffer Let what will be the Consequence. Youll be exceedingly carefull to have the flour as fast as made brought to Camp day by day let none remain in the Mills if possible 12 hours. a number of teams a detach'd with Major Mille[r's] party those you will employ so as to collect the grain and bring on flour to Camp in the most speedy and expeditious manner possible Should they not be sufficient for this purpose Apply to Major Miller to impress teams for this Service he will supply parties to execute and complete your requisitions—Conrad Hooff will accompany you he is a good Judge of Cattle and wish you to employ him in this business he will go where ever you direct and bring off Cattle and Hoggs

  For every article seized or taken, the owners may be Assurd that they will be paid a full and generous price as much as is allow^d. by Law— You will advise me as often as conveniency and Oppo^y. will admit of your progress in this business Assure the Farmers that a dispi^n. and readiness to part with their grain &^{c} provisions will not only be agreeable to his Excell^y. but will prevent his pursuing more rigorous measures which he undoubtedly will unless they on their part prevent It. I wish you success and am sir Your Very Hble Servant
Frame 1144.

Chaloner to John Campfield

Sir,   Head Q^{rs}. December 21st. 1777
  Inclosed you have a letter from Peter Colt Esqr. as the subject of which materially concerns you have sent it open for your perusal after which please to seal & forward as expeditiously as possible hope you will have it in your power to send Cattle more speedily and in larger droves than of late otherwise the army must suffer there not being sufficient in this department to support them one Month I am Sir Yours &c &c.
Frame 1147.

Chaloner to Blaine

Dear Sir,
I wrote you on the 20th Instant p[er] Express going from Col^o. Mifflins Quarters to Yorktown since which nothing material has occur'd The same reason for complaint still continues no supplies of Cattle as Yet come on the army clamoring hourly sending complaints to His Excellency and we have nothing to remedy or remove the cause Consequently we must suffer the Censure of His Excellency, and tho hard as this is it will be well should it stop here. We are now without one beast a live and am in debt to the troops some one day and others two of Beef what will be the fate of to morrow I know not. Inclos'd you have a Copy of complaint lodg'd with his Excellency and by him handed to Col^o. Stewart at the same time ordering him to attend to morrow Morning I could send you 1/2 Dozen of the same sort from Major Gen^{ls} & Brigadiers which as yet they have kept to themselves but Expect it all to be echoed to his Excellency in the most dismal manner to morrow. The fact is, our case is bad and owing to their sufferings being Real shall not obtain credit to any thing we may offer in our defence. Where is Smiths 1200 head of Cattle only one drove of Two hundred, and 3d come on Should they be as poor as those sent by him for Gods sake do not suffer them to come on they do more injury than Service. This day 44 head of Cattle was rec^d. from New England purchased by Reed and Campfield Extracts from each of their letters are as follows—If more Cattle should be wanted we will endeavor to send another Drove in Four or Five Weeks, you will please to let us know by M^r. Torrence the drover. The Purchasers for the Nothern departments have intefred and bought the live Beefs that we are not able to procure more yours &c.—Jno. Campfield—I shall only observe on the above Extract that the Bearer Mr Torrence says more may be easily purchased—Inclosed you have Copy of a letter from me to M^r. Colt I could wish to have said more to him on the subject but an convinced when you consider my station that you will be of opinion that I have said as much as I could with decency, this letter I enclos'd to Campfield open desiring him to peruse it & forward it to M^r. Colt as quick as possible—Col^o. Evans has been with me this day I beleive he would be able to procure some flour he has offered such prices as the Legislative of the state may affix for Wheat in doing which I have advis'd him to continue, he says there is no chance to procure Pork or Beef at the price. Kitts and Hoff are return'd not being able to do any thing sha[ll] send the one to Chester & Lancaster the other to Grahocken Kushahopen & that Neighbourhood where they both say

they can do something worthy of their time. Most of the flour from Lancaster is unfit for use and creates clamour hope Ludhwick will be able to manufactre it so as to render it more agreeable. I expected much from your presence at Lancaster & york but have had little from them since. The vast Consumption of Beef Cattle is owing to the diff^t rates of rations some 1 1/2 some 1 1/4 beef am surpris'd that a matter of that Conseq[uence] should be so neglected hope you'll do your utmost to have this matter regulated.

Decem^r. 22 1777 I delayd sending the Express in hopes to have had it in my power to have sent you something less alarming; instead of Which the Cloud thickens fast, the storm is gather'd to a greater pitch than ever known before, should be happy could I see but a prospect of its subsiding—I am in the most distress'd situation possible for man to be. Yours &c.

PS. The Express delay'd coming untill late in the evening yesterday which induced me to detain him in order to send you the result of A Board of Genl. Officers before whom Col^o Stewart Jones and myself had been summond to answer the Complaints of several Genl. Officers setting forth that their troops had been without provisions for three or 4 days—lucky for us that they advanced more than they can support, but we was obliged to confess that they had suffered and that we had nothing on hand nor no certainty of any thing within One or two days Journey of Camp to relieve their wants, this is the sad effects of not having a regular correspondence with all the Assistant Comissarys write them as often as you will no answer return'd and but little attention paid to the letters sent them—at my attendance on this Council I felt as I nor believe Man never felt before. Colonel Stewart only was admitted, who after a very long Conversation with the Genl. Officers they were reduced to the Necessity of executing his proposal Viz to send a Captain a Issuing Commissarys & twenty men from each Brigade to bring in from E. W. N. & South for 10 Miles distance a temporary supply Untill the fruit of their Labour is received the troops must suffer. Lucky for me Colonel Stewart was present, I may ad for you also, he being clear particularly as to the want of Beef and consuling their charges as to the want of Bread untill yesterday was able to face this Matter with a much better grace than I could have done our you had you been there—And for this reason facts were against us. Credit was given to his testimony, and the Genl. displeased at the Complaints and that they could not fully support their Charge however his Excellency declares that he will represent the matter to the Congress adding that all his plans have been disconcerted; attempt them he would for want of provision. that a large body of the Enemy marched into Spring field belo Chester the night before Easter[sic] that his Excellency had intelligence in the night of their move ordered the troops to draw two days provision and be in readiness to march that the provision could not be procured and all back on this Acc^t. is too true.

It being our duty to look and provide for the future admit the following supplies come to hand in the course of 5 days from the diff^t Guards sent out—150 head cattle or pork equivalent

    From Dunham   200
    From Smith   300
    From Huggins   300
    From Hugg   300
                     1150
From McGarmant   50
Consumption   1200 head ten days

where will more come from to succeed these, and here it is that I have no Assurance of any of the above being to be depended on Dunhams Hugg and the labour of this day excepted; have wrote Huggins by Express. Hugg left me Yesterday Dunham will be here to day or to morrow, & Smith can be informed thro you, so that they will all be acquainted with our want. and I heartily wish they may have it in their power to supply them but to Crown all our difficulties there. To you Sir who is so deeply interested in this important subject I need say no more—I wish not to distress you and have related the facts only shall exert myself and do all in my power to remedy our situation
Frames 1145-1146.

Chaloner to William Buchanan

Sir,   December 22^d 1777
Inclosed you have a letter to Col^o. Blaine the subject of which materially concerns the department and for which purpose have sent it open to you for perusal hope it will be forwarded without delay. I have ordered on what Pork is procured in Jersey to supply the present wants of the army, unless the Cattle purchasers send on more punctually We shall

be ruined. New England begins to cry out they are done as you will see by my letter inclosed I am Your Hble Servant
Frame 1147.

Chaloner to Unidentified

Sir,   Decr. 23^d. 1777
    Yours of the 16th was handed to me this moment I am exceedingly sorry it is not in my power to send you Cash—but am Assured shall be able to send the sum Request by the time you can possibly send or come forward with a drove—let me intreat You by no means to delay a single hour in bringing those you have collected to Camp and Ill answer for it that your wants of money shall be fully supplied I flatter myself that I shall have the pleasure of seeing you here in eight days by which time Colonel Blaine will also be here with his chest full I am Yours &^{c} &^{c}
Frame 1148.

Chaloner to John Patton

Sir,   Decr. 23 1777
    I have before me Mr Paines letter of 17th December and by it find that he was under the Necessity of Loading part of a Brigade of Teams sent to him by Colonel Jones with Q^r. Mr Tools instead of Provision—This indeed was mortifying and especially so as we have been call'd to Head Q^{rs}. to answer for the Sufferings of the Soldiers, who has been two days without Bread or Beef—We at the front bear all the blame—For Gods sake for your Countries sake exert yourself. I fear the department has suffered so much alredy that we shall never be able to retrieve our Credit—or be indulged to continue it longer. His Excellency was obliged to order out 16 parties to collect provisions. How oppressive this is you know well and as a Commissary of Purchas must sensibly feel. I am in distress Yours &
Frame 1148.

John Chaloner to Unidentified

Sir,
This serves to order immediately to forward to Head Quarters twenty Double Teams Loaded with Beef and Pork—If you have not received sufficient for that purpose from Bucklistown send of your own and advise me what you have on hand—I have seen receipt of yours to John Beacle of which the following is a Copy—
Received Flemington Decr. 18 1777 of John Beasle Waggon Master forty eight Barrels said to be pork not pickled which he says he bought from Bucklys Town for the use of the Army
Robert Dodd. Words so evasive (as said to be & he says) a Commissary of Purchases is by no means becoming the man of business & integrity, they at least betray negligence. You must in future satisfy yourself as to the Quantity and Quality of any thing you may receive, and hold yourself accountable for the delivery. by no means delay a single moment in Executing the above order as the Troops will want in a very few days. Yours & &
Frame 1148.

Chaloner to Thomas Wharton Jr. and Council

Gent^n Camp Valley Forge 24 Decr. 77
So great is the want of Beef and Bread in Camp that His Excellency has ordered out an Officer and 22 Men from Each Brigade in the Army to collect and send into Camp a Temporary supply they are now out in the Vicinity of the Camp, but this Country is drained and affords a very triffle—Another party will march tomorrow morning a greater distance & it is to be hoped be more successfull, this mode of collection provisions is very distressing to the Count^y. and by no means agreeable to his Excellency Yesterday last Night & this day about Seven Hundred Cattle are brought in by the Commissarys so that in Beef a Weeks allowance may now be depended on But flour is quite exhausted & Tho we know The Commissary General has a considerable quantity at Lancaster and York Town & Wrights ferry but a trifle has come in for many days, we have writ the different Commissarys to forward Flour from those Magazines their Answer is Waggons are not furnished by the Quarter Masters We beg your honour & the Executive Council to give

such Assistance to the Quarter Master as will enable him to furnish the Commissary at Lancaster with Teams sufficient to bring on 100 Barrels p[er] day from that Post which is most contiguous At present to our Camp one half that Quantity we have reason to think will come in from Jersey and the mills now here compelled to grind for us which will make good the daily consumption We beg your indulgence for application We are distressed beyond description and must in such cases apply to those whose power it is to Aid Us & we flatter ourselves it is in the power of the president & Council of the State to order Waggons sufficient to bring in the above supply daily We are with the greatest respect & Esteem
Frame 1149.

Wharton was President of the Supreme Executive Council of Pennsylvania. In effect he was the Governor and the Council his cabinet.

Chaloner to John Magee

Sir, December 24th 1777

By the Bearer we have sent Express to the Governor and Council writing them in the most pressing terms to Authorise & Empower the Q^r. Masters to furnish you with Teams to forward flour to Camp

For Gods sake for your countrys sake & yours & our reputation do exert Yourself or we all fall together—time will not Admit Us to Say more & obliges us to Conclude in a famishing situation Yrs & & A Hundred Bbls p[er] Day must come from you henceforward
Frame 1149.

Magee was an Assistant Commissary of Issues at Lancaster.

Chaloner to George Ross

Sir, December 24th 1777

By the Bearer we have sent an Express to the Governor and Council calling on them in the most pressing terms to give You aid & Assistance sufficient to Enable you to Impress teams to transport 100 Bbls of flour to Camp daily—We doubt not theyll readily do the Needfull—Our Necessities are such As obliges Us in the most pressing terms to Call on you to do your utmost to procure Teams without delay, As You regard

the support & union of the Army exert yourself We are in distress Yours & &c
Frame 1149.

George Ross was a Deputy Quartermaster at Lancaster, Pennsylvania.

Chaloner to George Kitts

M^r. George Kitts,
  You must immediately proceed with Captain Salen to Stadlers Tavern and from thence to Oley Pottsgrove, and the Neighbourood adjacent there collect all the fatt Beef Pork and Hoggs you can find leaving only such as may be necessary for their family. Captain Salen will supply you with a Guard to Assist where necessary. Give the people receipts estimating the Weight and assure them they shall be paid such prices as allowed by the law of this State. Exert yourself and forward all in your power. I wish you Success & remain
PS. Should you want Waggons you have authority to impress them get whatever Assistance you want and spare no pains or expences in procuring Cattle
Frame 1150.

George Kitts was a purchaser in the Commissary Department.

Blaine to Chaloner

Sir,   Carlile 26th December 1777
  I received yours the Evening from York Town M^r. Buchanan by some means forgot sending it with the other letters I am exceeding sorry for your Distressed Situation and have been one of the most Miserable Creatures Living since I received the Accounts of your Disagreeable wants, upon my way up used every arguments with the Quarters Masters of York and Lancaster they Assured me every Assistance of Waggons in their power, I have engaged sundry Mills in the Neighborhood of Lancaster to make Flour I have fallen upon every Method to procure Whiskey and hope to Accomplish it, that business Will delay me the day and to Morrow before I set out for Camp, I expect by to morrow noon to load three Brigades half with Whiskey the Other Flour and hope M^r

Buchanan will do as much at York Town, I wrote him some days past very pressingly upon that Subject—as to Beef Cattle a Drove or two may be purchased through the winter of Stall'd and all that Smith has fit for us are now upon their way to Camp say Four hundred head to Providence. We must depend for Winter beef and that will go but a very little way with the Army god only knows how they are to subsist. I am not Disappointed in the Accounts from Eastward for always had my doubts respecting those persons rendering their Supplys, though the army are in the greatest Distress for want of the Necessarys of life yet M^r. Buchanan will not be convinced but there are a great plenty in the Country and holds to the old prices.

I have sent Mr Pollock down with this and to carry what money the treasurey Office can advance to him for Your Acc^t. & Other purchasers which I hope will be considerable. I am to meet him in Lancaster upon his Return, but should you want them for any business in the Neighbourhood of Camp you had better detain him till I come, every method must be fallen upon to procure Beef, there is a great many fatt Cows in Lancaster & Bucks Counties those must be taken, make not the least doubt but you will adopt Every method you possibly can think of for the present, I shall have no ease 'till with you God only Knows what Service I shall be able to perform, present my Compliments to Col^o. Stewart and Jones, happy for you and more so poor Deputy Commissary of Purchases that Colonel Stewart was present indeed shall ever knowledge his Favour

I remain Sir. Your Most Obedient & Very Humble Servant

Frames 1150-1151.

Chaloner to William Buchanan

Sir,   December 28th. 1777

Inclosed is a letter from his Excellency to You which I am charged to forward by Express. embrace the Opportunity it affords of addressing you on a Subject that flatter myself I should not have had occasion for previous to receiving an answer from my last—but his Excellency has commanded me and I must obey—

You have also inclosed an account of Provision collected by the Parties ordered out for that Purpose of which I advised you in my last. an Accompt of daily Issues in Camp taken the 13th Instant also a state of the

Supplies for the army as farr as they have reached to my Knowledge, together with Copy of my letter to Mr Colt which I promised to inclose to Colonel Blaine but through the hurry of business it was omitted.

On the first I have only to observe that the provisions brought in was not equal to 1/3 of a days allowance. Should we be again reduced to the like necessity cannot expect an equal supply. the crys petitions and complaints of the inhabitants on this occasion is beyond description I sincerely hope the like may never happen. The State of Supplies delivered to his Excellency on which he observ'd that it was damn'd hard that the flour could not be brought on from the Susquehannah The expectation of Cattle as laid down if from Good authority those from Mr Hugg & new England only excepted the former promised Me to be here the 27th Instant he was well acquainted with our wants but have not heard of him or his Cattle since—And as those from New England it is suggestion only but so moderate that I hope it will be far exceeded—I now am in obedience to his Excellencys command to require of you what supplies are laid in for the insuing Year and what provision is made for the Winter contiguous to Camp supposing the worst of weather to happen to secure us from want

The Magazines for the purpose ought to contain at least three Weeks subsistance for the army—Colonel Stewart has appointed Pottsgrove and Downingstown for the reception of those Stores both places very contiguous and on public Roads leading from Lancaster and Reading.—

In conversation with his Excellency to day on the Subject of Supplies he expressed himself as follows—Damit what is that reason M^r. Buchanan is not here does he think to indulge himself at home whilst we are distressed and suffering for want of provision. This is Language that his Excellency is by no means accustom'd to use and you may Judge of the provocation when he is oblig'd to adopt. Where I to conceal it from you I shall be wanting in my duty—In consequence of General orders parties are now under the direction of Col^o. Evans & Mr Aston on purpose to compell the Farmers to thrash their Wheat and the Millers to make Flour, this together with the General orders to take the Straw with the wheat in it and pay for it as Straw may afford us some Assistance but have no great Expectations from this resource In this province. To the Bucks Counties only must we look for flour. We cant collect no great quantity in the Vicinity of Camp especially whilst the Forage Masters have power to take wheat in the straw. Colonel Stewart in justification of the Commissarys Department offered to produce the Letters from the

Commissary at York Town, Wrights Lancaster Easton & head of Elk which he had in his jacket in purpose of the General would not read them & sternly said the Commissary had power to impress, Stewart rattified they had but were restrained by the Quarter Masters. The General said those whose duty it was to supply ought to do it & all he wanted was a plenty for the army, if that could not be done now how would it be when the Army was augmented by draughts to fill the Regiments & the Militia brought out which perhaps would soon happen, In short sir You must to supply the Army this Winter either obtain a possitive Resolve of Congress What it is & shall be direct duty of the Quarter Masters to furnish the Commissarys with Teams on all Occasions or the army will Starve or dissolve for want should that happen Your Reputation & every person under you will be ruin'd & undone those in Camp especially pray prevent this by exerting your good sense in forming and carrying though Congress Such measures as will Reflect honour to Yourself and those You employ.

 I should have addressed some part of this Letter to Colonel Blain did I not flatter myself that on the receipt of mine of the 21. 22. & 23 he will immediately proceed to Camp His presence here is much wanted as well as in the several Districts of his Department—Permit me Sir to call your attention to the exertion of the purchasing Commissaries for this Six Weeks past to procure flour in the Counties of Lancaster Berks Northampton and part of New Jersey The supplie that all those Counties have afforded has not been able with the Assistance of the old Strores on hand to keep us a float If there be not more vigorous exertions to procure this article how shall we support the army when the old Stores are exhausted, this is a subject that cannot be to much attended to fear all the Industry our present Assistants of purchasers are masters of will not be equal to the task—You will I hope point out some effectual remedy.— Huggins enjoins me that has purchased a large Quantity of wheat that he has given Nine Shillings p[er] bushell I shall write him to proceed and purchase all he can. That Country and the neighboring Colonies must afford our Supplies of Flour. altho this province abounds in it, the disaffection of the people is such that they will not spare it at a reasonable compensation tho they have to detain or withhold it is destruction. Excuse Sir my freedom in this letter I mean not to dictate to you though I wish to see the present demand of Camp fully satisfied, on my part I trust I have done my duty, tho I am Assured If I continue here and matters remain as they have done for some time past I shall fall a prey to the prejudiced and Starved Soldiery—Another cause of our distress is the want of Cash every

Letter from the Assistant purchasers is full of Complaints that they are not supplied with Cash some say they could do a great deal more provided they could support their Credit and others again declare that the cannot do any thing for the want of Cash. If a large sum is not immediately dispensed throughout the Department it will be impossible to support the Credit of Purchasers or to render to supplies of the army. Col. Blain is sensible of this I wish to Conclude & Should be exceeding happy could I finish this with Assuring you that 500 lbls of flour were now in our possession. for a moment reflect on our situation without a Barrel of flour or Bread the feed the army none of which are served longer than to morrow and to ad to our distress the roads are so bad that it is impossible for Teams to Travel adieu and I remain Sir
Frame 1151-1153.

Chaloner to Unidentified

Sir,
      Inclosed you have a letter to the Quarter Master Genl. Copy of which is Included to M^r. Payne who has orders to Demand a Brigade of Ten Waggons daily to proceed on with provisions to Camp. I hope you will be able to Load them as they are Raised as the contrary his Excellency will be informed of and you must answer for the consequences—Should it be out of Your own power to comply with the above send The Teams to Wrights ferry or Lancaster for loading for your own sake I hope you will be able to compleat this order. I am Sir your Hble Servant
Frame 1153.

Chaloner to Thomas Huggins

Sir,   December 29th 1777
      I have in Charge from his Excellency to inform you that it is his orders that all the Stores from your Quarters be immediately removed to Camp, reserving only what is necessary for the Consumption of the troops in your Neighborhood, the more effectually to Complete this order, I sent you a warrant from the Quarter Master General authorizing you to impress Waggons—
      Your Method of doing business without invoice of Even a Memorandum of quantity or quality is by no means Excusable, the present

hurry is in Your favour, but should the Supplys through & from your Quarters continue as in all probability they will you must Employ proper persons to Assist you and to enable you to do business with method & propriety, Loose no time in forwarding on the Stores and particularly the Cattle, it is A Long time since we had any from you, I flatter myself they are now on the Road, If I am disappointed in this I shall be exceedingly unhappy, for the troops must want I have returned the Number you promised to send to his Excellency, and you must be Answerable for their arrival. Send a particular Acc^t. of the Stores you have on hand.—I am Sir Your Very Hble Servant
Frame 1154.

Chaloner to James White

Sir, December 30th
I have wrote M^r. Robert Dod of this Date to forward on all the salt provision he has in care have requested him to set in motion 30 Teams from your Quarter & in case he cannot Load them with salted provisions to send them to Pittstown for flour or Bread, I hope in that case they will not be Disappointed His Excellency desires to know what Supplies are laid up for the winter to enable me to do this You must furnish me with an exact Acct. of what Stores are in your possession fail not as It is of importance to His Excellency and by his order that I have dispatched the bearer I am Sir Yours & &
Frame 1154.

Chaloner to James White

Sir, December 30th 1777
I have wrote M^r. Robert Dodd of this date to forward on all the Salt provisions he has his in care, have Requested him to set in motion 30 Teams from your quarter and in case he Cannot Load them with Salt Provisions to send them to Pittstown for flour or Bread, I hope in that case they will not be Disappointed—His Excellency desires to Know what supplies are laid up for the Winter to Enable me to do this you must furnish me with an Exact Account of what Stores are in your possession fail not as it is of Importance to His Excellency and by his order that I have

dispatched the bearer & & I am Sir Yours & &
Frame 1155.

Note: The same letter, with minor differences is found three letters back in the manuscript.

Chaloner to Robert Dodd

Sir,   December 30th 1777
  I dispatch the bearer Express to Enquire what quantity of Stores you have in possession either of Your own purchasing or of other forwarded to Your care you will immediately on receipt of this forward to Colonel Blaine or myself a particular account therof as to quantity and specie.—
  You must also without delay send on to Head Q^{rs}. Thirty Waggons weekley loaded with Pork until the Whole is removed—Fail not in Executing the above order it is of vast importance and transmitted to you by order of his Excellency—
  At all events procure the Teams and in case You have not Salted provisions sufficient to load them send in flour or Bread from Pittstown this number of Teams must be kept in motion from your Quarter I am Sir Your Very Hble Servant
Frame 1155.

Robert Dodd was an Assistant Commissary of Purchases based at Flemington, New Jersey.

Blaine to Unidentified

Sir,   Yorktown   1st January   1778
  Yours of the 30th December to M^{r}. Buchanan I have had the perusal of and observe the contents Request your immediate Attention to the purchasing of Beef Pork & Whiskey those persons who are not satisfied with four pounds p[er] Cwt for Pork and four pounds ten Shillings p[er] hundred for the best Stall fed Beef and Ten Dollars for the Common Beef you have the Authority of the board of war to Seize the same and give Certificates to the owners specifying the Quality and Quantity so taken to be paid as the legislative Authority of the State or the

Congress may hereafter Regulate, Beg you may be active in Seizing all Beef Pork and Whiskey in the possession of Forestallers and forward the same by every Opportunity to this Place, have information of great Quantities of Pork in your Neighborhood pray secure all you Possibly can if you Could forward a Drove of Cattle and one of Hoggs in the course of a few Days pray do it as the army are in great Want. I am Sir Your Hble Servant
Frame 1155.

Chaloner to Unidentified

Sir,   Camp Valley Forge 3^d. January 1778
     There is at the other side of Correylls ferry Seventy Barrels of salt provision. The troops in Camp are in immediate want of it. You must immediately on receipt of this furnish waggons to forward on said provisions without delay use all the dispatch in your p[ow]er I am Sir Your Very hble Servt.
Frame 1155.

Chaloner to Unidentified

Sir,   January 3^d 1778
     You will immediately proceed from hence by the Warren down towards Marcus hook as far as Colonel Pierces within three Miles of the Delaware there wait the Comming up of an Escort from Wilmington to Marcus Hook. The Commander of which you must apply to for whatever aid or Assistance you may stand in need of—
     By the information received from Lord Stirling Copy of which you have inclosed you will discern the persons possed of the property affixed to their names which you are to seize and immediately bring off the Whole or as much as Your Teams can hall to Camp at Head Quarters—I would recommend to you first to proceed to the Warren down to Colonel Pierces within 3 Miles of Marcus Hook there Wait the arrival of a Party from Wilmington to protect you from any incursions that the enemy may make from their Shipping—as soon as You are advised of this proceed to John Moulders and there Load all the Spirituous Liquors you may find him possessed of also take an Inventorary of any other Stores You may find in

his possession that you cannot bring off If any Quantity of Salt or Salted provisions bring it of also then. on your return call on M^r. John Smith who also has a quantity of Spirituous Liquor salt Provisions & other Stores which you must also seize and bring off Should you receive further information of any Stores in that Neighborhood you will use Your utmost endeavors to bring them off with you but if impracticable take an Inventory thereof and an obligation from the owner not to conceal or remove them but deliver them up to the army when called for. If by this time you have Teams to spare take a party with them to William Ruses near Newton Square and bring from thence Whatever Rum or other stores you may find useful for the army.

In conducting this business you must be exceedingly cautious to keep Secret the information you are possessed of and to improve it as much as Possible. We have the most Positive Assurance that the articles in the list inclosed are in possession of the persons Whose names are affixed against them must therefore charge you not to be set of by evasion or artifice but fully satisfy yourself of the truth of their Assertions by peculiar demonstrations—

You will be exceedingly cautious of exerting the Authority with wich you are vested to the injury of the inhabitants those whose property you will be under the Necessity of taking treat with the greatest Civility leave them Certificates specifying the quantity and Quality of the articles you take from them and direct them to me for payment. do your utmost to Endeavour to prevent the Soldiery and Waggoners from plundering the inhabitants. I am Sir Your & &
Frame 1156.

Chaloner to James White, Robert Dodd or Gustavus Risberg

Sir,   January 4th 1778
Never was man so unhappy situated as myself left him to feed an army consuming 30,000 Bread & meat, deserted and deceived by almost every Assistant Purchasing Commissary—How they are to exist or to be kept together God only Knows—Must now call on you to exert yourself to forward all the Pork you can lay your hands on of New Jersey pay no attention to any ramour of troops being rationed there—Delay not a moment in forwarding an Express to Colonel Joseph Hugg—assure him that I think myself exceedingly ill used by him, and the publick more so.

When he boasted it was in his power to send 300 head of Cattle in two or three days, 15 are elapsed and not a line or Beast from him. He well knew our distress. I would write him but so very uncertain where to find him: demand the Cattle, inform him they are reported to His Excellency and he must answer the Disappointment. For Gods sake For your Countrys sake and the Reputation of the purchasing department do Your utmost to forward on all the Pork and Beef in Jersey be it in whatever situation it may defend it from the Weather in the best manner possible, and use all the dispatch in forwarding it that you and all the Assistants you can muster are masters off—Dispatch a line Az. Dunham Morristown & another to Nehemiah at I am in haste Sir Yours & & p Express
Frame 1157.

Gustavus Risberg was a purchaser for the Commissary Department.

Chaloner to Thomas Huggins

Sir, Camp Valley Forge 4 Jany. 1778
 Yours of the 30th was handed to me this afternoon am well convinced of Your trouble but you must employ sufficient hands to go through with it all, am much surprized to find the difficult in collecting Beef you must at all events send on the number promised—You must also on receipt of this send on as fast as possible all the salt Beef pork or other provisions You have in possession delay not a moment our wants are beyond comprehension and we shall have the army dissolved if not speedily relieved Apply to the Governor and Council and Request their Assistance—am Sir with Respect Yours & &
Inform me what Quantity of Wheat & flour you purchased and what salt provisions you have on hand p[er] Express
Frame 1157.

Chaloner to Robert McGermont

Sir, January 4 1778 10 oClock night
 Am much surprised that I have not received a line from you since You left Camp—Col^o. Blaine expected from Your promise to have received a drove of Cattle longer this. I reported It to his Excellency but am exceedingly sorry to find myself disappointed to him You must answer

but what is worse the troops suffer—I must now order you to do all in your power to forward the Whole of the salt provisions in your Custody by the bearer inform me of the quantity you have collected as also what you are like to procure. Let me intreat you as you value the union and existance of the army or regard the reputation of the purchasing department to exert Yourself—The loss of a day may be our ruin, and the fruits of a well employed hour save us from disgrace and the army from necessity—I am Sir with Respect Yours & & p. Express
Frame 1158.

Chaloner to Henry Fuller

Sir, Jany 4th. 1778
Information is given to his Excellency The Commander in Chief that there are in the hands of M^r. Oakley at Bethlehem belonging to the late Commissary 16 hhds of Rum & in the hands of M^r. Gordon 6 hhds Rum also that there is at Easton a quantity of Whiskey—The two first you are immediately to seize and the latter to purchase at the prices regulated by the State—and forward immediately to Head Quarters in this M^r. Frazer will Assist you. I am with Respect Yours & & p M^r. Frazeer
Frame 1158.

Henry Fuller was an Assistant Commissary of Purchases at Easton, Pennsylvania.

Chaloner to George Washington

Sir January 4th. 1778
The Assistant Commissary of Purchases hourly expects from Joseph Hugg 250 head of Cattle. from Azariah & Nehemiah Dunham daily 200 head—From Thomas Huggins in two days 250 head. from Anthony Broderick daily 200 head. From Robert M^c.Germant daily 100 head from all the purchasers in New England daily 500 head quantity am not certain of but am informed part are on the Road—He has also at Bombacks five miles distance from camp 20,000 W^t of salt Beef p estimation at Coryells Ferry which is order on immediately 70 Barrels of Beef. The pork purchasers in East & West New Jersey. The Several Counties in Pennsylvania Delaware & Maryland have not as yet reported their progress in this business nor does he Yet know what the parties sent to

Oley and Concord have collected, but expects daily to receive a quantity of Beef from them and to be informed what expectations may be placed on their collections. Large Quantity of Flour & Bread coming from Elk and Lancaster
State of provisions given to his Excellency
Frame 1158.

Chaloner to William Buchanan

Sir,
    Yours to Colonel Blaine of the 29 Instant was handed to me Yesterday evening have not heard from Colonel Blaine since the 26th. hourly expect him and for that reason omit writing to him—I have now to inform you that our distresses are not yet Relieved and our wants daily increasing the article of flour excepted. We have not one live Beast in Camp—Inclosed you have Copy of the State of our provisions as farr as I am acquainted with it I hope my last will induce you to make enquiry as to enable you to inform His Excellency the State thereof more fully—I am deceived by all the Purchasers they have far exceeded the time set by them for their arrival here with Cattle—Joseph Hugg at least 15 days in consequence of which I am charged by his Excellency with making false Returns, thus I am brought into disgrace and have forfeited my reputation at Head Quarters—I wish to give a full state of facts have attempted this in my letters to you & Colonel Blaine And now for that purpose send you the following Extracts —
    From Peter Colt New haven December 22 1777. Since my return (from Boston) have directed my People to push forward Beef Cattle for your Quarter; but they till me the supply will be much under your Demand. Mr Cuyler who supplies the Northern Department, I gave him up a large meat Country not contented with that, the people are driving of large droves of Cattle & Hoggs from that part from whence I expected to Afford you considerable aid. I am call'd upon for the supplies for all the prisoners in the Department as well Burgoines as the others—The troops at Boston Providence and North River look to me for their meat and the pork this year fall so much short of our former purchases that it will be absolutely Necessary to Barrel considerable quantities of Beef For these reasons must beg you to make as large purchases to the Southward as possible and lessen demands on us—Beef is here from Ten Dollars to 14

p[er] hundred He further informs that he has set the Salt in motion from Boston.—That the flour is wanted to Extremity at Boston and providence—and without cash having received no public money—
from Thomas Huggins December 30th received yesterday evening after Complaining of the difficulty of procuring Waggons to forward Bread and Flour he says, And to ad to the Whole The Governor and Council has sent for me for taking Cattle from the Damn Quacker [sic] Torys therefore you need not expect as many Cattle as I wrote you about Indeed will be with great Difficulty I will be able to get as many as will do the division at Wilmington The most of the Cattle are in the hands of a disaffected: I beg you will send me money as it takes no trifle to Keep Wilmington a going—From James White in Jersey Under is an account of what provisions have come under my notice as near as I can form a Judgement the Chief part of the pork being then in bulk —

Talmans near black horse	150 Bbls Pork
Bickles town	750 to 800 D^o
Trenton	100 D^o
Flemington	40 D^o
	1040 Bbls

I think there will be but little flour to spare—This pork I have ordered forward as also all that Huggins and McGermant has procured when it arrives shall only use it as Necessity obliges as to those Resources I cannot say whether they will arrive in time to releive our wants or whether they will come on as fast as consumed there being few or no Waggons in that Country Every letter I open is full of complaints for want of money if sufficient to pay of all arrearages cannot be obtained & that speedily it will be impossible to supply the army this would remove many difficulties render our business more easy & certain without it the worst may be of consequences may be justly feared and expected Thirty hours are elapsed since I presented to His Excellency the inclosed return and not one Bullock arrived, this day will consume the Whole of the Salt provisions Fish &^{c} God only Knows what will be for the troops to morrow—

By the Iclosed Resolves of Congress published in Genl. orders— you will see that the matter is like to become very serious—I am told that a Committee of Congress is to attend here to enquire into and remove the defects in the Commissary Department at which I hope and doubt not you will attend—and be ready to meet them with accounts of a large Quantity of Salted provisions being arrived from the Southward. Few of the General Officers have extended their views to that quarter could you prove that large quantities are collected there and that and that [sic] you have taken the necessary steps to forward them on also the Stores from Connecticut it will be certainly the best defence that can be made and for this purpose I send you an account of the Stages proposed by the New England Officers together with such alteration as I apprehend from the Conversations of the Generals and the situation of the country will be made—From the Eastern and Southern Departments must the army by supported through the Winter measures to forward supplies from thence cannot be to soon adopted or set in motion I fear we shall generally suffer before we can possibly receive that aid they have in their power to give us—no dependance is to be put on the middle department—it is quite exhausted, which with the Common and General disaffection of the people Cuts of all hopes from thence. I have sent parties to the South part of Chester County also in the lower parts of Berkes to Collect Wheat flour pork & Beef have received some assistance from them in flour & expect a little in the article of Beef and Pork—I should propose a method for collecting of pork out of the Counties of Berks & Northampton—where there is some quantity but with held from us by the disaffected—but should I be absent from here & nobody to supply my place I fear the remedy would be of more ill consequence than the relief would compensate for Another burden that the troops labor under is the want of Soap and Candles the inconveniences arising from this is beyond description—and will as the troops are got into hutts their Officers will expect them to appear on parade more cleanly than heretofore Mr Kenedys plea for the want of men is inexcusable and I fear shall not be indulged with their leave of absence for those persons he solicits—in a word our department is in such disgrace at Head Quarters that I dread to ask any favours—we not only risque denyal but run great hazard of a severe reprimand, immagine to yourself how disagreeable it is to do business in this situation—

  The procuring of flour casks is also become a matter deserving attention Coopers refuse to work and persons that are possessed of S[tu]ff holds it at so high a rate that it is improbably to procure it so as to furnish casks as a less price than 5 Shillings each—

  Inclosed I send you a draught in favor of John Pearson of Chester County tanner the amount of which please too Lodge in the Continental Loan Office for issue and take three Certificates for the same—transmitt to me p[er] the first safe opportunity. no doubt you will readily see the advantage of doing business in this way punctuality in this instance may induce others to follow the like Example

I have only to ad that I am ordered to send to Bucks for the purposes above mentioned with a person of any sort to Assist me. I conclude in great distress and shall be so untill relieved either by Blain or yourself I am Sir Yours & &
pr M^r. Meers
Frames 1159-1161.

Blaine to Chaloner

Sir   Lancaster   4th January 1778
Make no Doubt but you and M^r. Jones have had your own difficulties since I left you, but hope by this you are in a little better way, I have been doing every thing in my power, two Brigades are upon their way with Whisky and one with flour from Carlile, one with Whiskey and four with Flour are to set out this week from York town, one hundred Waggons will leave this in the Course of three days all loaded with Flour, I have purchased two small Droves of Cattle and some Hoggs which will come with the Waggons. have Contracted with three Men who have engaged to bring two thousand Hoggs from the South Branch Potomack and Redstone, am Seizing all the Whiskey, beef Pork Flour & Salt to be found in the Neighbourhood of this place; the Assembly have taken the Burthen off the Purchasing Commissaries and has appointed four Commissioners in each County two to secure all provisions Necessary for the Army, the other two all Kind of Cloathing, Inclosed you have the prices fixed by the Assembly which advise my Assistants in the Neighbourhood of Camp, this Keep to yourself till our people have set out to engage Wheat and flour that they may have all the advantages, I set out from this Early in the Morning with three Assistants and as many Officers and mean to take a Circuit of three days to secure Beef & Whiskey, after which may expect to see me, present my Compliments to Colonel Stewart Jones and all friends and am Sir Your most Obedient Very Hble Servant
P. S. Commissioners appointed for seizing Provisions for the purpose of Forming Magazines & &—

Phil^a. County   Peter Evans: Col^o. John Moore
Bucks County   Andrew Heighlen: & Jos: Green

Chester County   Thomas Haslip & La°. Cultbertson
Lancaster County   Thomas Edwards & David Watson
York County   Maj^r. Ja^s. Dill & Maj^r. W^m. Scott
Cumberland County   W^m. Blair & John Andrew
Northhampton   John O[r]natt & David Deshlar
  County
Bedford County   Robt. Cultbertson & Morris Reed
Northumberland   W^m. Gray & John Little Esqr.
  County
Westmoreland   Joseph Thorn & John Brannon
  County

Prices
  Flour 33/ p[er] Cw^t.
  Wheat 12/ p[er] bushell
  Rye 9/ p[er] bushell
  Corn 7/6 p[er] bushell
  Whiskey 8/6 p[er] Gallon
  Beef from 8 pence to 12 pence according to Quality
  Pork from 9 pence to 12 pences
  Neat Cattle and Swine as near as may be as above allowing the owner for the fifth Quarter in the Neat Cattle.—
Frame 1161.

Chaloner to Unidentified

Sir,
  When you reflect on your conversation here, your frequent declarations in the Hearing of several General Officers that you could forward 300 head in two days the time elapsed since and the very few brought on by your Brother and M^r. Morris you must acknowledge that you have not used me as you would wish to use an indifferent person— immediately after your departure from camp His Excellency a return of my expectations for the supply of the army: from the Assurances of you & the purchases of Live Stock gave me, I reported Seventy nine days beef this Season—was call'd on the other day by him to inform what quantity of Beef was on hand poor me answered two days at the elapse of which was call'd on again and not a Beast alive He confronted me with making false

returns—The truth is I made here returns from your information you desired me and they proved false—I must now call on you to exert yourself to Compleat the return of 300 Head—Your Honour and my reputation with his Excellency falls a sacrifice should I not be able to prove that my report it true, as you regard the Reputation of this department let me intreat you by no means to fail in this—

 His Excellency has call'd for a report of what expectations we have to feed the army this winter to enable me to do this you must immediately inform me what pork & Beef you have already procured its situation and what you can procure for this Two Months to Come—I must now charge you to forward all the Pork and Beef you can lay your hands on as expeditiously as possible no time must be lost in this business—

 p[er] M^r. Morris and your Brother can inform you My situation respecting Cash no Blain yet shall forward you your quota as soon as it come to hand In mean time remain Sir Yours & &
Frame 1163.

Chaloner to Azariah Dunham

Dear Sir,   January 7, 1778

 Yours of the 2 together with A very acceptable drove of Cattle have received this day I must again give you the Credit of saving the Reputation of the department and the Soldiery from the sad and fatal experience of Hunger. I am sorry to inform you that I have no money to send you—Colonel Blaine not yet returned tho expect him every hour am persuaded he will bring sufficient to Discharge all arrearages in the department Be Assured no time shall be lost in forwarding you your quota in the full amount of your demand—The New England Cattle does not come on as fast as we had reason to expect and experience teaches me that no dependance can be put on that Country for regular supplies of Beef Cattle this season From you Who has done so much and so largely in advance nothing else but a full persuasion of your attachment to the cause would induce me to expect more Assistance from you but my friend be Assured our Salvation depends on your exertions—destitute of Salt, provisions we must call on you to forward more Cattle. I know not where else to expect another Drove—

If your Brother approves of it I shall detain your Son to be the bearer of the needfull to enable you to render us further Assistance—

Must request of you to hurry on all the Cattle you have or can collect speedily as possible to camp together with an Acc^t. of what quantities of Beef & Pork you can send forward this Month, Shall be glad of it as soon as possible as His Excellency has call'd for it. There is a large quantity of Salt expected daily from New Windsor by way of Sussex Should it not be gone through Jersey you can detain as much of it as will enable to cure What pork you have or can purchase. In mean time remain.
Sir Yours & &
Frame 1163.

Chaloner to Blaine

Sir,
Yours of the 4th from Lancaster I this moment received, in answer to which I send the Bearer to inform you that I can stand the torment no longer. His Excellency has call'd for you, for Col^o. Buchanan, and no body there to answer but myself without the means of doing for the benefit or advantage of the troops tell your Assistants this day are gone home from hence without money; and declare they can do no more destitute of Cash or Credit.—I am thoroughly sick of my situation Colonel Stewart disgusted & well he may; The Board of War charging his Department with neglect and waste for heads & hearts—I have only to ad, unless you come yourself or send me money in three days, I must and will quit this Station.
I am thoroughly tired of the frowns of His Excellency and all ranks of people in and out of the army. am sir Yours & &
Frame 1164.

Chaloner to Blaine

Sir,
Just as dispatching the Express with the above Col^o. Broderick arrived with a small drove of Cattle and prevented my sending this on by declaring that he dare not go home and must see you before he returns, it affording me an Opportunity of more particularly answering your letter, I accordingly embrace it. In the first place must observe that it speakes of no

immediate supplys for the army flour and Whiskey only excepted two small droves of Cattle & some Hoggs with what little pork is already collected to feed the army untill the arrival of your Two Thousand Hoggs from the South branch of Potomack—From this Quarter New Jersey and the Eastern part of Maryland you must look for no supplies untill you send Cash sufficient to pay of all arrearages for be Assured you nor Your Assistants have Credit this side of Conneegocheague—I much fear you will find Yourself greatly mistaken in throwing of the burden of the Supplies for the Army of your own Shoulders on the Commissioners appointed by this state and am sure you will find it so unless they are to receive Pay & through you and become Accountable to you for their Conduct—If you cannot supply the army with Assistants appointed by yourself whose very existence in Office depends on their merits and your pleasure how will you support it with the Assistance of men over whom you have no Rule and they Accountable to those only who appointed them—I much fear you have the Authority which was vested in you taken away and put into the hands of persons who cannot (and perhaps are not disposed) to supply you and for neglect of Duty are answerable to no other Law than that which gave them existence. You well know the Weakness of Goverment in this invaded state, and I much fear their inabilities at this time are too great to do you service—Should this be the case instead of ease we shall find trouble & disappointments increase— You desire me to acquaint your purchases of the Regulated prices passd into a Law by the Assembly I shall do it but promises will not longer Answer without money. The want of which is our destruction and in the end will starve the army—I wish you seriously to consider this Material and important article in the light that I have Represented it—In the General orders of Yesterday the full allowance of Soap and Candles is ordered to the troops (none on hand not a Candle to write by even for his Excellency if wanted)—in case hard Soap is not to be had it is directed that they shall be supplied with Soft youll govern yourself accordingly. So for Gods sake Come to camp Relieve me or I must quit altoher. am Sir Your most Ob^t. Hbl Servant
PS If the Beefes you have purchased be such as was sent on by Smith I shall order the drover not to receive them they have been the cause of complaints & uneasiness in the army perplexity to His Excellency & have produced severall Issuing Commissaries to the Bayonett—
Frames 1164-1165.

Blaine to Chaloner

Dear Sir, Marhaim 11th January 1778
I have been in this County and Bucks this Eight Days purchasing and seizing beef Cattle and Whiskey, but meets with very little of the Latter have collected one Hundred and fifty good Cattle hope to make them two hundred, have to break open Stable doors windows &^{c} and a great Misfortune cannot speak German which Makes the business, am under the Necessity of doing very disagreeable. the Cattle I take this day they steal them to morrow, have got a party of Soldiers up from Lancaster and Keeps a Regular Guard, shall be obliged to Whip one of two of the Inhabitants or march down half a dozen to Head Quarters and make Examples of them. wish M^r. Jones and you would send out some Active person ten Miles above Camp to seize Whiskey the Dammd Forestallers are Stealing all out of the Country, it would give me pleasure to see half a Dozen of them Hangd you may expect me next Wednesday, my Compliments to Colonel Jones and all friends am in Haste. Dear Sir Your Hble Servant
Frame 1165.

Chaloner to Thomas Huggins

Sir, January 12th. 1778
I wrote you sometime past for an Acct of what Beef and Salt provisions you had purchased and what we may expect to receive in the Course of Winter—You will also furnish me with with an Acc^t. of what Wheat and flour you have purchased hitherto by no means delay as I want it for his Excellencys use underneath You have the Prices of sundry articles as regulated by the Assembly of this State—apprehend it will effect you as the price of pork and Beef which with all the Wheat and flour in your neighborhood you will still continue to Purchase as Cheap as possible not exceeding the prices Regulated by this state, apprehend your Legislative will not exceed 9 or 10 Shillings p[er] bushell—Forward all the salt provision you have be it of what sort it may as speedily as possible. I am Sir Yours &^{c} &
pr Capt. Sanderson
Frame 1165.

Chaloner to John Ladd Howell

Sir,   [January 12, 1778]
You will immediately proceed with the party ordered out under the Command of Colonel Stewart and do your utmost endeavours to purchase all the Fatt Beef Pork and flour that you may find in the Counties of Philadelphia and Bucks or such part thereof as Colonel Stewart may Judge to be in danger of the enemy subject to less lossd by their Excursions
You must give receipts for all Fatt Cattle estimating the weight and Rate them from 9^d. to 12 p lb—exclusive of the fifth Quarter according to Quality and the same Prices for pork or Swine—For good Wheat the owners delivering it at such Mills as Colonel Stewart may direct weighing 60 p Bushel 12/ and Flour 35 pr Cwt.—You must collect of each any every of those articles all such as may appear to you to be over and above such as may be Necessary for the Consumption of their Families and forward the same to Head Q^{rs}. as fast and expeditious as Convenience and circumstances will permit—persons having any of the above articles to spare & unwilling to part with them must be compelled Colonel Stewart will furnish necessary assistance for this purpose—You must be exceedingly careful Not to distress persons retired from the City and also to prevent the Soldiery from committing insults on the inhabitants or wantonly injuring them in their property. am Sir Your hble Ser^t.
Frame 1166.

John Ladd Howell, a purchaser with the Commissary Department, was later stationed at Middletown, Delaware.

Chaloner to John Ladd Howell

Camp Valley Forge   12th January
His Excellency having thought it Necessary to a Detachment from the Grand army to be joind by a party of General Potters Brigade of Militia to Proceed forthwith to that part of the Country of Philadelphia & Bucks lying between the Old York & Delaware river under the command of Col^o. Stewart in order to protect you and the Assistant purchasers of live Stock sent with you in driving & Conveying safely to camp, all the fatt Cattle, Hoggs & flour that you may purchase, or the inhabitants can spare allowing them sufficiency for their support—You are therefore Required

to proceed on this business & receive & take from the several Farmers all the Fatt Cattle Hoggs, Salt pork & Flour not for their Respective Familys use and send them the same to camp under such Guards as Colonel Stewart may furnish giving the owners Receipts for the same to be paid for at such Rates as the Legislative of this State have or may by Law affix & giving them an Assurance that all those who do agreeable to his Excellencys proclamation thrash their Crops and deliver the Wheat at such Mills as you fix upon should have protection for the Quantity Necessary for their support & Receive in Ready money the Rates p[er] bushell allowed by Law I am in behalf of Col^o Blaine D. C. G. of purchases Your most Obedient
Frame 1166.

Chaloner to Unidentified

D^r. Sir   Camp Valley Forge 12th. 1778
You will on receipt of this purchase as expeditiously as possible Two Thousand Bushell Indian Corn, and have it Manufactured into Meal for the use of the Hospital at camp. As there are a very considerable number of troops to be inoculated no time must be lost in forwarding the Meal to Head Quarters
You must immediately proceed on this business and inform Col^o. Blaine or myself of your progress therein by the very first Opportunity at Foot hereof you have the prices and Regulations passed into a Law by the Legislative of this State—I am Sir Your very Hble Servant

P.S. Flour   33/ Shilling p Cw^t
      Wheat   23/ p[er]. bushell
      Corn   7/6 p[er]. bushell
      Rye   9/ p[er]. bushell
      Oats or Spelts   5/ p[er] bushell
      Whiskey   8/6 p[er] Gallon
      Beef from   8^d to 12^d. according to Quality
      pork from   9^d to 12^d. — D^o. — D^o.

Neat Cattle and Swine as near as may be to the above, allowing the owner for the fifth Quarter in the Neat Cattle
Frame 1167.

Blaine to Mr. Dunham

Sir, Camp Valley Forge 12 January 1778
I have sent you by M^r. Byers twenty six thousand Dollars which I hope will not be too late to be useful to you, it was not in my power to procure cash sooner as there was large Demands on the Treasury Office from the Southerd & Eastern Departments, I need not point out to you the pressing Demand of beef for the army this make no doubt you have been well inform'd of however request you may procure Every hoof which are in any Killing order and forward the same without delay to this place, hope you have had it in your power to purchase largely of pork if you have not had a supply of salt from North River make application to M^r. Forman or Johnston at pittstown who can spare you some Congress have wrote to all Governors of the united States to adopt such Measures as will secure all provisions Necessary for the Army in each State—Beg you may apply to them shoud you want any Assistance the Board of War are to be in Camp next week, request you may prepare your Monthly Returns, as well your Bond of performance and the Necessary oaths of Fidelity and Office as I shall make preparation to settle my Acc^{ts}. and make Returns what provisions are on hand up to the first of January Inclosed you have copies the form of your bond & Oath of office shall be glad to hear from you by the bearer and what I may expect from you in Beef & pork am with much Esteem Sir. Your most Hble Servant
Frame 1167.

Blaine to Joseph Hugg

Dear Sir, Camp 16th January 1778
Our distress'd situation the want of beef in Camp induced me to have the greatest expectation of receiving at least Six or Seven hundred head of Cattle from your District, as the last time I had the pleasure of seeing you—you mentioned that Number & that your hopes from Cape May was very Great, as you had information of great Numbers of Cattle being in that Quarter and certain it is More Cattle might have been procured from Jersey—information has been made at head Quarters of the Enemy in philadelphia receiving great supplies from Opposite Chester and down that Shore (for god sake) my Reputation and Your own, procure every hoof of cattle anywise fit to Slaughter & all the pork you can meet

with make Application to the Commanding officer of the Militia and sweep that Whole Country Opposit & below Phil^d. of all the Beef Cattle stock Cattle in midling order fit for use, all Pork and Fatt Sheep.—in a General execution of this business you will do your Country essential service

   I have sent you by M^r. Steel twenty two thousand Seven hundred and Fifty Dollars woud have given you a Supply of Cash sooner but the demand upon the treasury Office for the Eastern and Southern Departments were so great I could not be furnish till their Orders were compli'd with and paid—The Board of War are to be here next week Must Request you to furnish me with your Monthly Returns up to the first of January as also your bond of performance and Oaths of Fidelity & Office. Inclosed you have copies of the Form,—you will also make me a Estimated Return the Quantity of pork you have taken in and what Your Assistants have reason to expect—and intreat You to Forward all the beef Cattle you possibly can, the pork you have in the Lower part of your district could it not be collected at Dun[kis]es Ferry or Burlington. Waggons coud bring it on to Head Quarters this inform me of by the bearer.

   You wrote me in your last your purchased me a small family of negroes but Mentioned it being Necessary my seeing of them before you would close your bargain if the Man is honest and the Wench Active & Acquainted with house Work they will suit you are Certainly a Better Judge than me and I am in great want therefore will leave in certainly to your Judgement I am Dear Sir Your Hble Servant
Frame 1168.

Blaine to Mr. Dunham

D^r. Sir,   Camp 16th January 1778
   I had the perusal of yours of the 2^d. of January till after the Inclosed was wrote, I know from daily experience that the pay of the purchasing Commissaries will by no means be equal to support them, much short of a Compensation for their Services this Complaint I have laid before Congress which they have promised to remedy and make not the least doubt but they will make generous allowances for the extravagance of the Times—however be Assured I shall lay a Memorial from the principle Commissaries of purchases before the Board of War for their Services reflection & hope they will take proper notice of the same—my

Dear friend I well know it is more from principale than Motives of interest you have Continued in your present employ and return you my sincere thanks for your study Attention to the publick service and the timely Assistance you afford us upon every occasion Indeed sorry I am to Acknowledge that but very few of my Assistants I can have that Confidence in the have Disappointed me so often, shall be glad to hear from you by M^r. Byers and am Dear Sir. Your most Ob^t. Ser^t
Frame 1169.

Blaine to Anthony Broderick

Sir, Camp Valley Forge 16th. Jan^y.
Request every exertion in procuring Beef & pork and forward all the Cattle you possibly can to Head Quarters by Droves, shoud you meet with any that is Beef & the owners are not disposed to sell seize the same & give Certificates for the Value of the Neat Beef, nothing would Justify conduct of this Kind but great Demands of Beef for the Army, shall be glad to hear from you by every Opportunity, and am Sir, Your Most Hbl. $Serv^t$.
Frame 1169.

Blaine to Robert McGermont

Sir, Camp Valley Forge 16 Jan^y.
Beg you may use Every Exertion to procure Beef and pork, what Beef you possibly can purchase leave your own prudence to Judge of also pork the price our Demand is very great, shou'd you be able to purchase any in the lower part of your District and the Distance to far to Drive up, have the Same Slaughtered there, and the Beef corned sufficient for present use and packed and forward the same by Every Opportunity to head of Elk, as also all the pork you have purchased, let no time be lost in forwarding all your Stores to the head of Elk as I want to remove the same to our Magazines and Head Quarters, so as to be out of Danger of the Enemy—(for god sake) my Reputation and your own procure Every hoof of midling Beef and all the pork you possibly can, if you can forward me One Hundred Barrels of Indian Meal you will greatly oblige me it is wanted for the Hospital, the sooner you can begin to send your stores to

the head of Elk the more advantage it will be to the publick Shall be glad to hear from you by every Opportunity and am Dear Sir Your Ob^t. Hble Ser^t
Frame 1170.

Blaine to William Evans

Sir,   Camp Valley Forge 16th. January 78
   I make not the least doubt by this you have engaged a large Quantity of Flour and purchased considerably of Beef and pork, the Legislative Authority of this State had allow'd the Following prices. Viz. for good Merchant Flour 33/p C^t. Delivered at such places as is agreed upon to fix Maggazines Wheat Weighing 60^{lb}, twelve Shillings p[er] bushell good beef sinking the fifth Quarter five pounds and from 9^d. to 12^d. lb for good pork, beg you may use every exertion in procuring all the beef and pork you possibly can, all contracts you make Convenient to camp let it be for Wheat, delivered at such mills as you fix upon, to grind, ordering the Bran Shorts & Midlings for the use of the Forage Masters, must be very Active in securing all the Wheat & Flour most convenient to the Enemy you possibly can, shoud you think it dangerous in removing such Quantities of Wheat and Flour as you may purchase or Seize make application to the Most convenient Commanding Officer who will Afford you the Necessary Guards such Mills as are out of danger of the Enemy will answer for Store Houses, than which are engaged in grinding near the Enemy's lines as fast as flour is made it must be removed to places of safety such Contracts as you make in the Lower part of your District for Flour you must engage such persons to Deliver the same near to such places as I shall fix for Magazines, One on the Hights below great Valley another at Downingstown, I will demand twelve or fifteen thousand Barrels of Flour from you, shall be glad to hear from you by Every Opportunity and am Sir Your Most Hble Servt
Frames 1170-71.

William Evans was a merchant in Chester County, Pa., who served as a purchaser for the Commissary Department.

Blaine to Nehemiah Dunham

Sir,   Camp Valley Forge 16 January 78
I make no doubt you have been at a Loss the want of cash so long, I have sent you by M^r. Byers thirteen Thousand Dollars which I hope will be of some Assistance for the present request you may use every exertion in procuring all the Pork you possibly Can as also Flour—will you have it in your power to procure us one or two droves of Cattle we never wanted them more, pray forward all you can to Head Q^{rs}. without delay and do not be so very nice in your choice Midling beef will pass the Board of War is to be hear Next week beg you to make out your monthly Returns till the first of January as I want to settle my Accts., favour me with a line and inform me what expectation you have had in procuring pork let not a fatt Hogg escape your Notice, as we shall be in great want. I am Sir Your Most Hble Servt
Frame 1171.

Blaine to Robert Dodd

Sir,   Camp Valley Forge 16 Jany. 1778
I hope eer this reaches you that you have had great success in purchasing pork & Wheat & have procured considerable Quantities of both pray use Every exertion to buy in all the pork you possibly can, I need not mention to you how great our Demand will be for that article before the summer, have sent you by M^r. John Byers Six Thousand five hundred Dollars which I hope will afford you some Assistance for the present, let me hear from you by first Opportunity and what expectations you have Respecting Flour, present my Compliments to Col^o. Lowrey's Family, and remain Sir Your most Ob^t Hble Servt.
NB should the bearer want Assistance of Hands you will make application to the Quarter Master for one
Frame 1172.

Blaine to Robert Hanson Harrison

Sir,   Camp 18 January 1778
the Information I hinted at to you Yesterday thought it my duty, the person who gave it was John Jones Inn Keeper near Windsor Forge, he

told me a Captain Reese belonging to one of the Pennsylvania Regiments his Brother and another man was present and that he M^r. Jones was astonished to hear a General Officer who aught to be a Gentleman express himself before a number of lay men as he did, the word I cannot well remember but, something to this effect, that General Washington was not the man people Imagined and by no means a great General, and if I can Remember shoud have said he was an Old Woman, however the Words can have wrote down by those people who heard that Gentleman Express himself would avise the Gentleman to take no notice of it for the present as very little time will discover those ill natured Malicious Men he may rest Assured nine tenths of the people are his Sincere friends and that persons are in Every Quarter who Knows him name and character & who will give the earliest Information, and am with much respect Sir Your Most Ob^t. & Very Hbl. Servt
Frame 1172.

Hanson was Washington's Military Secretary.

Blaine to Unidentified

Sir,   Camp 19 January 1778
    You will receive from M^r. Pollard Forty six Tierces of good rum ten Hhds of Ditto and twelve pipes of best manty Brandy shoud it not be safely stored you will please to order it to some secure place. M^r. Pollard informs me the Brandy is convenient to your town woud wish you could have it Brought there by the time the Waggons, I am preparing reaches you which will be next Week, have all the Rum & Brandy Gaged and give M^r. Pollard a Receipt for Quantity & Quality as also the salt his Excellency has informed me of a large Quantity of Rum being taken at Ready Island for the use of the army pray Enquire about it & if there have it removed to a place of safety under the Direction of some carefull person who will Keep the Carters from Aldulterating it let me hear from you by first Opportunity and am Sir Your Most Hble Servt
Frame 1172.

Blaine to Mathias Slough

Dear Sir,   Camp Valley Forge 20 Jany 78
    I hope you will be able to procure Sixteen thousand Barrels of flour and more if in your power You will make your contracts with the

Millers near town for as much Wheat as you possibly can, but when you cannot engage them in that way fix for flour any Assistance we can give the Quarter Masters in forage will be serving the Publick, yet they don't seem disposed to serve us. M^r. Bird of Reading is taking every method in his power to procure wheat ordering his Deputies to make out of each hundred Bushells Ten barrels of flour, by which means he will enhance large Commissions and the Commissaries will be obliged to buy flour from him at his price. Would return Col^o. Bird thanks for his Conduct if I thought it was to serve the publick. however this Keep to Yourself, and hold your own if Possible. I mean to contact with M^r. Bird for all the flour he will engage to Deliver me upon the banks of Schulkill or at such mills as may be convenient to our Magazine. He has employed Millers in Carnarvan Town. I heard you mention a M^r. Weaver who I beleive he has engaged. your own prudence will be sufficient to adopt such Methods as will procure the Quantities of Wheat & flour expected my Compliments to M^{rs}. Slough and am Dr Sir Yours & &
Frame 1173.

Mathias Slough was a purchaser for the Commissary Department at Lancaster, Pa.

Blaine to James Smith

Dear Sir   Camp Valley Forge 20th January 1778
    I hope eer by this you have procured a large Quantity of Beef Cattle and pork, need not point out to you the Necessity We have for those articles at Camp but doubt it will not be in your power to procure half sufficient for the magazines at Coreylls and furnish the numbers I expect from you at this place. Request you will forward all the fatt Beef you can and if M^r. Spears & you have been Successfull in purchasing Pork, forward five Hundred Head to Lancaster three Hundred to be Delivered M^r. Graff AC of Purchases there and the Remainder to be forwarded to Camp. I well Know Your Activity, therefore will not mention your exertion upon the occasion for the publick good am Confident you will do every thing in your power, use every Method to procure Whiskey, that article in Much Wanted in Camp my Compliments to all friends. am Dear Sir Your Most Hble Servt.
Frame 1173.

James Smith was a purchaser for the Commissary Department, west of the Susquehanna River.

Blaine to George Washington

Camp 20th. January 1778

May it please your Excellency—
The vast daily Consumption of Beef and the appearance of want of that article induces me to Present your Excellency with the under Mentioned Quiries—which if approved of may be of great Service to the publick—

Qu^s. 1 woud not a Reduction of the Rations of beef to the Soldiery be a great Service to the publick, suppose the Ration 1 1/2 Flour or Bread 12 Ounces beef or pork, and one Gill of Whiskey Flour is plenty and Whiskey may be procured to supply the army, and without great Assistance from the Southern & Eastern Departments it will be Impossible to procure beef—

2nd. A short address from your Excellency to the Farmers in the Middle Department, Requesting every Freeholder to feed one or more Oxen which they are to have in readiness to deliver to the persons appointed in the Respective Township to Receive them by next april or may for which they will be paid a Reasonable & Generous price this is the time the Collectors are gathering in the Publick Taxes, one of them papers Delivered each Collector will give general notice to the people, and your Excellency may be Assured it will be the means of procuring five or Six thousand head of beef Cattle in a Season of the Year when the will be most wanted for the army. I am Sir your Very Hlbe Servt.
Frame 1174.

Blaine to William Buchanan

Sir,   Camp Valley Forge 20th Jany. 1778
The vast expence in supplying the Army Makes the Demand of Cash in our Department very great I made a distribution of 208 Thousand Dollars which was but a mere trifle among them, half my Assistant Purchases are not above one forth paid they Complain the want of Cash is a great injury in their purchases and they have it not in their power to render the publick above one half the Service and this answers them to make apologies for theire not rendering the supply I had reason to expect from them. indeed this is a very heavy Complaint with M^r. Dunham and some of my Principle Assistants, wou'd request you to Procure an order

for three hundred thousand Dollars and without delay forward me 250 of it, I am this Moment without one Shilling six sheets only excepted and Croud hourly Applying, I hope you and the Board of war will adopt such measures as will draw supplies from the Eastern & Southern Departments of Beef and pork, otherwise the Army will suffer for want of that article, have nothing particular to write, the army are very well supplied for the present in Beef and Bread, beg you will make M^r. Echelberger exert himself in procuring us all the Beef and Whiskey he can.—

I have proposed to his Excellency to have the Ration reduced and add in L[erv] Bread & Whiskey which I hope will be done, this will lessen the vast daily Consumption of that Article, I expect you will look out some person to take my birth—so many Difficulties appear in the execution of the Business and the impossibility of supporting Character when a men uses every Exertion and studys every method of serving the Publick, those Reasons with sundry others have determined me upon Quiting the Service; shall be glad to hear from you and am Sir, Your Most Ob^t Hble Servt
Frame 1174.

Chaloner to Blaine

Dear Sir,   Camp Valley Forge 26 Jany. 1778
The first thing that occurred worthy of notice since Your departure was a letter from M^r. P Colt of the 10 of January in which he informs that he had sent on several droves of Beef Cattle but they were unable to pass the North River and consumed by the troops on that side contrary to his orders & Expectations. That the last drove of 100 he had not heard the fate off—He promises to continue sending supplies but Cautions you against putting too much dependance thereon, advising you to write to the Southward for all the Assistance that can be afforded. He is also exceedingly pressing for flour, and informs that the Salt is coming on & complains much of the badness of the flour Barrells—I have also received a letter from M^r. P. Schenck informing that he had recd. 2,200 bushell Salt, 500 bushell of which cross'd the River 8 days previous to the date of his Letter (January 4th) that the residue was coming on daily He Complains much of the great want of money and expects he shall be under the Necessity of declining if not timely supplied.—He Requests orders to load the teams from the Eastward with private property, back with flour—

On the first I have to observe, that no Cattle as yet arrived & on the Second no Salt—.

The urgent demand for Indian Meal & rice has obliged me to send the Bearer Express to Ja^s. White, to forward on those articles, many of the troops are taking the Small Pox the natural way, His Excellency desires the may all be immediately innoculated, but the Doctors say they have not proper food for the purpose—

I have received a Drove of Cattle of 120 from M^r. Patton; which with the drove from Azariah Dunham is the whole that has arrived since you left us—except the few you sent.—

I this day saw Colonel Sidney Berry of New Jersey who had been at Reading, He informed me that Mr Hooper had been there & show'd him a Certificate from the Board of War setting forth, that wherever Complaints has been alledged to the Board by R. Wilson, against R. L. Hooper it appeared by sundry Affadavids produced by the latter, that said complaints where vexatious & groundless—and that the Board of War has given R. L. Hooper further powers than he posses'd before, with which he was triumphantly returning home.

Col^o. Berry further informs that your Resignation is the town talk of Reading and the publick conjectures that Trumbull is to return to the head of the Department.—

I have received from M^r. Smith through M^r. Graff 39,000 Dollars in Loan office Certificates. M^r. Graff says that he is scarcely able to supply the troops at Lancaster with Beef; that M^r. Slough & himself had sent your orders to Mr Buchanan but both Returned without Cash.—

A few days past a Letter was bro^t here from Col^o Laurens A.D.C inclosing a Letter to his Excellency from J. Rodman complaining of the Conduct of Ge^o Kitts & Jno. Ladd Howell who had taken from him a large Q^{ty}. of Meat; Refused to Weigh the same and left rec^{ts}. for only about one half the Q^{ty}. His Excellency desires that the Complaint may be enquired into.

I have given you a Scetch of the most material things that have happened since your departure. I have only to ad that I wish you success and remain Sir Your very Hble Servt.
Frames 1175-76.

Blaine to Unidentified

Sir, York Town January 27, 1778
You will immediately proceed through the District or County And procure all of the Following articles which is much Wanted for the Army that you Possibly can Viz. Beef Cattle, Pork, Flour, Whiskey Wheat and salt, giving the Under Mentioned prices—for Good stall fed Beef Five pounds pr C^t sinking the fifth Quarter, for Midling Ditto Ten Dollars Good pork four pounds p[er] Hundred and a little over rather than Miss a good purchase Whiskey Fifteen shillings p[er] Gallon at this place Wheat Ten shilling p[er] Bushell Delivered at such Mills as you may order imported salt fifteen pounds p[er] bushell And this Country made salt Ten pounds— Those persons who are not satisfied with the above Mentioned Prices you are hereby Authorized to Seize the same and give Certificates specifying the Quantity and Quality of each article So taken to be paid as the Legislative Authority of the State or the Honourable Congress May Hereafter Regulate—I make not the least doubt but you will exert yourself in Every Measure to procure as much of the above mentioned articles as you possibly can, forward the same with all speed to the Army as they are much wanted Use Every [exer]tion to apprehend all Engrosers and Forestallers and seize all Necessarys from them Which the army stands in need off Shou'ld want Assistance to put those Directions into Execution You will make the application to the Board of War who will afford you the Necessary Assistance, I have wrote Colonel McPherson who I hope will give you all the aid in his power, all the Wheat belonging to the Publick stored in Merchant Mills in the Neighbourhood of this town you will have ground out immediately and forward the same to Camp without delay as also all the beef Cattle and Whiskey, you will engage one hundred Waggons and more if in your power which forward without loss of time, while you have so good a Bridge over the Susquehannah River let not one Hhd of Whiskey or a fatt Beef escape your notice and seize all of those articles you can meet with, without Respect of Persons—let me hear from you by every opportunity and am sir Your Ob^t. Hble Servt
Frame 1176.

Chaloner to Blaine

D^r. Sir, Camp Valley Forge 29 Jany 1778
I have this moment Received the Inclosed Letters and have dispatched the bearer with what Cash I have of yours to enable you if you

see proper to afford M^r. Wilson some Assistance—

I have also to inform you that at present we are entirely out of Cattle, do send us as quick as possible all that you have procured—The Salt Provisions ordered on from New Jersey is exceeding slack a Coming do write Hugg and White to be somewhat more vigilant—I am Assured If some provision more than I am acquainted with is not made for the army they must suffer for want of meat in a few days

I have also received from Col^o Buchan Patton Colt & Schenk several letters all of which calls for your immediate answers I could send them by the bearer but expect you hourly.

The Sum sent p[er] M^r. Reynolds is Six Thousand Five Hundred Dollars—of your own cash—

I have also paid M^r. Wilsons order on you in favour of Mr Reynolds for Eight hundred and Thirty pounds. 17/6 I am Sir Your Ob^t. hlble Servt.
Frame 1176.

Chaloner to Unidentified

Sir,   Camp Valley Forge 31 Jany. 1778

Inclosed I send you two letters this moment recd—finding them of importance I dare not detain the Bearer longer than to that I am Sir Your very Hble Servt.
Frame 1177.

Francis Dana to Chaloner

Sir,   Moore Hall January 31st 1778

The Committee of Congress now Setting in Camp, Request your immediate attendance here I am Sir Your Most Hble Servt
Frame 1177.

Francis Dana was a Delegate to Congress. He was part of the Committee at Camp, which was investigating the Army's supply problems.

George Washington to Chaloner

Sir   Moore Hall January 31st 1778

    This Letter will accompany one from Comitee of Congress requiring your attendance at this Place. In addition, I shall inform you that by a return from the Commissary of Issues we have only 90 head of Cattle in Camp, and the troops only served for this day; moreover that he Knows not of any supplies coming on. It also appears by the said return that there is only 560 Barrels of Flour this I mention for your Government I am Sir Your very Hble Servt
Frame 1177.

Chaloner to Unidentified

Sir,   February 1st. 1778

    You must immediately proceed to Correylls Ferry (leaving the Cattle with the Bearer) endeavour to fall in with any Drove that you may hear of on the Road and Charge them to proceed to Head Q^{rs} immediately without the least Delay, You must not return untill you meet with a Drove from Az^h. Dunham I am Sir Your very Hble Servt
Frame 1178.

Chaloner to Mr. Roberts

Sir

    You must proceed immediately towards Reading and endeavour to fall in with whatever droves of Cattle that may be on the Road to Camp order the Drovers to proceed immediately without the least delay to Head Quarters as they will for neglect be Call'd to an Acc^t. for their Conduct—I am Sir Your & &
PS. Should you not meet with Cattle you must proceed on with the Letter for M^r. Patton and deliver it to him yourself Should your horse fail you, you are hereby authorized to hire or impress one for the Journey
Frame 1178.

Chaloner to John Patton

Sir,   February 1st. 1778

M^r. Ottenhamer when here informed me that he had Collected a Considerable Drove of Cattle and that they would be here as on this day I have dispatched the Bearer to meet them & hurry the Drovers to come on without Delay should he not be successfull he is to proceed to Your House with this. So great is our wants that we must set every Wheel in motion if possible for Gods sake send those on and as many more as you possibly can Collect By a Letter rec^d. from W^m. Buchanan last night have some expectations of Cash in a day or two when shall send you a supply— Do for Heavens sake exert yourself or the army will suffer. I am sir Yours &
PS collect Flour & salt provisions on Schulkill Banks & send it down by water
Frame 1178.

Chaloner to James White & Robert Dodd

Gen^n.   Camp February 1st. 1778

From my very pressing letter of the 4th Ult, I expected you would have exerted yourselves in forwarding the Salt provision from New Jersey.—I observe by the entrys of the D.C.G. of Issues that no more than 65 Barrels of Salt provisions are arrived—and from time of their arrival I have little reason to Expect that they were sent of in Consequence of my letter of the 4th Ult.—
I am now to inform you that the Bearer Mr Risburgh is dispatched by the Express order of his Excellency the Commander in Chief & the Comitee of Congress now sitting here to order you immediately to adopt such measures as the Laws of your state require, to procure Teams sufficient to forward to Head Q^{rs}. every Barrel of salt provision in New Jersey— sufficient N^o. of Teams must be employed to bring the Quantity in Store at each post at one tripp Our wants are such as will not admit of delay or excuse—

His Excellency & the Committe have called for my orders to you on this Subject you must prepare Yourselves to answer for the Neglect or inatention thereto, a repetition of Neglect from this Notice will be increasing the Offence I expect ample supplys from you in 10 days from this & Conclude. Gentleman Yours & &
Frame 1179.

Chaloner to Thomas Huggins

Sir,   Camp Valley Forge Feby. 1. 1778

In obedience to the Command of His Excellency The Commander in Chief and the Comittee of Congress now sitting here, I must call on you to adopt every method possible to forward on the Stores from the Head of Elk and its Neighbourhood will all speed for which purpose You must procure all the Teams you possibly can—I am also ordered to desire you to exert yourself in procuring further supplies of Beef and pork— Mr Hollingsworth writes me he informed you of 100 head of Cattle for sale,—I hope you have purchased and forwarded them with what you have already procured to this Camp.—
Your post is now become of great importance to the supplying of this army and will be soon more so—For which reason it is absolutely necessary that you correspond punctually & regularly to this Office informing by letter once a Week the daily arrival of Stores specifying the Quality and Quantity also what you may from time to time purchase
Our wants are such as will require the greatest exertions to supply us with a sufficiency of Meat & Bread for the Army to effect which you must strain every Nerve.—I am Sir Yours & &
Frame 1179.

Chaloner to Sebastian Graff

Sir,   Camp February 1st. 1778

I am ordered by his Excellency the Commander in Chief and the Committee of Congress now sitting here to send Express to every Assistant Commissary of Purchases ordering them to forward on to Camp all the Beef pork and flour they can possibly procure without one moments loss of time—In obedience thereto I must call on you to make enquiry of M^r. George Ross to know what number of teams are now engaged by his direction in halling flour to Camp this number must be augmented to at least 100 which must be continued until 30 days provision are brought into the vicinity of Camp—You must also procure and send to the Head of Elk four Brigades of Teams to hall Stores from thence to Head Q^{rs}. for which they must apply to Thos. Huggins there who will Load and Dispatch them—You must pursue the means pointed out by the Legislative of this State to procure the Teams and inform Colonel Blaine or myself of your success therein as soon as possible—For Gods sake

loose no time in Executing this business & for warding all the Beef and pork you can possibly send—The army is suffering for want. I expect Col°. Blaine will be able to send you a supply of Cash in a few days in mean time remain Sir Yours & &
Frame 1180.

Chaloner to Robert McGermont

Sir, February 2^d. 1778
 I am ordered by His Excellency the Commander in Chief and the Committee of Congress now sitting here to procure an Acc^t. of what stores are purchased and to forward them as speedily as possible to Camp. In conformity thereto I dispatch the bearer Express to require of you immediately to furnish an account of what Pork or provisions you have on hand and to forward the same to Camp as Expeditiously as possible—
For Gods sake exert yourself in procuring Beef & pork and forwarding it to Camp, The wants of the army are such as will admit of no delay. pray be punctual in the above as much depends on it I am Sir Your most hble Servt.
Frame 1180.

Chaloner to George Echelberger

Sir February 2^d. 1778
 Yours of the 27 Ult. Just received with thirty five Head of Cattle Col°. Blaine Expected that you would have sent five times the number.—
I must request of you immediately on Rec^t. of this to inform Col° Blaine or myself the exact Quantity & Quality of Provisions & Stores now in your possession.
I am Commanded by his Excellency the Commander in Chief & the Committee of Congress now sitting here to order all provisions & Stores from every Quarter to Camp as speedily as possible In obedience thereto I must now call on you to procure a sufficient Number of Teams to transport all the Stores & provisions from York to this in two tripps, In executing this business no time must be lost—I shall lay your letters before Colonel Blaine when he arrives and am Assured he will be much Displeased at your discharging Waggons at a time provisions is so much wanted at Camp—Do your utmost to forward all the Beef Cattle you can

also Salt provision & flour as expeditiously as possible—At same time you vigorously execute the orders of the Board of War respecting Rum & Whiskey Joseph Carson writes me he has a Q^{ty}. in York Town. I am Sir Yours &c
Frame 1180.

Ephraim Blaine to James Smith

Sir,   Camp 3^d February 1778

Our demand for Beef Cattle as great as ever, must once More Request your immediate Assistance of all you can possible procure is not a number of your own good Beef, have you not purchased a Considerable number of beef Cattle in & about Potomack River, pray forward them all; I hope M^r. Spear and you have been very successful in purchasing pork, and wish a large Number of them might be brought on to Camp, this will leave you to your own Judgement & have reason to hope for One thousand, need not enlarge am Confident you will spare no pains and use every endeavour in your power to forward all the supplies you possibly can, pray favour me with a line by very first opportunity and am Sir Your Hble $Serv^t$
Frame 1181.

Blaine to Mr. Cox

Sir,   Camp 3^d. February 1778

I have reason to hope by this you have procured a Quantity of Pork some beef Cattle and Whiskey, our demand in Camp is very Great, pray use every exertion to procure those articles as they are much Wanted for the army, such persons as are not disposed to sell at the prices Stipulated by the Assembly Seize the Same and give Certificates, make application to the Nearest Quarter Master for the Necessary Waggons, shoud he refer an immediate Complyance make Oath before a Magistrate of your Application and send it down by first safe Opportunity, procure all the good Merchant Flour and Wheat you can and advice me of your Success, forward all the live Cattle & Pork without delay am Sir Yours &c,
Frame 1181.

This was probably Cornelius Cox of Paxton, Pa.

Blaine to Thomas Edwards

Sir,   Camp 3^d. February 1778

I hope by this you have procured a large Drove of Cattle, if upon Rec^t of this you have not forwarded them to Camp, pray do without one moments loss of time our Demand for that Article is very great—use every means to procure Flour and Wheat cannot engage sufficient for your Quota, and forward a Quantity of Flour as soon as the Roads will admit, as also Whiskey which is much wanted here, I shall write you next Week and furnish you with Cash, equal to your demand, pray write Me by first safe Opportunity and am. Sir Your Humble Servant
Frame 1181.

Thomas Edwards was a purchaser for the Commissary Department in Lancaster County, Pa.

Blaine to Alexander Blaine

Sir,   Camp 3^d February 1778

Expected long eer this to have Rec^d. a large Quantity of Whiskey from you hope you have Taken every Method to procure Largely, and forward the same without delay as its much wanted here, I hope You have purchased Large Quantities of Wheat and have the same Collected into the best Merchant Mills for Making Flour; after you have procured Seven or Eight Thousand Bushells of Wheat, advertise the Customary prices for Good Fresh Ground Merchantable Flour delivered at the Magazine at Carlile, let no time be lost with you and Captain [author's blank] in making out a Return of the Issues as also what provisions remain in Store, Beg you and my friends in Town may have an eye to my Woodland and try to Detect those low Villanous people who are stealing it daily sure you might in some Measure put a stop to them they have done me great injury—Remember me to all friends and believe your affectionate Friend
Frame 1182.

Alexander Blaine, Ephraim's brother, was at Carlisle, Pa.

Blaine to John Patton

Sir   Camp 3^d. February 1778

Request you may immediately upon your Return home order all the Flour you possibly can to the Banks of Schulkill & take the Opportunity of the first high Water to forward to this place youll make application to Col^o. Bird for all the Flour he may have ready This a very fine time to hurry down the Boats beg you may not neglect as there coming will be of great advantage to the publick at this time, as I need not expect many Waggons till the roads is better am Sir Your most Hble Servt. Frame 1182.

Blaine, Account of Cattle Expected

Account of Cattle expected from the Purchasing Commissaries in the Course of ten days from the 3^d. of February 1778—

James Smith	250 Head
M^r. Shigar & Comp^y.	150 Ditto
M^r. Dunham	300 Ditto
M^r. N. Dunham	75
M^r. Broderick	100
George Kitts & Major Edwards	100
	975 Head & no more

An Account of Pork & C^a
    Returned by M^r. White at Sundry Places
                                            1048 Barrels
    Joseph Hugg Gloucester C^o.   _400_
                                            1448

M^r. Huggins Elke	150
M^r. M^c.Germont Dover	_1000_
Ba^{ls}.	2598 Pork

Contracted with Sundry Persons for 3000 Hogs to be brought from Potomack & the back Parts of Pennsylvania Two thirds of which is to be

Salted up for the use of the Troops at Carlile & Lancaster,—Also engaged about 50,000 Barrels of Flour in the Middle district.
Frame 1182.

Chaloner to William Buchanan

Sir,   Camp Valley Forge 3^d. February 1778
Your letter inclosing Extract of a letter from M^r. Colt was put into my hands Just after I waited on his Excellency and the Committee of Congress that is now sitting here They call'd on me in the absence of Col^o. Blaine to inform what prospect of supplies I had to support the army for the Winter, Indeed I gave them but very little encouragement I had it not in my power to give them much expectation of ample supplies coming on in time, you may be Assured sir. It is a Truth and a Melancoly one that there is not one days allowance of meat in Camp and none of the troops longer served than for to day—The extract from M^r. Colt being on the Subject of supplies I thought it my duty to lay it before His Excellency as you directed and immediately returned to the Committee therewith where I had Just left him, He was returned home but the Committee call'd for the extract & the letter inclosing it which now lays before them and prevents my answering it as fully as I otherwise would wish to do—. However to enable you to answer to the Charge of immense qtys of stores & provisions being delivered Over by the late Commissary General I have inclosed you an account of Stores & received from him in the Middle department together with an Estimate of the time each article would serve the army as in December calculated by the Returns of the Issuing Commissarys for that Month. It needs no observation to show how far it removes the charge of immence Stores &c being deliver'd and in some measure Acc^{ts}. for the vast Expence for the present campaign in the Commissary Department—I expect Col^o. Blaine every hour I doubt not will immediately answer your several letters. In the Mean time. I remain
Sir Your most Hble $Serv^t$
Frame 1183.

Blaine to George Washington and the Committee of Congress at Camp

A few Quiries for Consideration of His Excellency General Washington and the Honourable Committee of Congress now sitting at Moore Hall February 4th 1778.

1st. as this is the Season for procuring the Stald fed Beef and a time we shall be Necessiated to issue Pork, would allowing the Soldier 1 1/2 Bread or Flour and 3/4 of Beef or Pork be a sufficient Ration till there is an appearance of a more plentiful supply

2^{d} of the article of meat ought not some method be immediately taken to induce the Farmers to put up one of more of their grown Cattle to feed which might be in good order for Beef by the month of April & May to Deliver for the use of the army—an Address from His Excellency to the people for that purpose might be of great advantage I will undertake to Circulate them through my District—and make not the least doubt it will produce three or four thousand head of good Cattle.—

3^{d} There a number of Cattle along the Beaches near Cape May & little Egg Harbour in Jersey are they in danger of the Enemy would it not be prudent to have them Collected without delay and places prepared to have them fed for Beef.—

4th. What ought to be given for Barreld Pork seized from the people near the Salt Works the value those peoples hold upon their salt and now obliged to give it will advance it far above what I can think of giving underneath is an Estimate I have made

    220 lb Pork at 5£   11 £
    1/2 Bushell salt at 20 Do^{s}.   3 15
    Barrel   15
                      15 10 one Barrel pork

5^{thly}. Should not some Method be taken to Secure a Large Quantity of Whiskey, the people pay no regard to the Law passed by the assembly of this State for Regulating the price & no spirited measures are persued by the executive authority to put those Laws into execution ought not large Quantities of Whiskie be purchased for the ensuing Campaign

6^{thly} ought not some Method be taken to rescue all the Beef Cattle in North Carolina & the back parts of Virginia for the Army, and stop Forestallers from bying any those persons have been a great injury to the

publick and have added to the extravagant prices of every article wanted for the army
Frames 1183-1184.

Blaine to Anthony Broderick

Sir, Camp Valley Forge 5th. February 1778
    Yours I received of the 28th. January and an exceeding sorry You had it not in your power to forward a larger drove of Beef Cattle—we are in the Greatest distress for want of Beef, must request your immediate Attention to that Business, & beg you may forward as many Cattle as you possible can without one Moments loss of time, has as yet received no Cash but by the Return of the Next drove hope to have it in my power to advance you largely, procure all the good Flour you possibly can—the hurry of Business prevents me answering you as fully as I would wish to do—the Laws of your State will support you in making Seizures, beg you may procure all the Cattle in your power & am—Your Most Hble Servt.
NB the Board of War are sitting: wish to have your Acc^{ts} as soon as possible.—
Frame 1184.

Blaine to Stephen Porter

Sir, Camp Valley Forge 5th Feby. 1778
    Yours I received the 2^d. Instant and have only to add, that with Respect to the Magazine I have not obtained the Gen^{ls} permission where to fix, or whether there will be new Stores erected or not, but believe one will be in your Neighbourhood and you may depend on being the person appointed to superintend the Same, as to large Stores being erected don't apprehended it will be Necessary, the Mills which grind Flour, (those only excepted near the Enemy) will answer for Magazines, the Stores will only be wanting for what salt provisions & hard Bread is expected from the Southward, and doubt it will be very triffling—
    I have not altered from my intentions of Quiting the Service, therefore will not stand in need of an Assistant, any service in my Power shall render you with great pleasure as soon as his Excellency determines in the place shall write you, have some thoughts of going to the Head of Elk and make your house on my Return, am Quite out of Cash therefore

have it not in my Power to Assist you at this Time but request you may continue purchasing all the wheat you can upon Credit, am Sir Yours & & Frame 1184.

Blaine to David Frazer

Sir, Camp Valley Forge 5th. February 1778

I am exceeding sorry to find your Magazine is so scarce of every species of Provisions; Certainly M^r. Fuller has not been Active or he might have done much more and had by this a large Quantity of Flour and Considerably of Beef & Pork, believe he has suffered in not being regularly supplied with Cash I have ordered Colonel Patton as soon as he received a larger sum which he has an order for, to send him a Considerable sum. I have a special order from the Board of War to seize all Kind of Provisions and Spirits, shall beg your assistance to M^r. Fuller, and wou'd request you wou'd spend two or three Days with him up at the Minisikns I want him to Contract for all the Flour he possibly can. Wou'd also wish this matter might be done with dispatch and Secrecy, M^r. Vancamp has been Recommended as a very proper person to contract with,—engage him 33 Shillings p[er] Hundred if delivered at Nicholas Pattersons on the River Delaware, and Coryells Ferry woud wish all the Millers who will engage upon those terms to be employed immediately. I need not mention my Reason to you for Keeping this matter Secret, you Well Know the great Consumption of Wheat. this I have not mentioned in fullers letter, but Request you would Caution him, a great trade of Whiskey has been carried on through your Country to the North River Request every Gallon may be Seized without Respect of Persons, and refer them to me for payment, do press Mr Fuller to do his Duty, and be a little more Active.—the Salt must remain with you for some time till we are in want at this place, wish you and Mr Fuller wou'd seize the best bake House in Town for which the owner shall be paid Rent. and engage a Baker who may be continued & kept in employ.

M^r. Magill presented me an Acct for salt delivered M^r. Means issuing Commissary, I have not money to discharge it at this time, but inform the owner he cant expect the price charged in the Acc^t., I shall properly reward you for what Trouble you have in Assisting M^r. Fuller in contracting for Flour & Seizing Whiskey, wish to hear from you as soon as You Return off the journey with Mr Fuller, and am Sir Your Hble Servt. Frame 1185.

David Frazer was in the Commissary Department at Easton, Pa.

Blaine to Henry Fuller

Sir,   Camp Valley Forge 5th. Feby. 1778
I saw a Letter to Col^o. Jones from M^r. Frazer Complaining of the supplies he has received into the Magazine from you—I expected you would have purchased a large Quantity of Pork & considerably of Beef Cattle, but find by M^r. Frasors Return there is very little on hand, request you may procure all you possibly can without loss of time, from those persons who are not disposed to sell, you must seize, & give the Owners Certificates for the same, hope you have engaged large Quantities of Flour, upon Receipt of this desire You may proceed up to the Minisinks, & engage with the Millers there for all the Flour you possibly can to be delivered at Nicholas Pattersons upon the Bank of the Delaware River & Coryells Ferry for which agree to pay them thirty three Shillings & the Casks (this business keep to Yourself) & you have special orders to seize all the Whiskie you can meet with without Respect of persons, am well informed, large Quantities is Stored in your Town, & daily passing through to the North River, pray let none escape your notice & refer the owners to me for payment. I have wrote M^r. Frasor to Assist you in making Contracts for flour & ride up with you to the upper part of Northampton. M^r. Vancamp has been Recommended to me as a very worthy Man; give him the preference for what Quantity he may engage for am sorry Colonel Patton has not supplied you better with Cash—He has received a large order for Cash the other day—when paid have ordered him to remit you largely; when your Man was here I had no money or would have sent you some beg your man procure all the Flour Beef Pork & Whiskey in your Power shall be glad to hear from you & am Sir Your most Hble Servt
Frame 1186.

Blaine to William Buchanan

                                  Camp Valley Forge 5th. Feby. 78
M^r. M^c.Germont having sent up the Bearer M^r. Emory for Cash am obliged to send him to you Request you may pay him the Amount of his Order which is thirty five thousand Dollars, and dont delay him one

moment if possible, as M^r. McGarmant cannot procure pork without Cash, & he has been the only Person in my District who has been Successfull in that Business. We are daily from Hand to Mouth with Beef and Pork, and without you order forward large Quantities of Pork from the Southward (and for the present M^r. Smith Echellberger & the Mr Guyer you engaged to supply us with Cattle the army will suffer for that Article) the Pork Collected in Jersey is but Very triffling & is all on its way to Camp, & will be but a few days of subsistance for the Army little supplies of Cattle from Mr Colt, not one fifth the number I demanded.—Chiefly all the Cattle taken, and but Very few left in my District those Circumstances ought to alarm you.—Wish how soon you can supply me with Money & as a large a sum as you possibly can procure ought to pay my Assistants Four Hundred Thousand Dollars to enable them to carry on the purchases of Wheat and Flour the want of Regular supplies of Cash is a great injury in their Purchasing forward by the first Opportunity a Number of the Account Books—have not time to Answer your several letters now, but shall in a day or two. & am Sir Your Most Hble Servt.
Frame 1186.

Blaine to Joseph Hugg

Sir,   Camp Valley Forge 5th Feby. 78
  Yours of the 23^d. and 29th. January I have received—I am greatly disappointed with Respect to the supplies, I flattered myself with receiving from your District, and the more especially as every Person from thence Assured us that Country could furnish large Quantities of Pork provided Active persons where appointed to the Service—this was a Matter left with you—It certainly appears there has been a Neglect in the purchasing Department as we now have no other remedy than by a more vigorous Exertion to this Duty—and on you I must Depend for it.—
I beg on receipt of this that you Capt. Hugg & M^r. Morris may adopt some Plan to secure all the Middling Beef, Pork and Salted provisions you can lay your Hands on, giving the prices the Law has stipulated for those Articles—think you ought to give £15.10 p[er] Barrell for Pork, hope you will have it in your power to procure large Quantities—For Gods Sake try to procure a large Drove of Cattle & bring them on yourself, if they could be Collected in a few Days you may Delay Steel to Assist you—by this time you come over shall have Cash to supply you with.—

From this to the first of April will be the only time we shall labour under much difficulty, as large supplies are on their way from Virginia; every exertion must be used in forwarding all the Salt provisions. call upon the Quarter Masters & left them Know the great want of provisions in Camp & demand a sufficient Number of Waggons for transporting all of you possibly can spare from the posts in your District—

M^r. Harvey complains greatley of not being regularly supplied, and the great Difficulty, he has been obliged to keep one of his Assistants daily engaged in collecting Flour and other provisions—The scheme you mention in your Letter of securing all the grown Cattle upon the Beaches lay before the Committee of Congress, would wish all that are Middling Beef might be brought on to Camp—Woudd wish how soon you can have your Accounts ready the Board of War are calling upon me daily

You mention Resigning, you must not think of it for the present, Allowances will certainly be made for the great Expence the purchasers are exposed to, therefore hope you will Decline any Such Thought—pray dont let the want of Money delay you for the present but use every Means to Render us every Assistance in your Power and as speedily as possible, would be glad to See you as soon as your Accounts are ready, pray engage all the Flour you can
Frame 1187.

Blaine to Henry E. Lutterloh

Sir,   Pawlings Ford 7th. Feby. 1778

  The demand of provisions in Camp is very Great, and the principle part of our supplies for the army must Come from the Head of Elk & Dover, Request you may Immediately furnish me with four Brigades of good Waggons for the above purpose, and oblige Sir Your Obd^t. Hble Servt
Frame 1188.

Henry E. Lutterloh was Deputy Quartermaster General and acting as the head of that department.

Blaine to Joseph Hugg

D^r. Sir,   Camp Valley Forge 7th Feby. 78

  The pressing Demand of provisions for the daily support of the army Obliges me to call upon you for every exertion in your power of also your Brother and Mr Morris, beg that one of you may have an Immediate Eye to the forwarding of the salt provisions without a Moments loss of time & the others attend to the procuring all the live stock possible, and salt provisions.—will expect a Drove from you as soon as in Your power to send—Inclosed you have a copy of an Order from the Board of War to me and hope you will adhere to it with respect of Beef, Pork & live Stock, all those Cattle you mention, upon the Beaches at and near Cape May, request you may have them Collected & such as are fitt for Immediate use forward to Head Quarters, those of the Inhabitants as have shown a Disaffection to the General cause give them Certificates, to be settled in future.

His Excellency is informed great Quantities of Pork are salted up by private persons in the Neighbourhood of Shrewsbury, Egg harbour and the County of Salem, this beg you may secure, paying such prices as I have Mentioned to you in mine of Yesterday, or wetheirn Your power to purchase, favour me with a line by Every Opportunity, and am D^r. Sir Your Most Ob^t. Servt
Frame 1188.

Blaine to Nehemiah Dunham

Sir,   Camp Valley Forge 7th. Feb^y.

Need not inform you how great our want is of Provisions, must therefore Request every exertion in your power to procure another Drove of Cattle & all the Pork you possibly can, do not stick to the Nicety of purchasing none but fine Beef our Wants will admit of Delivering the troops that which is Middling, therefore am Confident you can procure another Drove which forward without one Moments Loss of time, continue your purchases of Wheat & Flour shall want a great Quantity, M^r. Formans Mill must be certainly employed, the Flour Middlings and ship stuff all mixed together, any such other quantities as may be necessary to Bake done in the same Maner, immediately upon your arrival home you will forward all the salt procured in your District, there is a neighbour of yours one Col^o Stewart am informed he has four very fine Oxen you must take them and all others such. am Sir Yours Ob^t Hble Ser^t.
Frame 1189.

Blaine to Henry Schenk

Sir,   Camp Valley Forge 7th Feb^y.
         Your several Letters of the 20th. December & 4th. Ult are now before me and mark the Contents.—
I am much obliged to you for your exertions in purchasing Flour from the Eastern Department as also in forwarding Salt from the New England States—the Conducting of which Business must leave intirely to your direction; relying on your prudence not to employ more persons than is Necessary, and at the same time not to suffer the Stores or Provisions to be embezled or wasted for want of proper persons to take care of them.— M^r. Colt complains that the Carters could not bring on Flour owing to the Casks being in bad order & that it occasioned great waste in what was brought; to prevent which you must get the Casks made of seasoned Wood with three Hoops on each Head, & have them secured with good Linning Hoops—You must procure Nails for the Milers and if not to be had with you am of opinion M^r. Colt can supply you—
I expect a Quantity of Salt Provisions will be forwarded to Hudsons river from Connecticut must request your Attention in sending it on to Delaware where the teams from hence may take it up the Army is now suffering from want of that article and must call on you to loose no time in sending it forward—.
         I shall send you a supply of Cash p[er] the first Opportunity. You must continue your purchases of Flour only for the present Consumption of the Army to the Eastward endeavoring to reduce the price if possible; as soon as the Roads will permit I shall have it in my power to furnish them large supplies on much more reasonable terms—relying on your exertions.—I remain sir Yours & &
Frame 1189.

Blaine to Henry Champion

Sir   Camp Valley Forge 7 Feby. 1778
         Nothing could afford me greater consolation than hearing of your appointment as D. C G of Purchases for Live Stock in the Eastern Department. I have received undoubted information of your abilities in this Business as also of the Assistance You have frequently afforded under the Command of his Excellency General Washington—Never did there Necessities more loudly call for the vigorous exertions of the Purchasers of live Stock in your Department, when Inform you that the Army and its

dependances in this encampment only has drawn from 28 to thirty thousand Rations p[er] day for some Months past, and that they together with all out posts, Hospitals & Prisoners amounting to one third more, have been supplied with receiving only small assistance from your Government—I need say no more to Convince you that without your vigorous exertions we must soon suffer—The Provinces South of Hudsons River not very remarkable in raising Cattle &^{c}. are Quite drained of the few they have fed & in some parts their Stock Cattle are also Consumed which obliges us to look to you only for our Winter & spring support—The small aid your States have afforded in Companies with large Quantities of Beef sent last year gives me great reason to expect considerable from you.—

For the more easy and quick dispatch of bringing on Beef Cattle I have appointed M^r. Azariah Dunham one of my Assistant Purchasers to receive them at Morris town, and Mr Broderick at Sussex, also to provide forage for them on the Road this side Hudsons River and I flatter myself your droves [sic] will be able to inform you that this Business is already done with Judgement & propriety, any other Obstacles in the way of forwarding Cattle or salt Provision within my Department, shall be Removed if it lies in my power on the earliest information. our distress for meat has been so very conspeciuous that I am persuaded you will receive abundant Testimony of the Truth of the above Facts, by persons from hence belonging to the Army.—Resting Assured that the army receive timely aid from your spirited & vigorous exertions in this Business I conclude. Sir Your most Ob^t. Hble Servt
Frame 1190.

Henry Champion was in charge of purchasing cattle in the Eastern Department.

Blaine to Peter Colt

Sir,   Camp Valley Forge 7 Feby. 1778
Your Favours of the 24 of December as also of the 10th. January is received and now lays before me—I have not heretofore had time sufficient to attend to answering them, my presence being Necessary in almost every part of my department, to force from thence the necessary supplies for the existence of the army, daily looking for relief from your Quarter but found none till Yesterday. when a drove of Ninety seven head arrived—.The Army in this encampment has drawn from Twenty eight to

Thirty two thousand Rations p[er] Day for several Months past and have been supported in the article of Beef (off which none of the Middle States abound in) without much aid or Assistance from your quarter.—These states are now exhausted of all their Beef have put up very little pork for the want of salt, and the Communication in Chesipeak Bay stoppd, that we can have very little Hopes from the Southward, those Circumstances obliges me to look to you and your department only for the supply of that article—M^r. Dunham of Morris town & M^r. Broderick of Sussex my Assistants are directed to Procure Hay at the proper Stages for the Cattle & to receive them of your Drovers—

It gives me great concern to find that the Flour sent to your Quarter is not in order fit to be transported. I have given the Necessary Instructions to my Assistants in New Jersey to prevent the like in the future.—

You would have had more ample supplies in this article, had not Col^o Trumbles returns fallen short some Thousand Barrels which obliges is to Draw part of the Flour in Jersey from thence, but now sufficient Quantities are purchased, & will be in Motion towards your relief as soon as the Roads will permit.—

I flatter myself you will send us every Hoof you can possibly spare.—without a great Relief from you we cannot support the army many weeks, His Excellency has wrote General Putnam not to stop any of the Cattle as his Troops can be supplied with salt provisions—We have no news here worth Communicating great talk of French war but wish it may not be talk only—shall be glad to hear from you p[er] every opportunity—and to render you any service that be in my power. in the mean time remain greatly distressed for the Armys wants—am Sir Your most Hble Servt

Frame 1191.

Blaine to George Kitts

Sir   Camp Valley Forge 8. Feby. 1778

The scarcity of Beef in camp is so great that His Excellency has commanded me to use the most vigorous Exertions in procuring supplies for the army.—

In consequence of which you must immediately proceed With the Guard allotted to go with you into the Counties of Lancaster Berks and Northampton and there Collect all the Beef Cattle you possibly can procure For this purpose you have herewith [writer's blank] Dollars which

you must apropriate to the payment of the Cattle. Any person possessed of fatt Cattle for use and refusing to take a reasonable and Just price for them You must have them seized giving the Owners Certificates Certifying the weight only Such persons direct to me for payment.—
I must charge you to be exceeding diligent use every exertion in your power forwarding all to Camp you possibly can collect without delay. am Sir Yours & &
Frame 1191

Blaine to Azariah Dunham

Dear Sir, Camp Valley Forge 9 Feby 78
I acknowledge the receipt of yours this morning and am sorry the drove of Cattle was not thrice the number we are much distressed for beef some of the Troops only served for the 7th. Instant and no cattle expected but one small Drove except from you, for god sake and my Reputation use every exertion to forward with the greatest dispatch all the stock and other Cattle you possibly can without one Moments loss of time, (as I dread our situation before they arrive) the Roads being so bad have little hope of receiving any salt Provisions by waggons—I have given a Just state of our district to his Excellency and what subsistance in meat he has reason to expect from us, can we Keep up an ample supply for this Month, will be able to support characters. have had advice from M^r. Hugg, Dunham & Broderick, and am sorry to inform you that my Hopes from them is very triffling, on you M^r. Smith and M^c.Garmont Must I place my Confidence & make not the least doubt but you will adopt such measures as will afford a speedy and temporary supply.
Must Acknowledge your supply of cash has by no means been equal to the demand but hope in future it will be more Regular I have had great reason of Complaints against Col^o. Hugg and those of his district in the purchasing Department, their supplies at Head Quarters has been very tardy and triffling and very far short of what I expected—shoud be exceeding sorry to find any of my Assistants spending their time and laying out the public money for private advantages, so soon as this can appear to me no longer shall they continue in the department.—Youll oblige me by a further hint of this matter. I have sent you by your Brother twenty Thousand Dollars in cash, and fifteen thousand in Certificates which I hope will arrive safe and in some Measure remove the Difficulties you labour under—such Quarters I enjoy in Camp shall be chearfully welcome

to Col° Dunham, but Request he may fetch plentiful of Beef Cattle with him and he will find his Lodging more Comfortable have laid our grievances before the Committee of Congress and they have given me every satisfaction with respect to the expences the purchasers are exposed to, and have every reason to beleive they will make proper allowances, I have made them a list of the faithfull in the purchasing department and am satisfied proper encouragement will be given them to continue My good Friend exert yourself this time to relieve us from our distressed situation and you will ever lay me under a particular Obligation and am with great Respect. D^r. Sir Your Most Obd^t. & Most Hlble Servt
Frame 1192.

Chaloner to Azariah Dunham

D^r. Col°. Camp Valley Forge 9th. Feby. 1778

Never did supplies arrive more timely than the Drove of Cattle brought this day by your Brother Some of the troops had been without meat for two days and the consequence of another day in this situation I fear might have proven fatal to the Existence of our army.—

To you who have so repeatedly manafisted more than the common regard for the welfare of this army by your repeated exertions and timely aid, a bare recital of our wants is sufficient without further stimulation to produce your accustomed aid.—

In greater distress than ever we before experienced we look to you for relief—exert yourself for a short time and enable us to rub out this Month plenty & let what will happen we sustain our credit—but if the Contrary we must fall with the Army.—

Col°. Blaine has sent in his Resignation to Congress and they by letter from the President solicits his continuance promising to remove every obstacle and render the department as agreeable as Circumstances and seasons will admit of—From this arrival as from the frequent interviews he has had with the Committee of Congress now here I have reason to believe our department will be fixed on a footing both respectable & profitable—Be assured Sir he has a High sense of your services and wishes to reward them by a punctual remittance and adequate Compensation which soon he hopes to have in his power—Your Brother brings you a further amittance also Loan Office Certificates for 19093 Dollars more of which may be obtained if required—

[author's blank] has received [author's blank] on your Acc^t all which shall adjust with you when you to Camp—.

I have only to ad that I wish most heartedly for another drove of Cattle from you For gods sake send on those from New England without delay or the army must disband. To you only do i look to with any degree of Certainly for our support and by your exertions must we stand or fall.— Resting Assured we shall receive the Necessary relief from your bountious hand that we stand in need off. I conclude D^r. Sir Your very Hble $Serv^t$
Frame 1193.

Blaine to Thomas Huggins

Sir, Camp Valley Forge 10 Feby. 1778
When you were last here I informed you of our distressed situation with respect of Beef, and requested you to forward us every Assistance in your power after supplying General Smallwoods Division, which you Assured me you had done before you left home, the Day after you left complaints from the General to his Excellency came to camp informing him that his people had been without meat two days you must also Remember that I gave you a very particular order to forward all Hudsons salt Beef to Head Quarters, but to my great surprize when I returned from Bucks County to Camp found that a Considerable quantity of Pork, and forty five head of beef Cattle, from M^r. M^c.Garmont was stop'd for the use of General smallwoods Division, and only thirty seven Barrels of the Beef forwarded, you had my orders Respecting Indian Meal I think one Hundred Barrels, this you have also Neglected though very much wanted for the sick in the small pox, such conduct and Neglect is pardonable [*sic*] in persons who are appointed to purchase for and feed the army, I have often found you guilty of Neglect of Duty therefor is future must insist upon your complyance with instructions from time to time—upon receipt of this desire you to forward the above Mentioned Quantity of Indian Meal and one Hundred Barrels more, as also all the salt provisions sent from Baltimore to your care, and such other quantities of Live stock and Provision of your own purchases as can be spared from General Smallwoods Division this I desire you may Immediately comply with all the Waggons you can press have them loaded without a Moments loss of Time to come one trip to Camp, M^r. Howell will inform you how great our demand is, therefore need not inlarger, must insist upon you making out your Acc^t. of Purchases to the first of March at which time hope you will have them ready for Settlement, let me hear from you by the very first opportunity and am Sir Your Very Hble $Serv^t$
Frame 1194.

Blaine to Robert McGermont

D^r. Sir   Camp Valley Forge 10th. Feby. 1778.
    I have sent the Bearer M^r. Howell down on purpose to hurry forward all the Stores of Salt Provisions and Indian Meal without one moment loss of time as we are in the greatest want of them, if in your power to procure waggons beg you may and what stores are Convenient to water Carriage forward them with dispatch to the Head of Elk when waggons will be ordered to receive it, I have sent three Brigades forward with some empty Barrels do forward them without loss of time, as soon as more waggons come to Camp shall forward them with more empty Barrels, my good Friend I need not mention to you how great our Demand is for Beef and Pork pray forward a Drove of good Cattle and all the salt Pork you possibly can procure M^r. Howell will acquaint you our situation, shall be glad to hear from you and am D^r. Sir Your Most Ob^t. Very Hble Servt
Frame 1194.

Blaine to Alexander Hamilton

Sir,   Pawlings Ford 12 Feby. 1778
    I have the Misfortune of Being this day out of Beef, but there is plenty of Flour and bread and Considerably of spirits, the Commissary must be to blame the want of bread in General Woodfords Brigade, inclosd is a return from him he complains the want of waggons, indeed there is but very few in camp, but such as Col^o. Biddle has engaged in hawling Forage and he seems determined to Keep them, and every hour looking for a supply of beef Cattle and salt Provisions, but believe Providence is determined I shall have no Assistance by Waggonage, the roads have never been so bad, shall cross the River in the Morning to hurry on some waggons with salt Pork am with respect Sir Your Most Ob^t. & Very Hble Servant
Frame 1195.

Alexander Hamilton was one of Washington's aides-de-camp.

Blaine to William Evans

D^r. Sir, Camp Valley Forge 12th Feb^y.

The Badness of the Roads and the Difficulty that will attend waggons coming a great Distance distresses me and obliges me to call upon you for every exertion. a few days to procure all the good Teams in your Neighborhood to bring two trips of Flour on to Camp. assure the owners they will not be delayed for any further service and shall be amply satisfied for their Trouble. we shall be ashore without your immediate Assistance, pray be here the fourteenth with all the Flour you possibly can, shall be able to supply you with cash, when you come here, let not a single waggon escape you, load and send on all in your power, we have not a single waggon in Camp, therefore to you we look for relief no person can hinder you from taking waggons upon this Occasion, and hope every of your Neighbours will show a williness to let their teams come out, coud mention two or three Reasons however the bearer will inform you, am with esteem Dr Sir, Your Most Ob^t & very
Frame 1195.

Blaine to Thomas Wharton Jr.

Dear Sir Camp Valley Forge 12th Feby. 78

The neglect in the Quarter Master department not keeping up a continual supply of waggons from the Magazines with provisions renders it difficult for me to support the Army, have not Received one Brigade of Waggons from Lancaster or the Bucks Counties this three Weeks—the Quarter Masters complain they have no power to press and have great Difficulty in procuring a single Team—wou'd request your honour Immediate Assistance to adopt such measures as to your prudence may effect drawing out the Necessary supply of teams, two Hundred and odd will be wanting in our department—if this salutary measure cannot be put in execution very shortly the army will suffer, there is flour and Whiskey in every County sufficient to load such Waggons as may be demanded, the Badness of the Roads have deprived a single waggon from coming to Camp this several days am with great respect your Honours. Most Obedient & Most Very Hble Servt
Frame 1196.

Blaine to Mathias Slough

Dear Sir,   Camp Valley Forge Feby. 12th. 1778

I hope eer this reached you that your success in procuring Wheat and Flour has been very considerable—I have two or three reasons which obliges me to call on you to adopt every Measure to purchase all you possibly can and beg you will use every exertion till the first of March—Cant you take in sundry millers by Contract for such Quantities as they will engage such Mills as are twelve or fifteen Miles round Lancaster can be very good magazines—for your Extrodinary trouble in the transaction of this Business be Assured you shall be amply rewarded.—shall have the pleasure of seeing you in a few days—No News worth Communicating have hard work to keep our army afloat in Beef—Please to present my compliments to M^{rss}. Slough, & am with respect Dear Sir Your Most Ob^t. Hble Servt
Frame 1196.

Blaine to Peter Aston

Sir,   Camp Valley Forge Feby. 13. 1778

You will immediately proceed to Newton Bucks County and adopt every prudent Measure to procure all the Wheat and Flour you possibly can, and without one Moments loss of time, beginning as near the Enemys lines as you can with any degree of safety. Major Murray is appointed by his Excellency to afford every assistance in his power, which make not the least doubt he will, all expence of carting thrashing &^{c}. must be stopp^d. out of the price of the wheat, every Exertion to have it removed to places of safety must be used.—there is a Number of people who have Certificates and Receipts from James Pollock for Pasturage of Cattle you will please to settle them in the following maner, for every night or twenty four Hours in Meadow Pasture ten Pence p[er] Head and in upland pastures five pence and no more. M^r. Frat who lives Near New Town has an Acc^t. but no Receipt, you will please to have this also settled wish you great Success, and am Sir Your Most Ob^t Servt
Frame 1196.

Blaine to Francis Murray

Dear Sir,   Pawlings Ford Feb[y]. 13. 78
Inclos'd you have a few lines from His Excellency Gen[1]. Washington requesting your Exertion in obliging those people who are not disposed to thrash their Grain to an immediate Complyance—your general Acquaintance with the Inhabitants of Bucks County will be a great Advantage, tis his Excellencys desire that all the Flour and Wheat contigious to the Enemys lines should be mov'd to places of safety— Please send me the Preachers Piece of Cloth, but first if possible have it valued, I want it very much, also Cap[t] Parrs Gun, M[r]. Ashton & you will continue Some method of forwarding them Immediately, Please make my Compliments to M[rss]. Murray & Miss Kitty—am with respect, D[r]. Sir
Frame 1197.

Major Francis Murray was at Newtown in Bucks County, Pa.

An Estimate of Provision in the Middle District, February 14, 1778

Magazines
Head of Elk, 5000 barrels of flour, 2000 barrels of bread, 500 barrels of
     beef and pork, 300 barrels of Indian meal, 60 hogsheads of rum,
     10 hogsheads of whiskey, 10 barrels of rum, 6000 bushels of
     wheat.
Dover &ca., 1200 barrels of beef and pork, 15 hogsheads of rum, 300
     barrels of peas, 6000 bushels of wheat.
Chester County, 5000 barrels of flour.
Philadelphia County, 1500 barrels of flour.
Bucks County, 4000 barrels of flour.
Northampton County, 3000 barrels of flour.
Berks County, 4000 barrels of flour.
Lancaster County, 10,000 barrels of flour, 100 barrels of beef and pork,
     5 hogsheads of rum, 5 hogsheads of whiskey.
York County, 5000 barrels of flour, 300 barrels of beef and pork, 20
     hogsheads of rum, 50 hogsheads of whiskey.
Cumberland County, 6000 barrels of flour, 800 barrels of beef and pork,
     50 hogsheads of whiskey.
Jerseys, 10,000 barrels of flour, 3000 barrels of bread, 1000 barrels of
     beef and pork, 1000 barrels of fish.

Totals:
53,500 barrels of flour
5000 barrels of bread
3900 barrels of beef & pork
300 barrels of Indian meal
1000 barrels of fish
100 hogsheads of rum
115 hogsheads of whiskey
10 barrels of rum
300 barrels of peas
12,000 bushels of wheat

   Large quantities of Provisions expected from the Southward to the Head of Elk.—
   Suppose thirty five thousand Rations p[er] Day issued in Camp and its neighbourhood that will be Two hundred & fifty Bbls p[er] Day, suppose two hundred & fifty Waggons each to carry Eight Bbls. and upon an Average make a Trip each Week, the amount will be Two thousand Barrels, suppose Fifty more employ'd at a greater Distance and bringing forward Stores—
   This Number of Waggons will scarcely be sufficient to support the Army—
Frame 1198.

Note: The information above was in chart form, and could not be reproduced in the same format.

Blaine to Thomas Huggins

Sir,   Pawlings Ford Feby. 15th. 1778
   Nothing in Camp but the greatest Distress, for the want of Beef His Excellency Genl. Washington has ordered Several officers out to press Waggons to go down to Dover & your Town to bring on all the provisions, upon Receipt of this request you may send an Express to forward the 100 Barrels you purchased & have it ready to Load upon the arrival of the Waggons, hope by this you have received a large Quantity of salt Pork & Beef from Baltimore and also some from M^r. M^c.Garmont—If you can Spare any Cattle from General Smallwoods Division forward them.—there is a quantity of Rum you will receive on my Acc^t from M^r.

Todd & Company have it Examined & Guaged immediately upon its Arrival. Pray be very Active in forwarding those stores and Secure all the flour you possibly can and without one moments delay, this done Shall be glad to here from you and am Sir.—Your Most Hble Servt
Frame 1198.

Blaine to Joseph Hugg and Israel Morris

Sir, Pawlings Ford February 15th 1778
The distressed Situation of Our Army in Camp for Want of Beef & Pork obliges me to call on you to use every exertion, without one Moments loss of time to forward all the Salt Provisions & Beef you can possibly procure by every means; have to inform you that the Whole Army has not had One Pound this two Days. Its very hard I should be disappointed in large Supplies from you. Can we Support the Army 'till the middle of March, my Character & yours will be Supported—
His Excellency has Sent Officers out to every Quarter to procure Waggons & Teams of force in What Provisions is collected in my district with all dispatch. Wish you may follow the same Example & have all forwarded imediately. have looked these three days for a drove of Cattle from you but as Yet none appear, procure all the flour you can, let me hear from you by first Opportunity, & am Gentlemen—Your most Obedient Servt.
Frame 1198.

Blaine to Henry Hollingsworth

Sir, Pawlings Ford Feby. 15th, 1778
The great Scarcity of waggons in Camp not above one eight Waggons sufficient to bring on supplies for the Army and the Appearance of the Army suffering for want of Beef has obliged His Excellency to send out Sundry Officers to press & secure all the waggons in their Power, would request your immediate Assistance in this Salutary Business, your Known Character in that Country will have great influence with the people, therefore have great Confidence in what Assistance you can afford me in this Business & forwarding the publick stores from the Head of Elk, which Service shall acknowledge a particular Favor & am Sir Your Mos^t. Ob^t. Servt
Frame 1199.

Hollingsworth was a Deputy Quartermaster General at the Head of Elk, now Elkton, Md.

Blaine to James Young

Sir, Camp Valley Forge Feby. 17th

Being informed you are appointed Waggon Master General for this State, am under the necessity of Demanding Three Hundred Waggons from the Publick, and as you are appointed for that purpose, request my proportion of all the Waggons you order out from the different Counties. Without immediate relief the Army must undoubtedly suffer—There is flour and Stores in every County sufficient to load any Number ordered; The Commissary of Purchases will furnish the loading Your attention to this request will greatly Oblige Your Mos^{t}a. Ob^t. & Mos^t. Hb^{le} Se^t.
Frame 1199.

James Young was Waggon Master General for the State of Pennsylvania.

Blaine to John Patton

Sir, Camp Valley Forge Feby. 17th 78

We are in great want of Flour, when you left this gave it in Charge to you to forward by the Reading Boats every Barrell in your power Since your Departure have not received one, (a few from Col^o. Biddle excepted—Youll please make application to James Young Esqr. Waggon Master General for this State, for all the Waggons you can Load have wrote him on this Subject—Have the greatest expectation from you respecting Flour make not the least doubt you will have Several Thousand Barrells. your Reputation and mine greatley depends in the quantity you have purchased. Therefore will leave you to Judge how much you ought to exert yourself upon this Occasion—Inclosed you have a Letter for Major Edwards which please forward by Express—I mentioned to you the procuring all the Beef Cattle you possibly can dont leave a single Hoof you can purchase to go Easton and see what M^r. Fuller is about; Doubt he has not done much, he Complains greatley not being supplied with Cash. am in great haste Sir Your Mos^t. Ob^t. Hble Se^t.
Frame 1199.

Blaine to Robert McGermont

Dear Sir,   Camp Valley Forge 18 Feby. 78
M^r. Fineys coming prevented me sending an Express, therefore upon his arrival request you may purchase twenty thousand Bushells of wheat provided you can procure craft to have it Brought up to Rock Run in the susquennah some few Miles above Elk, where there is store houses belonging to a M^r. Johnstone which I shall take on purpose for the Wheat, will fix some person there to Receive it and have it sent to the Most Convenient Mills for grinding Flour, (if no danger from the Enemy Part may be sent to the Head of Elk) you will I make not the least doubt be able to purchase it very Reasonable. shoud you find it easy to procure craft to transport it up the Bay extend your Contracts to thirty thousand Bushells let no time be lost in the execution of this Business as I want you to compleat it by the tenth of March at which time I am appointed to settle my Acc^{ts}. with Congress the first Boats you can send to the Head of Elk can return Loaded with empty Pork Barrells there is One thousand now at that place belonging to M^r. Huggins order such quantities as you may stand in need off—The Waggons who go from here shall be loaded with the best barrels in the Magazine. never did I receive a Drove of Cattle which afforded more relief the army has been in want this Six Days not half allowance. continue your purchases of all the beef, Pork and pease you can meet with dont let an ounce escape you upon any account whatsoever, and use every Exertion in forwarding all Provisions and Stores in your District with the greatest Dispatch to the Head of Elk where waggons will be fix'd to Receive them, such as you have in your District not convenient to water Carriage make an Estimate the Number of Waggons sufficient to fetch it up and they shall be sent you Captain Lee of the Light Horse is gone down to assist you in procuring waggons, such of your neighbours as are not disposed to take Continental Currency for their Provisions it will be an excellent Opportunity give him the Hint, he is a Soldier and a Gentleman and will do every thing in his power for the good Service loose no time in forwarding all the Stores in your District, be Assured my Dependance on you is very great therefore will not add—I have sent you all the Money I have in bank dont decline your purchases for want of Cash be Assured I shall pay particular Attention to your Demand and forward you such sums as you order from time to time woud wish to see you hear with your Acc^{ts}. the tenth of March—Will leave Camp to Morrow for York Town and take the head of Elk and Baltimore

in my way there, will leave you a few lines in Charge with M^r. Huggins to forward by Express whence will give you the Necessary Instructions Respecting the Stores hope to have fifty waggons down with me shall procure proper places then to store the Provisions there and the wheat at Rock run landing cou'd Potatoes be forwarded by water without being Injured by frost woud wish you to purchase some, you must procure three hundred Barrels of the Indian Meal & this must be forwarded the very first have it well Bolted—it is for the use of such of the army as are to be Ennoculated with the small Pox—Am exceedingly obliged to Captain M^c.Lean for sending you what assistance in his power for which as well on Acc^t of the Publick as myself Return my sincere thanks, will be glad to hear from you by every Opportunity and am Dr Sir Your Most Ob^t. & Very Hble Servt
Frames 1200-1201.

Blaine to Joseph Hugg

Dear Sir,   Camp Valley Forge 18 Feby. 78
    Your favour of the 11th. Ulto, I acknowledge the Receipt of and am exceedingly sorry you had it not in your power to forward there the number of cattle hope with the Assistance of your Brother & M^r. Morris you will be able to procure a large drove fit for Immediate use and One thousand that will be beef one Month or Six weeks hence, the army are in a Dreadful Situation but half allowance of Beef this six days, beg you may use every exertion to forward us every Assistance in your power, hope you will have it in your power to purchase large quantities of salt Pork and woud wish you to Confine your selfe to £10..10 p[er] Barrel and at most not more that £16. Inclosed you have a few lines for M^r. Crispin, please Deliver it yourselfe and charge him not to exceed the price given by you, such of the Inhabitants as are not satisfied with the above mentioned price Seize the same and give them Certificates, beg you may not let one Ounce escape your notice, and forward it by Every opportunity. the Acc^{ts} the bearer presented me of salt from M^r. Potts have nothing to do with it you must Settle all those Acc^{ts} woud not allow him a farthing more than Six pounds p Bushell for the Country salt, those other debts for waggonage must be settled with the quarter mastr, if the Boston Gentleman will take two hundred of flour for one Bushell for salt deliver at Egg Harbour bargain but upon no other Terms am D^r. Sir Your Ob^t Hble Servt
Frame 1201.

Blaine to William Buchanan

Sir   Camp Valley Forge 18 Feb^y.

My distressed situation this Six days has made the most unhappy Man living, the army reduced to Quarter allowance of beef and an hourly appearance of Mutiny with the soldiers in two Brigades, those circumstances making his Excellency the most unhappy man in the world. was obliged to appear upon every Complaint three or four times a day at Head Quarters his insisting to know the reason why more regular supplies was not laid in to support the army—what provisions you had made for the ensuing campaign, how you had ordered Your supplies from the Eastern and Southern States—those Questions I cou'd not be particular in answering but Assured him I believed you had taken every method to lay up large Magazines of salted of Provisions & to have them forwarded to the grand army, then what Magazines I had laid up in my district gave him for answer but a very few days supply of Beef and Pork, but a great Plenty of Flour, am sorry on many Accounts you have not given More Attendance at Head Quarters and been here with the Committee of Congress Certain it wou'd have been a great advantage to your department the Genl. refflects your being here oftner. Have the Board of war consulted you upon this late Regulation, they have taken no Notice of any those under your Appointment, the pay allowed those Superintendants are very Generous, hope they will procure large Quantities of beef & pork and Relieve the army from their wants, you are in a great Measure to blame the supplies not being larger, all the purchases limited far under the Market price, put it out of their power to procure large Quantities—Am ordered to the Head of Elk and will make Baltimore on my way to York Town shall hurry on all the salt Provisions there to Head of Elk whose waggons are ordered to Receive them, please procure me a large sett of Books by the time I come up, I want them very much. I wrote you several times about a Chest but have never Rec^d any from you press M^r. Echellberger to forward all the flour, Whiskey and salt provisions in York Town without a Moments loss of time shall be with you in a few days and am Dear Sir Your Most Ob^t. & Most Hble Servt

Frame 1202

Blaine to Henry E. Lutterloh

Dear Sir,   Pawlings Ford Feby. 18th. 78
I am ordered to the Head of Elk to forward Stores of Provisions from thence to the Grand Army—Youll be so kind as to furnish me with forty of the first waggons which comes to Camp and Send some Active Person with them, they will receive their orders from Col^o. Jones and Col^o. Chandler and proceed with the greatest Dispatch to the head of Elk where Indian Meal and other provisions will be ready for them to load—Your immediate Compliance will greatly oblige, Dr Sir Your Most Ob^t. Servt.
Frame 1206.

Blaine to Major Armstrong

Sir,   Camp Valley Forge Feby. 19 78
You will proceed to Genl Laceys Quarters & See what provisions are made for his people—A M^r. Rush was appointed for that purpose but find he has not been Active therefore do order him to Head Quarters to settle his Accounts—Request you may attend General Lacey & use the utmost Exertion to procure the necessary supplies for the Militia. those persons who refuse selling you will make Application to the General for an orderly Officer and Party who will make seizures but Guard against any kind of Abuses, and pay for the people the under mentioned prices. Viz. for good Beef sinking the Fifth Quarter Five pounds p[er] Hundred weight. Pork salted Five pounded Fresh Four pounds ten shillings,— Wheat Merchantable Twelve Shillings p[er] bushell Flour merchan[t] Thirty three shillings, good Common Thirty Shillings Casks. 3/9 Whiskey any Quantity that may be taken what the Laws allows, and Five shillings p[er] Gallon, Carriage, purchase all the wheat & Flour you possibly can but dont interfere with those people or Mills M^r. Ashton has contracted with, great Numbers of Stock cattle in Bucks County are fit for immediate use—The Superintendant of Slaughtering Cattle (if Calaghan is not faithfull discharge him immediately) is very Active & will take great care about camp & must observe such instructions as you give him from time to time should you find it difficult to support the Militia you will make application to M^r. Chaloner who will Afford you Assistance for your Transaction of this Business you shall be properly rewarded by Your Most Ob^t. Servt.
Frame 1203.

John Chaloner to Mr. Rush

Sir, Camp Valley Forge 19
Colonel Ephraim Blaine D. C. G of Purchases has appointed Major Armstrong to supply the Militia under the Command of Gen[l]. Lacey with Provisions—And has directed me to order you immediately to desist in purchasing in Consequence of your Appointment and repair as expeditiously As Possible to his Quarters to settle your Accounts—Any Contracts or Engagements made by you for the supply of the Troops must be immediately transfer'd to Major Armstrong as no other will be deem'd valued or complied with I am Sir, Your Most Ob[t]. Serv[t]
Frame 1203.

Blaine to George Ross

Dear Sir, Camp Valley Forge 20 Feb[y]. 78
How it happens we have no waggons with Flour from your Country cannot imagine our applications have been every hour for large supplies weekly but scarcely a Barrel this four weeks is arrived. Upon Rec[t]. of this Request you may forward team in your power Loaded with Flour else shall be ashore pray pay some atention to this my request Your Horse is in good order, will send him to You to morrow he is a very footless Carran only fit for the draft shall have the pleasure of seeing you in a few days and am D[r]. sir Yours & &
Frame 1204.

Blaine to Unidentified

Dear Sir, Camp Valley Forge 20th Feb[y]. 1778
Yours of the 4th. February Rec[d] Yesterday and am sorry its not in my power to give you an Explicate answer. The Honourable Congress have it now before them to fall upon some Method to put a stop to the Monopolizing of Cattle in Virginia & the Carolinas and believe will appoint purchases for the Army as soon as the place is adopted will give you the information, and will have a particular pleasure in rendering you any service in my power, is there any fated Cattle in your Country, does the people stall, if so woud wish you to appoint some person immediately to buy them up and bring them to Head Quarters, where they shall be

handsomely paid for their service no news worth your Notice to Communicate am with much respect D^r. Sir Your Most Ob^t. & Most Hble Servt,
Frame 1204.

Blaine to Francis Dana

Hon^d. Sir   Camp Pawl^s. Ford 20 Feb^y
    The great Consumption of Wheat in the Quarter Masters & Forage Masters department alarms me exceedingly they seem disposed not to leave a single Bushel in the Country was it in there power to procure it they have taken it upon them to Tax whole Townships for all the spair Grain, the Inhabitants have, they have had the Impudence to take Grain out of Houses & a mill that my Assistants had purchased, was this waste of that valuable grain only in the Vicinity of Camp would not think so much about it, but it is a general practice all over my District.—
There was a letter or a Resolve of the Honorable the Congress respecting Colonel Hoopers not buying any Wheat for horse Feed; but be Assured nine tenths of all the Forage which comes to Camp is of that kind choped for Forage—I could wish this Destructive practice to subside, else I fear a famine will ensue, am convinced from every Acc^t a sufficient Quantity of Indian Corn might be procured at the head of elk which is but forty five Miles from Camp & waggons have come Eighty Miles with chop'd wheat in Bulk in their wagons—
I wish the Commissary General to have the Intire Direction of purchasing of Wheat & the Quarter Masters & ca. confined, but when there was the greater necessity then be obliged to Bolt, taking Ten Barrels of Flour every Seventy Five or Eighty Bushells of wheat, the Offals with other Small grains will make extrodinary Horse Feed—
A Number of Mills about Camp are now engaged in that Business, Four in the Neighbourhood of the Potts grove.—wish the Honourable the Committee of Congress wou'd put an immediate stop to this practice, all my advantage from grinding Flour shall go for the benefit of Forage; I am determined to seize all the Wheat I can meet with let the consequence be what it may—Be Assured those are all Facts which can be easily proven— am with much respect D^r. Sir Your Most Ob^t. Hble Servt
Frame 1205.

Blaine to John Cox

Sear Sir, Pawlings Ford Feby. 20th. 1778
Yours of the 3^d Instant p[er] M^r. Booryhell I received & am greatly obliged to you for the Cattle, Am sorry they were not six times the number; you will give what Assistance of Beef Cattle you can to M^r. Graff in Lancaster as he cannot support the Troops there; A doubt will be a little distressed to supply them, let the Beef and pork remain in store till further Orders; Purchase every Barrel of Flour and Bushell of Wheat you can & that Immediately give the following prices Viz Flour 33/ p[er] C^t. for Mercha[nt] Flour & Twelve shillings p[er] bushell for good Wheat 12 Shillings p[er] bushell delivered in the Mills you appoint to Grind, hope you can procure 2,000 Bbls—Will be at York Town & Carlile in a few days at which time will furnish you with the Necessary Cash, Am sorry you cant purchase Whiskey, had hopes of your laying into the Magazine at least fifty Hhds, Request you may seize every Gallon you can lay your hands on.—
Am informed Monopolizers have purchased large Quantities up the River which is to be Delivered in Middleton, this will be an excellent opportunity, if you keep a Good look out large Quantities are distilled in your Township. Seize all you can & secure every of those forestallers you get information of—
M^r. Borryhill will inform you the News of Camp, am with great regard D^r
Sir Yrs & ca
Frame 1205.

Cox was a Colonel of the New Jersey Militia.

Blaine to Peter Aston

Dear Sir, Camp Valley Forge Feby 21st
Am extremely glad to find you have made So lucky an escape of which Acc^t. I give you great Joy am very sorry for the unfortunate Major Murray and the Distress it must leave his Family in—What fools the Light horse Men were, why did they not go upstairs in M^r. Thorntons New house, a Commissary & Doctor would have been a great Prize—Our Demand for flour is very great send us every Assistance in your power—Inclosed you have an order from Col^o. Lutterloh to the Waggon Master of your County for all the Waggons he can procure had discharged Rush and

given Instructions to Major Armstrong to attend the Militia & try to procure all the Flour and Wheat he can, your own prudence must direct you in the Execution of this Business, be carefull not to be in the power of the Enemy employ some good Active person to Assist you while the Wheat is Collecting in Bucks County, which wish may be done with all Dispatch, as Soon as you can leave that Neaghbourhood woud wish you to go through your own District, am greatly afraid you are loosing large Quantities of Wheat through Oley & the Country round Potts Grove am Sorry you delayed Sending my Cloth was pleased with the Thoughts of a New Coat—the Disappointment is very great, have been waiting this two days for the return of my Boy, what in the Name of good sense has kept him wish you would hurry him without loss of time, am Just Setting out on a Journey of three hundred Miles, which will employ me two weeks, make not the least doubt of Your exertion & adopting every Method in your power to procure all the Flour & Wheat you can—Wish you great success and Am D^r. Sir Your Most Ob^t. hble Ser^t
Frame 1206.

Blaine to Jacob Anderson

Sir, Commissaries Office Feby. 21
    I am informed that the Mills in and about Potts Grove are Choping Wheat for the Forage Masters without paying any attention to the Resolve of Congress Requesting them to make Ten Barrels of Flour every Eighty Bushell—You will please to examine said Mills and enquire the Quantity Sent to Camp or elswhere as forage Regardless of the above Resolve and the Quantity of Wheat now in the Mills for that purpose, all which you must seize, provided the Forage Masters, refuse to comply with the above Resolve—Desire M^r. Murray to grind the Wheat sent him by M^r. Ashton, and send the Flour to Camp with all expedition—Your compliance with the above Request will oblige Sir Your Very $humb^l$. Servant
Frame 1207.

Jacob Anderson was Assistant Commissary of Issues at Pottsgrove, now Pottstown, Pa.

Blaine to James Young

Sir,   Commissaries Office Feby. 23^d
    Yours of the 18th. Instant to Col^o. Blaine is Rec^d. thank you for the information Respecting the mode of calling out the waggons which in future will be attended to—Some of Your Assistants has taken Account of Waggons which I have employed for some time past in hawling provision for the Army, and say they must take those waggons in their Rotation, to compleat the Number called for at Camp—this will effectually destroy the Brigades, now employed, and it persisted in will oblige us to make large requisitions—Col^o. Blaine will be glad to be advised respecting this matter, as speeding as possible—The Army being in want of provision shall be much obliged to you to order your Deputies to make application to the following persons for Loading the Teams Coming to camp—this measure if adopted will render essential Service to the Army and particularly oblige Sir Your hlbe Servant

James Smith	York town
John McCalister	

Major Thos. Edwards	Lancaster
Robert Purdy	D^o.
William Evans	Yellow Springs
George Simpson	Correyls ferry
John Patton	Reading—
Frame 1207.	

George Simpson was an Assistant Commissary of Issues at Coryells Ferry. John McAllister held the same position at York, Pa.

Chaloner to Joseph Hugg

Sir,   Commissaries Office Feby. 24
    I embrace this opportunity p[er] return of the Bearer of yours of the 20th. to inform that the supplies have not as yet come on equal to the Consumption—Your Assembly now sitting it is highly Necessary the impediments & difficulties attending the Execution of your Business be made known to them—I hope you will particularly exert yourself in purchasing salt pork in the hands of the Inhabitants, which as well as that

you have already procured send on to Camp with all expedition—I wish you a Speedy Recovery of your indisposition and Remain Dear Sir Your Hble Servt
Frame 1208.

Chaloner to Henry Fuller

Sir,   Camp at Valley Forge Feby. 25
    Yours of the 21st. to Col^o. Blaine was this moment handed to me, am exceedingly sorry that Col^o. Patton suffered you to be so long neglected—He has been wrote to on this subject and I flatter myself will speedily relieve you with an ample supply of the needfull to discharge your Contracts and enable you to procure the Supplies your County affords—I have not plenty of Cash or would Assist you, however must urge you to exert yourself and extend your Credit untill Col^o. Blaines return from Maryland at which time I doubt not but he will fully reimburse you with satisfaction—Forward all the Flour you can and send a Brigade with salt to head Quarters. Send your Acct in as speedily as possible I am Sir Your hble Servt
Frame 1208.

Chaloner to John Coryell, M^r. Robinson and John Sherrard

Sir,   Commissaries Office Feby. 27. 1778
    Should any teams arrive at Your Ferry with provision or any number of cattle You will please to direct them to dispatch a person to General Lacey for an escort. and not to proceed without Neglect or inattention to this order by direction of his Excellency The Commander in Chief will be at the risque and peril of the disobedient, I am Sir Your most hble Servt
Frame 1208.

These men ran ferries on the Delaware River between New Jersey and Pennsylvania.

Chaloner to James White and Robert Dodd

Gentlemen, Commissaries Office Feby. 27th. 1778

I must request of you to forward with all diligence the Indian Meal you was directed to procure for the Soldiers under innoculation—Many of The Troops are now in the small pox and like to suffer for want of that Necessary article—You must also forward all the provision and Stores of whatsover kind you have in Custody, to Camp without loss of time, directing the Waggon Masters to keep above the Militia and apply to General Lacey for an Escort, in Case of neglect they must answer for the Consequences as it will be at their Charge I am Gentlemen Your Most Ob^t. hble Servt.
Frame 1209.

Chaloner to John Lacey Jr.

Sir, Feby. 27. 1778

Inclosed is a letter rec^d. from Head Q^{rs}. on the subject of supplying persons coming with provision to Camp with a proper escort for their security—This order is occasioned by the loss of 130 head of Cattle on their way hither. shall take it as a particular favour you could forward a letter to Sherrad and Robinsons Ferry which will be delivered by the Bearer—I am Sir Your Most h Servt.
Frame 1209.

Chaloner to Azariah Dunham

Dear Sir, Commissaries Office Feby. 27

I expected long e'er this to have received from you a Considerable drove of Cattle and doubt not but you have forwarded them—Shall be exceedingly happy if it should lay in my power hereafter to inform you that they are not fallen into the hands of the Enemy but certain it is that a Drove with four men were taken near Shrolls, on Monday last Consisting of about 130 head—From this information you will be able to Judge whether they are from you—I sincerely hope it will prove Contray to my expectations, but be this as it may, I must Request you to supply their place as speedily as possible—It is not easy to conceive our wants, this loss has added to our distress, and hope you will do your utmost

notwithstanding this misfortune to Relieve us, directing the droves to keep higher up the Country and cross above Correylls Ferry—It is a Neighbourhood much disaffected and which we may Justice ascribe the loss—I have only to add that I shall make strict enquiry after the persons taken with the Cattle. Should they have come from you shall use my influence with some Citizen or other to Relieve that distress; their present situation must occasion—In the mean time Remain D^r. Sir Your Most Hb Servt
Frame 1209.

Chaloner to William Buchanan

Sir,   Commissaries Office Feby. 27. 1778

    Col^o, Blaine is now on his way to the head of Elk, Baltimore and York Town, he enjoined me to write to you p[er] express to have his Books ready for him against his arrival—

    When you were at our Quarters at White Marsh you was an Eye witness to the many inconveniencies Col^o. Blaine and myself laboured under; for the want of proper Chest to secure our Cash—convinced of our necessity you was kind enough voluntarily to offer to remedy our distress by sending two Chests made on the same Construction that your own was—Under this promise I have hitherto contented myself with the old Box, tho it exposes my Cash to the whole mess, and to the honesty of the Waggoners when Travelling—tired of this Confidence of the World, I must quit and cannot Continue here without proper accommodations to Render the Publick Property secure and somewhat Commodiuos to myself—You well know that we are without Books the Accounts are demanded but it is impossible they can be rendered, untill first put in proper form which without Books cannot be accomplished—must request You will send twelve blank books as soon as possible—Colonel Blaine doubtless has informed you of the great wants of the army has been reduced to some few days past it has been better supplied but a prospect adequate to the present Consumption has not Yet reached us—a sufficiency of Hogs for a few days are on hand Which when exhausted God only knows where we shall look for more—It is with pleasure I inform you that the Industry of Col^o. Evans one of Col^o Blaines Assistants has rendered the supply of Flour beyond a doubt by purchasing and securing 10,000 Barrels in Chester County one third of which is now

ready for delivery and no greater distance from Camp than 45 Miles, the residue will be ready as soon as casks can be procured to contain it.—
I expect by the latter end of this Week he will augment it, to near 15 or 20,000 Barrels, this together with what Col^o. Blaine will procure. I trust will secure a plenty of that article—The Bearer of this Colonel Blaine desires may be detained untill he arrives—I only wish the prospect of Meat was as good as that of Flour both for your satisfaction and our ease—Much Disatisfaction has taken place in the Army, through your not complying with the Resolve of Congress which directs that you shall inform the Commissary General of Issues of the Cost of a Ration by which he shall certify the Acc^t of retained Rations, this neglect has prevented the Settlement of many Regimental Acc^{ts} and greatley biassed the officers against Your Conduct—I sincerely wish a matter so easily attained as this is may not be suffered to continue neglected when it is so much to your prejudice—It is said you have proposed 1/7 this has added to the disaffection as being short of the Value—The confidence you have put in M^r. Kennedy has injured your reputation as Purchasing Commissary General and his indolence & inattention to the wants of the Army sufficiently Justifies a Suspicion of his want of common honestly, Pity it is that he should be suffered to monopoly the whole Tallow to your prejudice and the injury of the Soldiers. His whole supplies has not exceeded 900 W^t of very bad run soap—indeed the Army has been reduced to such straints as to get Candles made by the Halves I am sir Your Hble Servt
Frames 1210-11.

Chaloner to William Buchanan

Sir,   Commissaries Office Feby. 78
Since my last I have met with a very Considerable Loss of Beef Cattle, Dunhams brother and Son and two others on their way to Camp with 133 head of Cattle were beset by Enemys Light Dragoons near Shrolls Tavern and Captivated—It is said that his Son has made his escape but I fear it is not so—as he has not made his appearance here—
I have only to inform You that the Clamour of the officers and soldiers respecting Retained Rations increases Daily and the want of integrity in M^r. Kennedy appears to glaring to pass unnoticed, Since my last he has furnished us with 26 Bbls Soap and Seven of Candles the latter is all which

he has yet sent us of that article and of worse quality cannot be—the Colour of Beeswax—& not Tallow the former is not Accompanied with Invoice or even Computation of the Quantity I am Sir Your most Obt h Servt.
Frame 1211.

Chaloner to Unidentified

Sir,
Colonel Tilghman informed me Yesterday that he had been in Jersey and obtained an Acc^t of what pork there was there and to my surprize he informed me that the whole did not exceed 225 Bbls of Pork—I dred the wants of the army which will inaivitably ensue—do exert yourself to Collect what may be in the hands of the Individuals. General Waynes being in Jersey will afford an excellent opportunity to bring to the disaffected and punish the Monopolizers—They too well deserve it & i doubt not they will feel your Just resentment Confident of your endeavours. I Remain in all hopes that you will be successful I am Sir Your & &
Frame 1212.

Chaloner to Robert McGermont

Sir,   Commissaries Office Feby. 28th 1778
M^r. Emorys favour of the 24 Ult Was handed to me this moment accompanied with 85 Cattle the Residue he left at Wilmington p[er] Rec^t.—It would be well to send the salt Pork to those troops and forward all the Cattle you possibly can to this place, as more convenient to transport—
For Gods sake forward all the Indian Meal you can the troops are innoculated and I fear will suffer for want of that article—If you can purchase Peas & any vegetables on Reasonable terms delivered here do it—I am Sir Your Very Hble Servt
Frame 1212.

Chaloner to Anthony Broderick

Sir,   Camp Feby. 28. 1778
        Yours with the Cattle I rec^d. lament they were so few it is a Melancholy Circumstance considering our distress—By the Bearer youll receive 16,500 Dollars left here by Col^o. Blaine for you The present Drove has by no means answered his Expectations he looked for three times the Number—I must call on you to exert Yourself for us, unless supplies come more speedily we must sink, not only our Reputation but the great and General cause will be ruined unless some Masterly stroke of Industry in the Purchasing Assistants save us—130 head were unfortunately taken by the Enemy a few days ago—strive to remove the difficulty this will occassion by a vigorous exertion of your abilities—Flattering myself that you will Afford speedy relieve—I Conclude Sir If any Cattle from New England comes youll forward them without delay procure hay at the proper Stages and direct them all to Cross at Easton and keep up the County as high as the Trapp
Frame 1212.

Chaloner to Mark Bird

Sir,   Commissaries Office March 1st
        The Roads have been so very bad and likely to Continue so that I much fear the army will want flour unless a quantity should be sent by water—I should be glad you would forward p[er] first opportunity all you have on hand also of Indian Meal, thank you for the last sent from Bishops and shall be glad if you can procure more—
You will much oblige our family by sending us Two or three Barrells of Beer such as you sent Col^o Biddle one of which he has been good enough to spare us—I am Sir Yours & & &
Frame 1213.

Bird was a Deputy Quartermaster General at Reading, Pa.

Chaloner to Henry E. Lutterloh

Sir,   Commissaries Office March 1st. 78
        Above you have Copies of Letters written by Col^o. Blaine before he left this, one to Yourself the other to James Young W. M. G.—In

consequence of which no Waggons are as yet Rec^d.—The W M G writes that You have ordered out four hundred and Sixty waggons the purport of this is to Request that a proportion of said Waggons be allowed the Commissary department as also that the Number of Waggons demanded of you and the W M G, be furnished as speedily as possible, in case of neglect the army will suffer for want of provisions, Resting Assured of your Compliance—I remain Sir, Yours & &
Frame 1213.

Chaloner to Henry Champion

Sir, Commissaries Office March 1st 78
The bearer M^r. Lemuel Stores has delivered me Your first drove of Cattle consisting of 107 head, they arrived most seasonably We being much in want—The Middle Department having supported the Army for several Months past, is now entirely exhausted, there whole dependance is on your Exertion owing to the Enemys preventing salt provisions coming from the Southward
This has been Represented in a proper manner by his Excellency General Washington to General Putman Governor Trumbull and Mr Colt of which no doubt you are advised and I flatter myself will exert you to do the Needfull—I am Sir Yours & &

North River
From Fishkill to Chester   From Kings Ferry to Ramapo
to Sussex Court house   Mount hope Iron works
Sherrads ferry   Suckesunny plains
Hackets town   Union Iron works
Col^o. Robinsons   Sherrads Ferry
Camp V. Forge   Col^o Robinsons
                             Camp V. Forge
Frame 1213.

Blaine to Chaloner

Sir, Dover 1st. March 1778
Since my Departure from Camp have been at Wilmington Head of Elk, head of the Tide Johnstons Ferry Susquehannah River, Stephens

Ferry Coles Mills Charles Town and Northeast looking out for a place of more safety to store our Southern supplies than Elk, find them all inconvenient no Wharfs or store houses only at Charles Town, there I have engaged a person and have ordered a Quantity of provisions to his Care, shou'd you have occasion to send there direct to Mr Patrick Hamilton—there is a large Quantity of Flour in the Neighbourhood of Middleton which I have seized as also a very large Quantity of Wheat which will be in the power of the Enemy should they send a party with Boats up the apoquiminy Creek to Cantwells Bridge have wrote his Excellency and Requested him to order down all the spare waggons in Camp, there is above One thousand Bbls of Flour and twelve thousand Bushells Wheat, have left M^r. Howell at Middleton in order to receive the Waggons, Load and Dispatch them, you will Direct them all to him at that place, pray let you and Col^o, Jones use every art in procuring waggons for the above purpose. the Distance from Camp will not exceed fifty Miles— Before this reaches you suppose you have Received sundry droves of Cattle from Captain Lee and M^r. Howell, doubt a great many of them is very poor, such as are not fit for immediate use have them sent under the direction of some carefull person Where hay can be procured, and Convenient to some of the Mills which is grinding Flour that they may be fed with the Offals,—beg you may keep up proper supplies of Flour and Indian Meal and let no Cause of Complaint in our part happen for the want of those Articles—M^r. M^c.Garmont has been exceeding Active and procured a large Quantity of pork and have not seen him, the Road I have to travel and the delay I shall meet with add to this a Lazey horse & very bad Roads will make my Journey very Disagreeable, shall write you from Baltimore, my Compliments to M^r. Jones and all my friends am Sir Your Most ob^t & Most h Servt
Frame 1214.

Blaine to Robert McGermont

Dear Sir　　　　　　　　　　　Dover 1st, March 1778
　　　was exceeding sorry I had not the pleasure of seeing you at this place, many things which will not occur to write woud have had an Opportunity of communicating to you—in my last omitted mentioning to you any thing repecting the purchase of Flour, if you find any wheat very reasonable upon the Eastern Shore will not limit your purchases of that

Article, and where you have it in your power to Contract for any Quantities of Merchant Flour, convenient to water Carriage on Chesepeck wou'd wish you to do it, suppose you can engage Flour from 20/ to 25/ p hundred at those places, you will use every exertion to forward all the pork, have Rented Stores from one M^r. Partrick Hamilton at Charles Town I look upon it as place of more safety than Elk, & wou'd wish you to order your pork to his Care. I wrote you to apply to M^r. Huggins for Pork Barrels he has one thousand, now wish You had them at Your Magazines, is not Chester and Below that a fine wheat Country, does it afford many good Mills are the Convenient to Chesepick, if so this will be your part of the Country to Extend your purchases of Wheat and Flour— Have left Directions with M^r. Emory to pay for the Cattle taken by Captain Lee and others, and have furnished him with Cash to Discharge those Certificates about Dover and as soon as possible will send you Cash sufficient to Discharge the Whole—Am obliged to go to Anapiolis and up through Maryland dont expect to be at Camp before the middle or 20th. of March at which time shall be glad to see you there with Your Acc^{ts} & pray if in your power procure me a good Negro Wench and one or two Stout men—wou'd have no objection to a family with two or three Children provided the parents were young—however will leave you to Judge of such as will suit me—am with much respect D^r. Sir Your Most Ob^t Servt Frame 1215.

Chaloner to James Young

Sir   Commissaries Office March 2^d. 78
    This is accompanied by a letter from Col^o, Lutterloh, calling on you to stimulate the D W M. G of the Counties to Forward the waggons ordered for the Commissaries Department as Speedily as possible; The Army will Assuredly suffer for want of provision and the publick Stores will be exposed to emminent Danger if not soon removed, to places of safety—I am unacquainted from what Counties the waggons are ordered but would beg leave to hint that Very few if any can be expected from Phila^a, or Chester C^{os}, Suffer me again to repeat our Necessity Assuring You that not one of the 180 is yet arrived, which should they be detained much longer the Army will be reduced to the disagreeable Necessity of impressing, to avoid which I doubt not You will exert the powers you are vested with and in which hope you will succeed—I am just now informed that a number of Country Waggons Coming from Lancaster loaded with

flour have laid down their Load on the Horse shoe Road and gone home, a practice so destructive to the Publick Wealth as this I doubt not You will do your utmost to prevent by bringing the offenders to Justice. I shall endeavour to obtain their names and if succeed thereon shall inform You I am Sir Yours & &
Frame 1216.

Chaloner to Henry Fuller

Sir   Camp March 3^d. 1778.
  The very urgent necessity for salt at Camp obliges me to dispatch the bearer on purpose to Request you will immediately without the least delay, forward to camp two Brigade of Waggons loaded with Salt. It is much wanted and delay may prove fatal to us I must urge you to overcome all difficulties and loose no time in forwarding this Necessary Article—
  I should be glad you would render to M^r. Patton Your Acc^{ts}, as speedily as possible to enable him to settle with Col^o. Blaine for the first 6 months
  Resting assured of your immediate attention to this business—I remain sir Yours & &
Frame 1216.

Chaloner to Robert Dodd

Sir,
  Yours of the 28 to Col^o. Blaine was handed to me Yesterday in answer to which have to inform you that is Col^o, Blaine most anxious wish that You should procure all the Wheat and flour possible that your Country affords and the latter forward to Camp without loss of time— Another important part of your business in which he most assuredly wishes you to succeed in the purchasing a large quantity of salted Pork or Beef—The Price to which he has limited Jos. Hugg £15..10 P[er] barrel and by which you must govern yourself untill further orders from him Do not miss one Barrell that is in your power to obtain—The army will want it, and of Col^o. Blaine and his Assistants It will be required—I expect e'er this comes to hand all the Indian Meal is forwarded we want it much—and I doubt not as you have been aprized of the Necessity that you have

attented to sending it—I must also request of you to send to Camp P[er] the first teams that leaves Jersey, all the Salt you have in charge we now have only 1 Barrell and Your post is the first that we can supplied from—
A few good Gammons for the use of his Excellency and the General officers are much wanted—Your must procure them as cheap as you can & forward them as soon as possible—Wish they may arrive before Lady Washington leaves Camp and meet her approbation—Nothing is more scarce in Camp than Cash and Ink powder—of the former expect a supply in a few days when Col^o, Blaine will doubtless forward you a considerable sum—
He wishes for your Acc^{ts}, to enable him to compleat a Settlement with Congress for the first 6 Months, Your sending them as speedily as possibly will be exceedingly pleasing to him—I have only to Request your immediate attention to forwarding the Salt Meat & flour by way of Sherrads ferry which is now the course all provisions, should come I remain Sir Yours & &
Frame 1217.

Chaloner to David Desher

Sir March 3^d. 1778
I have this moment Rec^d. yours to Col^o. Blaine informing that in Consequence of an appointment from Congress and Assembly you have procured Number of Beef Cattle & desiring to be informed whether they should be drove to Camp or Salted down for Stores—
In the absence of Col^o, Blaine I must direct You to forward to Camp as speedily as possibly all the Cattle and other provision you can procure Shall be glad at all times to receive supplies and remain Sir—Your Very h Servt.
Frame 1218.

Desher was at Allentown, Pa.

Chaloner to Robert Wilson

Sir
Yours P[er] M^r. Hamilton to Col^o. Blaine of the 27th. Instant I rec^d. this day—Col^o. Blaine being absent I cannot give you so particular an

answer as you desire or that I cou'd wish you to receive—The accounts you inclosed I have examined and laid before the Inspective of Col°, Blaine, but must observe thereon, that Notwithstanding they afford a very good view of your transactions, they are sort of what Col°, Blaine stand in need off preparatory the general Settlement demanded by Congress at the 1st March—You will please therefore, in addition to what I have now rec^d. to send a particular and General Account Current setting forth the prices of each article, the persons name & place of abode purchased from together with Rec^{ts} of the delivery and to whom—In respect to the dispute between Col°, Hooper & you—I can only Say that I think you are exceedingly ill used and shall be happy to hear that You have obtained Justice—Col°, Blaine I expect not to be wanting to afford you any Assistance necessary to effect this end. He conceives it to be his duty and will I am Assured chearfully embrace an Opportunity to convince you of his Sincerity to support you—How Col°. Hooper will feel after his large boasting to find the Authority vested in him by the Board of war, disanul'd by Congress—he only Can be a Judge of—Individuals will conceive it to be mortifying—However disagreeable it may be, he is reduced to the Necessity of experiencing it—The Carting of Wheat from the Farmers is a new thing to me, I would not be willingly advise thereon without Consulting Col°, Blaine. but am of opinion, if others in the Publick employ pay them for this service you ought to do the same—I should be glad you would send a Brigade or two of flour to Camp as speedily as possible— The distance will render it necessary that the Casks should be made very strong—your order in favour of Col°. Stewart has met with due honor. On the arrival of Col°, Blaine whom I expect in 12 or 14 days doubt not but you will receive a very considerable sum of Money—In mean time remain sir Your Very Hble Servt
Frames 1218-1219.

Chaloner to Jacob Anderson

Sir,   Commissaries Office 4th March
I exepct [sic] e'er this Col°, Biddle has wrote to the Forage Master at Potts grove to grind forage on the Terms that Col°, Blaine wrote to you about, if he stills neglects or refuses to comply with them terms must trouble you to inform me or Col°, Blaine P first opportunity—The purport of this is to Request of you to call on M^r. M^c.Caskey Forage Master at the white Horse. deliver the inclosed, enquire how many barrels of Flour he

has and urge him to forward them to Camp as speedily as possible—M^r. Aston has been with you lately he doubtless has set the Mills to Work & must request of you to forward the flour as speedily as possible to Camp where it is much wanted,—I am Sir Yours &
Frame 1219.

Chaloner to Alexander McCaskey

Sir, Commissaries Office March 4th. 1778
Yours of the 1st. Instant to Col^o. Blaine inclosing a letter from John Lesher of the 27th. Ult was handed to me this day In answer to which must request of you to forward the flour down to Camp P[er] the first boat that Comes this way the army is in great want of it and I expect after this information, it will be no longer detained by you—I am Assured Col^o. Biddle will have no objection to its coming allong with Forage however if opportunity offers shall procure his order for this purpose—You will please to forward the inclosed as speedily as possibly and you will oblige Sir—Your Very h Servt,
Frame 1219.

McCaskey was a Forage Master at Oley in Berks County, Pa.

Chaloner to John Lesher

Sir, Commissaries Office March 4th. 1778
I am not little surprized to observe the round about method you have adopted of Corresponding with Col^o, Blaine through the hands of M^r. M^c.Caskey F M at Oley—the Consequence of which is your letter of the 27 Ulto came to hand this day—In answer to which I must inform you that M^r. Jacob Anderson at Pottsgrove will receive any flour you have ready to Deliver Col^o. Blaine—He wishes not to store any at Oley nor will the Army admit of Magazines been laid up till the Roads grow better—You will therefore immediately on Rec^t. of this forward to camp or to M^r. Anderson at pottsgrove as speedily as possible all the flour you have on hand—Any persons having Beef to dispose of by delivering it to M^r. Anderson will receive ample compensation for the same—It is expected that you pay strict attention to the above order and shall expect to Receive

from you a considerable quantity of Flour shortly in mean time I remain Sir Your Very Hble Servt.
Frame 1220.

Lesher was at Oley in Berks County, Pa.

Chaloner to Henry E. Lutterloh

Sir,   Commissaries Office March 4th
    The bearer Capt. Moland is arrived with 4 Teams in Consequence of the late Requisition made to the Waggon Master General—We are now without a Barrell of Flour and plenty around us, yet likely to starve for want of Teams to hawl it—shall be much obliged to you to order those as well as any others that may speedily arrive to the use of our Department until the Number called for by Col^o, Blaine is completed—Sure I am no Department is more distressed from want of them than ours—Your Affording us the first relief in your power will particularly oblige Sir Your Very h Servt,
Frame 1220.

Chaloner to William Evans

Dear Colonel,   Commissaries Office 4. March 78
    When you was here last, you carried away with you your return of flour and the Copy of it in our present scarcity of flour is great, and must request of you to Send it me P[er] the bearer—also beg of you to direct the Millers not more than 20 miles distance to deliver their flour, on Col^o, Jones or my order taking Receipts from the Waggon Master to deliver the Same to Col^o, Jones, D.C.G of Issues at Camp—this will Save both you and us much trouble. We are much distressed for Flour the Roads are so bad that it is impracticable to bring it any great distance must beg of you to hurry all that is in the Neighbourhood of Camp—do if possible employ some Teams for this particular purpose—Your Sending the Cloth [per] the bearer will particularly oblige Sir Your Most Hble Servt.
PS Buy a hundred or two of Quills and send us we are all Idle for want of them
Frame 1221.

Chaloner to Alexander Hamilton

Sir, Commissaries Office March 4. 1778
I am apprehensive that the information given to the General has arisen from the Circumstance of a Number of Cattle passing through the great Swamp on their way to Camp—Shall immediately dispatch a person to make enquiry and remove them should any be found there—I am Sir Your Most Obt Servt
Frame 1221.

Chaloner to Thomas Smith

Sir, March 6th. 1778
This is to inform you that the Certificates sent to Col^o, Blaine is all disposed of, and has opened a door for many applications—It is in the Power of him to dispose a Number of them to a very large amount, and he will be much obliged to you to furnish him with a quantity P first Opportunity—The bearer Azariah Dunham Esqr. is one of Col^o Blaines Principal Assistant Purchasers of Live Stock and is very largely in advance for the Publick—He now waits on you for a considerable sum in Loan Office Certificates—If convenient for you to spare him to the amount of Twenty Thousand pounds on Acc^t. of Col^o, Ephraim Blaine D.C.G. of Ps, it will particularly oblige him & render essential Service to the Army—I am for the Gent^m Sir Your Very h Servt.
Frame 1221.

John Chaloner to Henry Echart

Sir, Commissaries Office Camp March 8th. 1778
The Bearer having delivered a small drove of Cattle for the use of the Army, purchased by you in Consequence of an Appointment rec^d. from the Legislature of this State—He informs that you are Solicitous to know where you shall send future supplies and how to dispose of them to the best advantage for the Army—
In answer to which, after thanking your for your present Assistance—I must urge you to forward all the Flour, Beef and Pork you possibly can— When any of those articles are coming forward particularly live Stock, it will be well that on their arrival in the Neighbourhood of Camp some one

person come forward to Col°. Blaine or myself that they may receive instructions where to carry their Cattle, this if attended to will save the Drovers much trouble and loss of time—Our present situation respecting the article of Flour is such as will require all the aid your most speedy and vigorous exertions can possibly afford, owing to the badness of the Roads in one instance, and the delay of the waggons order to Camp in another, we are suffering for want, and have plenty all around us—After this information your own good sense will readily point out, the property [sic] of embarking all you possibly can by water which directed to Thomas Jones Esqr. D.C.G of Issues at Camp will be thankfully Rec^d, and properly recited for—I should be glad your Purchasers of Live Stock be Confined to that which is full grown as the Slaughtering of Cattle under Size is destroying of Beef and will render the Supplies of another Year more difficult to avoid which, ought to be the particular attention of all concerned or engaged in the present dispute—I am with respect Sir Your Most Hble Servt.
Frame 1222.

Chaloner to Henry E. Lutterloh

Sir
    I am sensible the W. M. appointed by the State has made a misrepresentation of facts to You the person appointed by M^r. Ross W M was appointed previous to the Acc^t. of Assembly pass'd by the Legislative of this State and with which the W M appointed by that act has nothing to do with as you will see by the Inclosed letter from the W M G of the state to Col°, Blaine on that Subject, it is their duty to bring waggons into the Service not to take away those which were in the Service previous to the Act and are still Continued in the Publick employ—The person appointed by M^r. Ross W^m S[ki]les—was on his way to Lancaster with Teams for flour they were loaded with Tallow belonging to the Publick—This M^r. Moreland Seized his Teams left the Tallow on the Road to be embezled by any body that pleases and carried them to Lancaster which with 5 he had of his own he brings to Camp & charges the Army with 11 Teams furnished by him as W. M. to the State, when the fact is he only furnished 5—I have only to observe to you that if this Conduct is admitted contrary to the intention of the W.M.G of this State. as you will observe by his Letter and Contrary to the expectation of Col°, Blaine when he applied to you to order out 180 Teams for this Service—I must call on you to order

out One hundred Teams more than those already ordered for the Commissaries Department If the W.M, appointed by the State does not interfere or take away the teams already engaged in the Service then in that case not notice is to be paid to the above order but if the Contrary they will be wanted immediately—Must beg of you to order to our use the first Teams that arrives as we are much in want of them to haul flour of which there is none in Camp—I am Sir, Yours & &
Frame 1223.

Chaloner to Blaine

Dear Sir,   Commissaries Office—
It is with the greatest pleasure I now inform you that Since your departure there has been little or no complaint in our department, nor have we been likely to want for any thing but flour and Salt, and this owing to the delay of the Waggons ordered out by order of the Q M. G agreeable to the late Act of Assembly of this State—The consequence of this delay if continued, will be the Total neglect and overthrow of that Salutary law—for the Army must not, nor will not suffer whilst the power is in their own hands—Inclosed I send you Copies of several letters received from the Eastward as they are of importance to you, if you continue in the Business, I thought it best to give you the earliest intelligence thereof—
General Green rendered us but little assistance from the lines. tho Captain Lee from the Southward has sent us two droves, consisting of more than 100 head each. Colt and Champion has sent from N. England two droves amounting to 248 and Broderick brought in 55—General Wayne has also sent us from J. Huggs district 126 head; the enemy having left that quarter expect he will soon do more for us—I have ordered the Major part of them Cattle a very considerable distance from Camp, cannot Slaughter them for want of salt—I am in hopes that those supplies, together with what the New England States will be able to afford us, will prevent cause of Complaint in future—Amongst them there are Some very large Cattle not fit for the knife I wish you could provide fodder and early pasture for them it would be much more profitable than to Slaughter them in the present condition. Had we not experienced the fatal loss of Samuel Dunham, his Son Nephew and other drovers together with 130 head of Cattle we should have been tolerable happy—but unfortunately for us and more so for them—they have fallen a prize to the enemy tho

hope soon to get them exchanged—Col^o. Evans has made a return of 12,000 lbs of flour, he has purchased and of which 3,000 are ready for delivery, it is very convenient none of it being more distant than 50 miles from Camp and a great part within Thirty miles. Notwithstanding which we daily suffer for want, whilst there is abundance provided thro the neglect of the W M Department—All of Jos. Huggs late Letters is full of complaint of the conduct of Wm Crispin Commissary of the Navy of this State in Delaware, that he still continues to raise the price of provision and now is giving the immediate price of 20 £6 P[er] Barrel for salt pork, and no Regard is paid to your Late Letters to him on that Subject, I think it would be well if his Conduct was represented to the President and Council of this State, desiring them to put a stop, to a practice which if persisted in will prove exceedingly injurious to the publick, and very detrimental to the Commissarys Department—Robert Wilson has wrote largely respecting The Board of War in Justifying M^r. Hooper without giving a hearing to the party accused. He has also inclosed an Acc^t. by which it appears that he has procured 788 Barrels of flour & 15,6000 Bushells of Wheat exclusive of 535 Barrels of flour already paid for which with the Money given by him to the Millers for procuring Wheat, leaves him in advances £383.5.6. He observes that it will be necessary for him to be furnished with Twelve Thousand pounds, to enable him to procure the wheat that the district offered—Azariah Dunham left here Yesterday for Reading & Lancaster he informs that he is now in more than Thirty pounds [sic]in advance on your Acc^t. Twenty thousand of which he Solicitous to have in Loan Office Certificates; I have given him a Letter to Thomas Smith desiring him to supply him with that sum on your Acc^t. he cannot return without a very large Remittance—Hugg has also wrote pressingly for 20,000 Dollars in Loan Office Certificates as a part will be very agreeable—I have paid Roderick the sum left in my hands for that purpose, and expect he will also want more I have already spoke of Col^o. Evans purchases—They are extensive and for which he has engaged to pay the Cash. By him we have been entirely supported of late in the Article of Flour and you must of Course be very largely in Debt—It is necessary that he be well supplied to fulfill his engagements The General Scketch of the situation of your department with the Knowledge you will obtain from the Southward, will I flatter myself enable you to demand a Sum adequate to the Supplies engaged and expected—I have lately wrote to Col^o, Buchanan on the subject of Retained Rations & the Conduct of M^r. Kennedy, his own neglect in the former Case & Kennedys in the Latter is

daily growing more and more injurious to his Reputation as C. G of P—I sincerely wish him to remedy these matters, and Sure I am if he heard as much as you or I do, he would soon do the needfull to remove Complaints—do exert yourself to obtain this for your own peace and Contentment when you return—Robert Dodd writes he has got the Millers to Work and if supplied with Cash can provide plenty of flour—James White is arrived and for want of your Books can make no progress in your Acc^{ts} he also is in advance for you, and myself am destitute of Cash—I now beg leave to Conclude by desiring you to cast about for some Person to Succeed me in Office Should you continue to hold your appointment, as I am determined on no Consideration whatever to enter into the ensuing Campaign in my present Capacity I hope this Notice will be sufficiently in time to prevent any inconveniences arising from my Resignation, as it would be exceedingly disagreeable to me to be the author of the least disadvantage to you in your business, to promote which in any other Situation than of Residing at Camp, will give me pleasure—I wish to see you return speedily, as does all the family, who are well and desire to be considered with me as your Ready Friend & Very Hble Servt
Frames 1224-25.

Chaloner to Henry Champion

Sir,   Commissaries Office March 9th 78
    Yours of the 28th. to Col^o. Blaine was handed to me this day by M^r. Wells—To answer thereto I would observe that the Intention of Col^o. Blaine in desiring the Cattle to be delivered at Morris was solely with [or i]row to render the business more eligible and easy to your drovers—He I am sure will have no objection to their coming forward with them if equally convenient to you and them—
    I am exceedingly sorry that any impediment should be thrown in the way of your business, for at present our whole dependence is on you and will be so untill Grass Cattle can be obtained, the demand for which will increase as the Army augments, which already is very conspicuous—Confiding in your abilities and exertion I flatter myself the Army will be supplied with plenty of Meat the want of which is our only dread, and I doubt not but your earnest wishes to avoid—I can enjoy no greater pleasure than to inform you of the good success of your endeavour and

embracing the first Oportunity of Acknowledging the aid you may afford, in the mean Time Remain Sir Yours & &
Frame 1226.

Chaloner to John Ladd Howell

Sir   Commissaries Office March 9
 Yours of the 5th. was this moment handed to me, and glad to here of your Success in procuring supplies—I must urge you to do all in Your power to forward every Barrel of flour to Camp, you can possibly procure teams to haul, I had hopes of making a Brigade or two for that purpose but the Execution of the Law of this State for that purpose is so relax that I have my fear of obtaining a sufficiency to haul the Necessary supplies as fast as wanted—do try to get a Brigade or two raised for that purpose for we now are without one barrel of flour. I am Sir—Yours & &
Frame 1226.

Chaloner to Henry Hollingsworth

Sir   Commissaries Office March 9
 I Rec^d. a letter from you without date p[er] M^r. Mullen with Fifty nine head of Cattle—I am glad to hear of the large purchases you have made for the Army and wish you to forward to Camp with all possible expedition as much flour as you can possibly procure Waggons to Load, the delay is not only strge [sic] but attended with the most fatal consequences—Notwithstanding the W. M. G. has been early acquainted with the necessity, few or even none, are, as yet come on when they do shall send some your way—Your mode of feeding Cattle, no doubt will be approved of & for this as well as your exertions for the supply of the Army, I return you my sincerest Thanks & remain Sir Yours & & do forward some good Hams & Bacon for the use of the Genl. Off^{rs}.
Frame 1227.

Chaloner to Blaine

Sir
 The Bearer having first noticed me that he is on his way Carlisle—I detain him on purpose to Request Your immediate attendance at Camp

where Your presence is much wanted to support the Credit of your Assistants who for the long want of Money has now lost all they formerly where possed of—The large Q^{ty}. of Stores on the waters to the Southward demand your attention they are at too great a distance from the Army and much exposed to the Enemy—I have made some efforts to have them removed but whether of not they will Succeed is to me doubtfull I should long eer this had not expected you here have wrote you a Volume but as the bearer cannot stay I shall conclude with informing you that we are much distressed for Teams but have plenty of Beef and Flour for the present—Your Most hServ^t
PS Send or bring Cash speedily in case of Failure I must desert and all your Assistants leave the Country they reside in
Frame 1227.

Chaloner to Joseph Hugg

Sir,   Commissaries Office March 15th. 1778
The bearer is desirous of bringing a number of Teams to Camp & wishes to load them with Salt of Jersey Manufacture. this is an Article much wanted, the method of transporting it such [ ] is our Interest to encourage, you'll therefore please to deal with them on the best terms you can, for which purpose they now wait on you—I am Sir Your Most Obt Servt
Frame 1227.

Chaloner to John Lesher

Sir,   Commissaries Office Camp March 1[7]th 1778
I am again informed by M^r. Ohl that you still Persist in preventing the flour purchased by Peter Ashton A. Comm^y. of Purchases coming to Camp—The nature of your appointment is to procure & forward Provision & not to delay or prevent its coming to Camp be it purchased by whom it may & I must now inform you once more, that M^r. Ohl is employed to haul flour to Camp for the use of the Army under the Command of His Excellency General Washington Also that M^r. Peter Ashton is employed as A. Comm^y. of Purchases under the authority of Congress—to purchase in the district of Northampton and Berks—To

whom after this information, I expect you will give no further opposition or instructions. Nor by any means pretend to seize or impress Wheat or flour purchased by Peter Ashton or prevent M^r. Ohl loading his teams with the same for camp—
    Your Immediately desisting from a practice so injurious to the United States, will prevent a Regular Remonstrance being presented to the Council & Governor whom I have no doubt will Reprobate your proceedings, to avoid which is the Sincere of Sir Your Most hServ^t
NB I shall be glad to receive any supplies you have to send. The Army is much in want of flour for immediate use
Frame 1228.

Chaloner to Henry Champion

Sir   Commissaries Office March 17
    The absence of Col^o. Blaine your letter of the 5th Instant was handed to me, wherein your appear to be anxiously concern'd for the difficulties, with which You are embarrass'd by the Immediate operation of the Regulating act—I embrace the earliest opportunity of laying the Same before the Committee of Congress now sitting here—The President of which was pleased to Say that they had seen a letter of the like nature to His Excellency The Commander in Chief and as you had wrote Congress, he had no doubt but they would do the needfull on this occasion & advise you thereof—
I heartily thank you for the Cattle you have already furnished us & earnestly solicit you to continue your supplies and if possible to increase the number—160 head P[er] week now the Army is reduced & divided in Winter Quarters, have sufficed, but Recruits are daily coming in & in a very short period the whole force of our Army will be collected here, must advise you very soon, nay immediately if in your power to enlarge the Number—If they are more than what is necessary for immediate Consumption—it will be easy to salt them, which will preserve the Meat, without loss of Quantity or Quality—You doubtless have seen His Excellencys address to the inhabitants of Maryland Pennsylvania & N. Jersey, calling on them to prepare all the Beef Cattle they possibly can for the spring of the Year & notwithstanding his very pressing & earnest Solicitation on this occasion I do not expect to Reap any very Material advantages therefrom; These States, having already supported both

Armies for two Years, it is not in their power to do much now.—You observe that you have Rec^d, no particular directions from Col^o. Blaine with regard to the Quantity or posts to send to; In answer to which must inform you that the Quantity must not be less if possible than 200 head P week & the grand Army, the only post we are most anxious to supply—in a word the Quantity cannot be too great nor to soon forwarded—
  Confident of your combating every difficulty & embarrassments that may oppose or obstruct with that Vigour, exertion & perservance necessary to insure Success & afford the needful supply I remain Sir. Your Most Ob^t Servt
Frame 1129.

Chaloner to Unidentified

Hon^d. Sir   Commissaries Office March 19
  Inclosed I send you Copy of a Letter from Col^o. Tench Tillman received this day, informing that General Clinton has forwarded a Large quantity of pork, for the use of the Army in the Middle Department & that it is his Excellencys desire the same be removed into this province—
To enable me to comply with the above Request must beg the favour of you to grant me the assistance of a presswarrant to raise the Teams—The provision is much wanted in Camp—& I flatter myself I shall not be disappointed in my expectation of your aid—Mr Azariah Dunham will receive the pork at Morristown & deliver it to the Carters when called for—I have the honor to be Sir Your Most Obet Servt.
Frame 1229.

Chaloner to Thomas Huggins

Sir,   Commissaries Office March 19
  Yours of the 18th. Instant was handed to me this Moment, In answer to which must inform you that the Teams Col^o. Blaine expected are not yet arrived, as soon as they do & can be conveniently spared you may depend on receiving them—
I am very sensible of the impropriety & risque of the Stores in your Neighbourhood & wish them speedily removed—Depend on receiving all the Assistance in our Power to Afford but fear it will not be competent to the Necessity—Must urge you to do your endeavours to procure as many

Teams as you possibly can. I doubt not but M^r. Saunders will be able to collect his Old Brigade or raise a new one—I wish you would endeavour to hire 2 or 3 Brigades & am persuaded if proper Men are appointed to conduct them they can be procured—Their pay shall be the same as is allowed by the Legislature of this State, unless alternated by your Assembly—Col^o, Blaine is not yet returned from York Town when he does expect he will bring a Supply of Cash & no doubt he will send sufficient to answer your demands I shall be glad you would Send an Acc^t. of the Stores on hands Specifying the exact Quant^y. & Quality as near as in your Power—I am sir Your Most Obt Servt.
Frame 1230.

Chaloner to Andrew Boyd

Sir,   Commissaries Office March 20th. 1778
    M^r. Saunderson informs me that your Assistant have taken Sundry waggons from his Brigade of Teams, employed in the publick service previous to the Act of Assembly under which you are appointed—In order to explain to you Your duty respecting this Matter. I enclose a Copy of a letter from James Young Esqr. W M G & must request you immediately to conform thereto—A large number of Waggons have been called for the Camp from this State, doubtless a part are expected from you, none are as yet arrived but Teams actually employed by the publick are prevented from doing that Service which they have been Accustomed to render— This certainly is an abuse of the Act—I am informed that Capt. Gardiner one of your Assistants has been hauling flour to Dowings Town—It is an Article much wanted at Camp & must beg you to order him to proceed here with his Teams as his leaving it on the Road is accumulating the expence & disappointing the Army of that Necessary Article—I must beg of you to attend to the conduct of your Assistants & prevent that delay they are too apt to be guilty of—On their dispatch & integrity much depends—I am Your Most Obt Servt
Frame 1230.

Boyd was in the Quartermaster General's Department in Chester County.

Chaloner to Azariah Dunham

Sir,   Commissaries Office March 20th. 78
    The General has Rec^d. information that Governor Clinton has forwarded towards Morristown between three or four hundred Barrels of pork, you will please the receive the Same of the Carters & load them back with flour. The Pork forward to Sherrads ferry immediately by waggons from your State. Should you not have flour sufficient to load the Teams back to York you will if you arive in time write to M^r. N. Wilson of Hacketts Town to supply you—Must urge you to purchase & forward on all the Beef Cattle in your power & do your endeavours to procure pasture & feed for a Considerable number of poor Cattle, 200 of which you may have whenever you please to send for I am Sir Your Very Hble Servt
Frame 1230.

Chaloner to Henry E. Lutterloh

Sir,   Commissaries Office March 20
    When you left this place I was confident that in a very short time we should have been supplied with Teams sufficient to transport the provision to the army & remove much as are in danger, I must inform you that all the Stores purchased from Maryland & virginia, which are very considerable is transported to the Head of Elk by Water—& now lays there for want of Teams to bring forward—Their situation His Excellency thinks is by no means safe & had ordered them to be moved immediately—not more than Thirty Teams from the State are as yet arrived to our department & to Col^o Biddle less—for want of which both our departments Suffer & had it not been for the Small supply we have Rec^d. down Schuylkill, the Army would have been without Bread This will in a few days be the case if not properly furnished with wagons—I must desire of you to call on W M G of the State acquaint him with our Situation & demand the immediate endeavours to supply us, which if not speedily complied with we shall for the preservation of our own Caracters be under the necessity of representing this matter to the president & Council praying them for redress, I am Sir Your Most Obt hble Servt.
Frame 1231.

Chaloner to James Young

Sir,   Commissaries Office March 20
  I have wrote several Letters to you informing of the great injury our department has experienced for want of the Teams ordered out for the Army, more than Thirty are not as yet received for our department & less for the forage department Many of your deputies Assistants have broke up several Brigades engaged in the Service, previous to the passing of the Act of Assembly under which you Act—This has added to the distress occasion'd by the delay of the Waggons out—I must beg of you if in you power to Stimulate the Waggon Master to come on & to be carefull that their Teams stay to do the Necessary duty untill relieved, and unless they can be depended on the Army will soon suffer, I am Sir—Your Most Ob^t. Hble Servt.
Frame 1231.

Chaloner to George Washington

           Commissaries Office Camp March 21 78
May it please Your Excellency
  I take the liberty of informing you that there is Large Quantities of Flour, salt provision, & other stores at the Head of Elk & Middletown in the State of Maryland & daily expectations of more arriving there, That by the laws of that State for procuring Waggons for the Army—their service is confin'd to the removal of the Baggage of Marching Troops, as your Excellency will more fully see by the enclosed Letter; by which means the transportation of the provisions to the Army is greatly impeded & cannot be brought on for the consumption of the Troops—As many inconveniences to the Army may arise from the Stores not being timely removed, I have thought it my duty in the absence of E Blaine D.C.G. of Purchases to give your Excellency this information to prevent any blame that might hereafter arise to the Commissarys Department from being silent—I have the Honor to be Your Excellencys Most Ob Servt.
Frame 1232.

John Chaloner to Nicholas Patterson

Sir,   Commissaries office March 21 78
  The season for procuring shad is nearly arrived You must do your utmost endeavours to procure at least 1,000 Barrels & more if possible, you must do your endeavours to provide sufficient number of Barrels to cure them—& salt shall be timely ordered you—I apprehend the Fisherman will readily part with them at 9 a piece, should any of them not have hands enough to carry on their fishery you may engage a Sufficient Quantity of Militia Men to work who shall as a Compensation for their Labour be exempted from Military duty in the Militia for the Same time that they are at work at the fishery—For which purpose you must keep account of all such employed & do your utmost to prevent Idlers reaping the Benefit of this proposition of His Excellency & transmit to me when the work is compleated a full Acc^t. of all such persons so employed & the time of their Service in order that I may procure His Excellencys exemption—
  The Commissarys Department being in want of a number of good Teams must request of you to raise & hire for our use two Brigades of waggons consisting of 12 four horse Teams each to be continued in the Service for the space of 6 months or longer if agreeable—Their pay shall be the same as established by Act of Assembly of this State You will have Teams valued & forward them to Camp with all possible expedition, loaded with flour, or Fish—You must be carefull that the Conductors & Drivers be men of Integrity, as much will be entrusted to their care I am Sir Your Most Hble Servt.
Frame 1232.

Patterson was at Sherrard's Ferry on the Delaware River.

Chaloner to Henry Hollingsworth

Sir,   Commissaries Office March 2[2]
  Your several Letters to Col^o. Blaine & stewart is Rec^d. all of whom are absent, In answer to which I have to inform you that the great want of flour at Camp will by no means admit of Teams being employed in any other Service, untill a Suficiency is procured to remove every kind of danger of the Army being in want of that article, which owing to the badness of the Roads in one instance & the neglect of the W. Masters

coming to Camp in another has nearly reduced us to this Situation—You omit mentioning what Country it is that Col°. Blaines Assistants have engaged the Wheat, employed the Mills & selling the Offal—They were directed to grind & deliver the Forage to the Forage Masters, but were not convenient for the Forage Master to Receive to dispose of it—However Sir as I am persuaded Col°. Blaine is exceedingly desirous of fattning a N°. of Cattle you may rest Assured of any & every Assistance in the Power of him or any of his Assistants to Afford—If you will send me a list of Millers grinding for Col°. Blaine, convenient for you to fatten Cattle with I will give you orders on them, for the Offals, for this Purpose, I think it would be well to hire Waggons for the Removal of Stores from Elk into the Country, Farmers will more readily adopt this, than come to Camp Downingstown is a Suitable place for a magazine &^{c} as mentioned by the Board of War. I am Sir. Your Most Ob^t. Hble Servt.
Frame 1233.

Chaloner to George Morrison

Sir   Commissaries Office March 2[3] 78
You must proceed from Hence to Wints Tavern, from thence to Shrolls & Robinsons, enquire for a drove of Cattle has been seen there or on the Road you must at all events find the Cattle & deliver the Inclosed Letter to the person who has charge of them I am Sir Your Hble Servt.
Frame 1233.

Sir
His Excellency having Rec^d. information that the enemy are out of Phil^a. has ordered me to dispatch the Bearer to meet you with the Cattle, to direct that you immediately on receiving this intelligence push for pawlings Mill or above it & keep as high up the Road as Pottsgrove you must keep a strong Guard over the Cattle & keep further up the Country if you heare of the enemy being out—Cross the cattle at Pottsgrove & leave them at French Creek Bridge in care of Michael Crouse who is at B. Waggoners house, the North side of the Bridge I am Sir Your Hble Servt.
                                                John Chaloner

For Off^r. of the G^d. who has the Care of the Bullocks or Droves
NB Alex^r. Steel rec^d. Copys of the above likewise M^r. E[arns]t Foster French Creek Bridge who went different Roads—
Frame 1234.

Chaloner to Henry Hollingsworth

Sir,   Commissaries Office March 24th. 78.
I wrote you an answer to your several Letters Rec^d. P[er] express on Saturday last since which nothing material has occurd. The Bearer has a Letter indorsed to J. L. Howell from his Excellency the Commander in Chief to Governor Johnston on the Subject of Removing Stores from Elk Middletown & & by Teams from Maryland I should be glad you w^d. accompany M^r. Howell to deliver this Letter & with him Consult His Excellency on the most eligible & expeditious mode of removing the Stores to a Safe Country; as also to forward them to Camp Be Assured Sir of every Assistance in our power to promote the feeding of Beef Cattle & only wait your pointing out the Names of the Millers to Send them directions to deliver to Your order the Offals of all the Flour. I am with Respect Your Most Obed^t Servt.
NB shall be much oblig'd to you to inform me the price of good bright Muscavado sugars—
Frame 1234.

Chaloner to John Ladd Howell

Sir,   Commissaries Office March 24, 78
In consequence of your last I waited on His Excellency with Col^o. Henrys to you & solicited him to write Governor Johnston on the Subject which he has complied with & I doubt not press'd him to exert his influence to forward the Stores from Maryland to a place of safety must request of you to present this Letter & let it be accompanied by an exact List of what Stores & Provisions are exposed to danger either at Elk, Middletown or elsewhere—I have desired Col^o. Hollingsworth to accompany you in delivering this Letter in order that Teams sufficient may be procured to Remove the Stores in his Possession as well as Yours—I doubt not you will See the propriety of this & readily acquiesce in his

accompanying you, I am Sir. Your Most Obed^t. Servt
NB Inform me what good Muscavado sugar will fetch
Frame 1234.

Chaloner to Tench Tilghman

Sir   Commissaries Office March 24 78
I have this moment rec^d. certain intelligence that there is at Sherrards Ferry five hundred head of Cattle, One Hundred & forty of them have cross'd the River & is coming forward—
One Driver writes that General Lacy has promis'd to send a guard to meet them at Col^o. K[al]ilens & another writes that no Guard has come on & that he should not come forward untill an escort met him, or the person Return'd that he had Sent forward to look for a Guard—
I am Just dispatching a person to General M^c.Intoshes agreeable to His Excellencys order this Morning—I have ordered the Drovers to keep as high up as Pottsgrove. If you think this not safe shall be glad of your advice—I am Sir Your Hble Servt
Frame 1235.

Chaloner to Lachlan McIntosh

Sir,   Commissaries Office March 25, 78
The above is a Copy of a Letter I rec^d. this morning from Col^o. Tillghman in Compliance therewith must inform you that I have Rec^d. certain intelligence of 500 head of Cattle being arrived at Sherrards ferry part of them crossed the ferry Yesterday & part of them not Yet got over—We daily have droves of Cattle crossing the Country above you & doubt not but they will pass with much more Security now you are Station'd there I am Sir Your Hble Servt.
Frame 1235.

Chaloner to Thomas Huggins and Robert McGermont

Sir   Commissaries Office March 27, 78
This morning I Rec^d. an order from His Excellency The Commander in Chief to procure a sufficient quantity of Indian Meal for the

support of a Very Considerable number of Troops whilst under innoculation in Camp—You must therefore on Rec^t of this purchase 2,000 Bushells of Indian Corn, one half of which send to Camp immediately in the ear & the residue have manufactured into meal & forward with all expedition—

  The Troops about to be Innoculated are Recruits who cannot be capable of Service until recovered & as the General is desirous of having the Army early in the field much depends on this Article being provided in time, all business whatever must give way to this and you must hold yourself accountable for the want of the Necessary Supply should it not arrive in time I am sir Your Very Hble Servt.

Thos. Huggins Esqr. at Elk
Robt M^c.Germont   Esqr. Dover
PS to M^r. McGermont

  Inclosed is a letter from M^r. Tenant, a Young Gentleman much noticed by his Excellency, must request of You to comply with the Contents thereof & forward the Things mentioned in the Inclosed list by the first waggon from you, Since his Arrival at Camp I have been particularly acquainted with him & shou'd be exceedingly sorry if any disappointment should arise—You must be careful that his Books &c are so packed up that they will receive no damage, as a loss or Injury to them will be a great disadvantage to the publick—Order all Waggons from you to come directly to camp & not to call at or near Wilmington
Frame 1236.

John Chaloner to Mr. Harnett

Sir,   Commissaries Office March 30, 78
  You will call on M^r. George Kitts & receive from him as many Cattle as he may have in his possession not fit for Slaughtering take them to M^r. Azariah Dunham at Morristown, there is a number about 200 head—If any of them are so poor as not to be able to drive leave them at Some of the Farmers Houses to Recruit untill another Opportunity offers to carry them on I am Sir Your Very hServ^t
Frame 1236.

Chaloner to Azariah Dunham

Sir,   Commissaries Office March 30, 78
    The bearer bring you a number of Poor Cattle, You will please to Acknowledge the Rec^t. of them & dispose of them for the publick to the best advantage either by putting them to pasture or Selling them to private persons, If the latter they ough to be obligated to give the preference to the publick—I am Sir Your Hble Ser^t
Frame 1236.

Chaloner to John Phillips

Sir,   Commissaries Office March 30, 78
    There is to meet to morrow or next day Commissioners at Germantown for the purpose of Setting a General Carteel am desirous of Feeding those who go from us with the best the Country affords—Must therefore request of you to send me per Bearer a Loaf of Double refin'd Sugar if you have not Double send me single & by the first Waggon or other Conveyance a Keg Containing 5-10-or 15 gallons of best Madeira Wine, rather than fail Send a Quarter Cask—I am Sir Your hServ^t.
Frame 1236.

Chaloner to Nicholas Patterson?

Sir,   Commissaries Office March 30th. 1778
    I doubt not but you have & are adopting every measure Necessary for procuring a large Quantity of Shad His Excellency Strongly urges that a large Quantity be procured—I would wish you to extend your Views beyond your own Neighborhood Securing all the Fish wherever Barrels can be obtained for which purpose you will appoint such persons as you can confide in to Assist you in Superintending that Business—I wish all the shad as low as Trenton to be Secured & Barrelled—By the first return Waggons I shall send you Salt & empty barrels, of the latter but few—Do use every exertion to get as many Barrels made as possible—Should any difficulty arise as to the price of Fish, You are not to Consider yourself limited but left to Your own Judgement to act as you think best for the Service—I hope by this time you have raised the Teams I wrote about in my last, they are much wanted & I hope Some of them are on their way

here, Shall be glad if you can procure 500 Bushells of Shell'd Corn & forward here for Indian Meal—If casks can be got Shall be glad if would be Manufactured it is much wanted & you will do us essential Service by forwarding a Quantity. I am Sir Your Most Ob^t. Servt
Frame 1237.

John Chaloner to The Committee of Congress at Camp

To the Honble The Committee of Congress now Siting at Camp—
 The Memorial of the A C of Purchases in Camp—
Sheweth—
 That the different purchasing Commissaries in the Middle Department, having procured large Quantities of provisions which from their scattered situation do no afford that relief to the Army they were intended for, but are also much exposed to the incursions of the Enemy— That the Removal of Said Stores have been & are greatly delayed by the Waggon Masters of the state of Pennsylvania, breaking up several Brigades of Teams employed in Removing of Stores notwithstanding Said Teams were previously engaged in the Service & the owners of them willing to Continue for the space of three Months & more—To you to prevent that Blame which may hereafter arise to the Commissary Department from the Stores not coming forward in time—Your Memorialist hopes that measures will be adopted to remove the inconveniency & to prevent A. W. M. of the states taking cognizance of any Teams hired by the Commissary General or his Assistants during their Continuance in the service
Frame 1237.

Chaloner to Patrick Hamilton

Sir,   Commissaries Office. March 31 78
 Yours to Col^o. Ephraim Blaine of the 21. Instant was handed to me Yesterday, the first information that I have had of Stores being in your possession Am exceedingly surprized to hear of a quantity of Beef in such situation as you represent that in Your care to be—On Rec^t. of this make application to the nearest Assistant Commissary of purchases or Issues for a sufficient Quantity of salt, which obtained you must loose no time in

overhauling & Securing all the Meat you have in Care—Use Your utmost endeavours to procure Waggons for to forward the Meat when repacked to Camp—As also the flour as speedily as possible or at least part of the way—You may draw on Col^o. Blaine for Cash to defray the necessary expence attending the perserving of the provision to accomplish which it is expected You will spare no time or trouble—I am Sir Your Most Obe^t Servt.
Frame 1238.

Hamilton was in the Commisary Department at Charlestown, Md.

Blaine to Unidentified

Sir   York Town 31 March 1778
  Upon examining the new regulations in the Commissaries Department find the Provision made for a Deputy not equal to support him much short of rendering him an Acknowledgement for his Service upon making the Under mentioned allowances Viz—one P[er] C^t. upon all Disbursement agreeable to your own plan—An allowance of a Clerk and my traveling expenses paid while upon Publick service the Middle District continued Mine of which I am to have the whole Direction, only subject to orders of the Congress the Com^r. in Chief or Commissary General upon that footing I am willing to continue and render the publick every service in my power
Frame 1238.

Chaloner to Henry Champion

Sir   Commissaries Office April 2^d. 1778
  Yours of the 25th. came to hand this Moment in the absence of Col^o. Blaine in answer to which I have to say that the Colonel is confident of your exerting every nerve to serve the General Cause—
After thanking you for the supplies you have rendered the Army & which whilst dispersed & in Winter Quarters have been sufficient for the support—I must add that it will be necessary to increase the number of Cattle very speedily—As His Excellency purposes bringing the Army into the field very early—Recruits daily arrive & our Numbers in the course of a Month will be greatly augmented—His Excellency has desired me to

write to you to order the Drovers to cross the Delaware at Easton this Road will afford more Forage & is So high up the Country as will prevent the Fatigue of the Troops escorting them—I Shall comply with your Request in Showing your letter to the General & forward it to Col^o. Buchannan, your Scheme of securing the Fish will be of essential Service & hope you will procure a large quantity, we have adopted the Same measure to the South. I w^d. recommend Shad Fish only, Sir I am Yours & &
Frame 1239.

Chaloner to Azariah Dunham

Sir,   Commissaries Office April 2^d. 78
  His Excellency has desired me to write you to direct all persons with Cattle coming to the army either from yourself or others to come by way of Easton, this Road will Afford forage & prevent the Fatigue of the Troops escorting them—
I shall be glad you could Send to Capt. N^s. Patterson all the tight Casks you can procure for putting up of Shad—I left at Middle brook in a Slaughter House near to Phil Vanhorns a Considerable number of Beef Barrels which would answer the purpose with a little Assistance from the Coopers—They are worth enquiring for and Sending forward, do all you can to get a number made—Col^o, Blaine not yet arived, hourly expected & doubt not but he will bring the needfull with him—I am Sir Your Hble Servt.
Frame 1239.

Chaloner to Thomas Richardson

Sir   Commissaries Office April 4. 78
  Yours to Col^o. Blaine of the Ulto inclosing return of Purchases for the Month of Feby. I rec^d. in his absence, In answer to which I have only to inform you that it is his Excellencys wish that you procure, and put up all the Fish you possibly can—it is of material consequence to the Army especially So, a Cattle [sic] are greatly exhausted in these Middle States— Much depends on the salt provisions from Col^o, Aylett arriving in time & as Governor Johnson has been wrote to by His Excellency of the Subject of providing Waggons, to transport the provision now in the province of

Maryland as well as what may hereafter arrive I doubt not but he will take the earliest Opportunity of laying the Same before the Assembly—It would be well for you frequently to remind him of it & to report to him the very pressing necessity there is for forwarding to the Army every Barrel of Provision within our reach. without very ample Assistance from the Southward States both in provisions & Waggons the Army must suffer—I hope you will Succeed in procuring a much larger Quantity of shad than which you mention & remain Sir Your Very Hble Servt
PS   Inclosed you have a Letter to Lud Washington Esqr from M^r. William Miller late of Phil^a. desiring him to deliver you all his Barrells &^{c} a which he says will amount to 800, as also 200 Hogsheads—I wish him to go down & Superintend the Fisheries, he is better acquainted with the River & the Business than any other man & have put up the most Fish of any person there. If I can prevail on him to go shall send him, his Scenes Boats &^{c} & will be usefull—
Frames 1240-41.

Chaloner to Joseph Hugg

Sir,   Commissary Office April 4th. 1778
     I have rec^d. Several Letters from you in the absence of Col^o. Blaine on the Subject of procuring of salt Pork & collecting the Cattle on the Beaches of Cape May & Egg harbour In answer to which I can do no other than refer you to Col^o. Blaines Letters of 5th. & 7th February in which he has wrote on this Subject—The purport of this is to reply to yours of the 30 Ult informing of the arrival of a Prize at Egg harbour Loaden with Butter Beef Pork Tongues Potatoes & Claret & you are to consider this as His Excellencys orders to you to Secure the whole Cargo for the use of the Army & immediately remove the Same to a place of Safety by no means Suffer it to lay exposed to the excursions of the Enemy, after it becomes the property of the publick Condemned or not condemned, I wish you to strike immediately with the owners of the Prize on Conditions of her Cargo being condemned & this will admit little or no doubt you must immediately adopt measures to remove it to the Army, as also a place of more security
     On this Subject I have wrote His Excellency Govr. Livingston & doubt not but he will render you every Assistance in his power—You will take special care that none of the Cargo be embezzled or stolen & that

none of the Cargo be embezzled or stolen & that the Tongue particularly be preserved for the use of his Excellency's Family—this is his request—Sir this is a matter of great importance to the Army. Rest assured of your utmost Vigorous exertions not only to procure this Cargo but to have it transported to a place of security & forwarded for the Assistance of the Troops with all possible expedition—You may depend on Return of Col^o. Blaine to receive a supply of Cash sufficient to discharge the Amount of this Cargo as also to extricate you in part from the difficulties you now labor under—For Gods sake your own Reputation & Col^o. Blaines Secure this Matter and render your Acc^{ts}. he cannot with propriety request another payment until his Acc^{ts}. are presented for the 6 Months & Sure I am if he does It will be denied him this being the case I flatter myself you will not disappoint him effect it be the Cast [sic] what it may—You must forward to Camp Country made salt for immediate use of the Troops for the want of which we are now using foreign at double the Cost, having rec^d. some from you this is a matter of importance pray attend to it—If any tight casks or Pork Barrels in your power to procure & forward to Captain Nicholas Pattersons at Sherrads ferry for the purpose of Securing Shad will be doing essential Service—I am Sir Your Very Hble Servt

P.S. I have seen the Governors proclamation which you allude to and am of opinion it Strenghtens your hands than relaxing them Duplicate of this you will receive by my Messenger to Govr. Livingston whose directions respecting this Matter you will obey—In my letter to Govr Livingston I have mentioned in Sherrards ferry as a proper place of storing the Butter &^{c}a. & as also to cross the Delaware on its way to Camp. Should he disapprove of it you will follow his directions on that Subject.
Frames 1240-41.

Chaloner to William Livingston

May it Please your Exc^y
Sir,   Commissaries Office Camp 4th 78
  Your favour to Col^o. Blaine of the 21st. Instant was handed and Should have done myself the Honor of Acknowledging it eer now had I not expected the arrival of Col^o. Blaine who is now absent on business with Congress on his Return I doubt not but he will procure & forward to your Excellency the Affadavids required respecting the salt seized from M^r. Leaming—I have the Honor of informing you that it is the order of

His Excellency the Commander in Chief to the purchasing Commissary of the Middle Department to purchase the Cargo of the prize lately arrived into Egg Harbour consisting of Butter Beef Pork &^{c} &^{c} to have the same immediately removed to a place of safety & brought on for the future use of the Army with all possible expedition & as the effecting of this with that dispatch the nature of the case requires may interfere with the Laws of the state of N. Jersey in two Instances first that of Removing the goods before legaly condemned & 2dly. of detaining the Waggons more than 3 days in the Service—His Excellency has desired me to solicit your aid to Justify Jo^s. Hugg Esqr. Col^o. Blaines Assistant for purchasing the Cargo before condemnation as also to advise with you the respecting of the Continuance of the Waggons in the Service for this Necessary duty—
I have thought of Sherrards ferry as a place of safety and convenient for transporting the above mentioned Cargo to the Army, If it Should not appear So to your Excellency I shall esteem it as a particular favour you would please signify to Col^o. Hugg the most proper place for that purpose your orders to whom the Bearer is directed to wait for Col^o. Hugg instructed to Comply with—I have the Honor to be your Excellencys Most Ob^t Hbl Servt
Frames 1241-42.

Livingston was Governor of New Jersey.

Chaloner to William Buchanan

Sir,   Commissaries Office Valley forge April 5. 1778
    Yours of the 18th Instant lays before me I Should have answered it eer now but have been much taken up in preparing my Acc^{ts}. for Settlement as well as attending to forward the Stores from the different posts & purchases to the Army. in the former I hope to succeed but am Sorry to Say notwithstanding all my endeavours the prospect of succeeding in the latter is but small, Owing to the neglect of the W M G^s. Department in the state of pennsylvania & which if not soon remided will Prove the Overthrow or neglect of the act of Assembly, besides the loss of many of our Stores. I am not a little Surprized that you should take offence at my mentioning to you the Complaints of the Army respecting the Retained Rations—I am much at a loss how you Conster the Sentence to make it involve yourself as a principal in the Clamour against you I assure you Sir it was not my intention to make a Charge, or do anything

more than to repeat the Language of the others—had I attempted more than this, you might with Justice have Loud I was deficient in Candour— Whether or not your Reputation depends on the conduct of Tallow Chandlers or any other employed under you is only matter of opinion. I firmly believe that your Reputation may be injured by the Ill conduct of any employed under you even Tallow Chandlers—& If the murmur and complaints of the Army is Sufficient testimony of this injury I certainly am Right and it becomes my duty to inform you of the cause But as you have already convinced yourself that no foundation of Complaints existed I should be very Justifiable as far as it relates to your Reputation. So ado no more on the Subject but it is now fallen on my Shoulders to Support the Charge—Inclosed is copy of a letter from M^r. Kennedy to Col^o. Jones a part of which I must confess does not a Little Surprize me, I went to York and it appeared to the Board of War, that the aspersions against me were without foundation. I ask was any body noticed to prove the Charge—I should have most chearfully have met Mr Kennedy & have proved my Assertion by exhibiting his own Goods in evidence against him, But from the delay in this transaction it appears as If intended that I shou'd be deprived of this proof & the partial determination of the Board of War, confirms that the suspicion, I hope You will do me the Justice to enquire of persons qualified to give evidence in this matter who know the Quantity & Quality sent—be assur'd Sir to hear the echoing complaints of the Soldiery on the one hand, is no grateful sound & the partial determination of so respectable a Body as the Board of the War, on the other is highly mortifying to avoid which in Future I am determined to render my stay with the Army so short as possible perhaps I shall not have occasion to make any more complaint—I have only one remark more to make on M^r. Kennedys Conduct that is not Satisfied with falsely denying the charge of the Quality of the Soap he had, I have Supplied the Army with 11,000 bls good Soap. this I trust is proved false by the inclosed Acc^t. which at the time of my Writing did not exceed 5,304—I flatter myself I have Wrote the truth respecting M^r. Kennedy. You Sir may reward him with your Countenance as far as he merits it, & I sincerely wish you may not be deceived in him—
The Bearer M^r. Robt Stevenson will hand you my Draft on Acc^t. of Col^o. Blaine for 4160 as it is for salt & Rum, imported & Seized by one of his Assistants. I hope it will meet with due Honour, the delay of payment has already been considerable & I should be exceedingly sorry if he should be disappointed, as he is now on his way to Baltimore to remit his

Correspondent—I am Sir Your Most Obt Servt
NB   The Army is tolerable well supplied with Beef Bread and Flour we have been able for some weeks past to Secure the troops three of four Days at a time & have now in Camp provision for four Days Col^o. Blaine arrived at Camp last night & purposes writing you by express to morrow—Understand he has brought but little money with him, for want of which every Assistant in the employ is much distressed. I am Confident if Waggons enough could be procured that the Magazines of flour would be Seen filled & a considerable Quantity of salt provisions Collected— Frames 1242-43.

Blaine to Joseph Hugg

Sir,   Pawlings Ford 6th. April 1778
    I was handed sundry Letters of yours this Morning which Mr Chaloner Received since my absence from Camp am exceeding sorry to find by yours of the first of this Ins^t that the enemy had it in their power to take the advantage of you in your own District when every fatt Oxen and Owner of pork might have procured and Mov'd to a place of safety long eer this—
The 28th. January I had the Information of Large Quantities of salt pork and Beef Cattle in the possession of sundry of the farmers, the Seventh Feby. last I wrote you respecting those matters and the Cattle on the beaches near Cape May, with the Copy of a special order from the Board of War to seize from such as is not disposed to sell. it gives me the greatest uneasiness to find you have neglected so good an Opportunity and which might have been a great advantage to the publick, the Board of War & Commissary General reflect much my not bringing in my Acc^{ts}. for settlement to the first of March nor, will I ask a single shilling till I have my Acc^{ts}. ready for settlement—and know what footing I am on with the publick & purchasing Commissaries, will expect you in a few days prepared for settlement as I am to be with Congress the 20th. of this Ins^t. M^r. Foster whome you seized a Cargo of salt Rum & Sugar from, has been with me at York Town and Receive the amount of his Cargo of salt—[seems] he did not Act like a Gentleman or Man of honour shoud any part of the property Remain with him Desire you may immediately secure the same, and order with the Other Stores to a place of safety M^r. Chaloner wrote you expecting the prize Cargo at Egg Harbour beg you

may punctually Comply with his Excellencys order and have what part of the Cargo answers for the Army removed to a place of safety as also all other Stores upon Land—you will procure a Quantity of Country made Salt agreeable to the price fixed by your Legislature and forward it to Camp by the first waggons. we are obliged to use the imported Salt daily which is a great loss—which doubt I shall want a Negro Man and Woman long if I wait for your purchase, am Sir get your brothers Accounts with. Your Most Obed^t & Very Humble servant
Frame 1244.

Blaine to Israel Morris

Sir, Pawlings Ford 6th. April 1778
    Am ordered by the Board of War and the Commissary General Immediately to prepare for setling my Acc^{ts}. will have to attend at York Town the 20th. this Instant for that purpose, request you may bring in your Monthly Acc^{ts}. of purchases properly Vouched for settlement before that time, shou'd any salt provisions or Beef Cattle remain in danger of the Enemy wou'd wish you to have them Removed to places of safety, advance the price of good salt pork to [writer's blank] p[er] Barrel of 220 lb hope you have considerable Quantities yet on hand, we shall be hard Kept to it, to Keep the army in Beef and pork every exerion must by the purchasers to Keep up the supplies, expect Col^o, Hugg daily with his Returns and am Sir Your Most Obed^t. & Very Hble Servant
Frame 1244.

Blaine to Unidentified

Sir, Pawlings Ford 6th. April 78
    Yours of the 2^d. Instant I have received & am exceedingly sorry to find you have had so much difficulty respecting the purchase of Wheat, & more so, as I have every study'd to keep up the Credit of the Department, yours is the first instant in the last Campaign of either Quarter or Forage Masters taking the Credit of paying cash, your application to me for Cash without an order from M^r. Hugg, is Singular, as I have had no information of your Contract only what Conversation passed between us when you were here, & my payments of Cash are confined to those Assistant who

have to Settle there Acc^{ts}. however as you Seem much distress'd for want of Cash & hope it will be of advantage to the publick have sent you 3250 Dollars in Cash & Three Thousand Dollars in Certificates which will in some Measure relieve you for the present, let your future Applications be to Col^o. Hugg for such supplies as you may want Am Sir. Your Most Hble Servt.
Frame 1245.

Blaine to Robert McGermont

D^r. Sir, Pawlings Ford 8th. 1778
Am hourly called upon for settlement of my Acc^{ts} with Congress. Would wish how soon you could Attend with your Acc^{ts}. and Vouchers to the first of March, Am now prepared to Begin my settlement with the purchasers And hope you will be with the first of them have been very unwell this Week past. If i dont get Better shall be obliged to leave Camp Am with much Regard D^r. Sir Your Very Hble Servt.
Frame 1245.

Blaine to Unidentified

Sir Camp Valley Forge 8th. April 1778
Yours of the 8th Ins^t came safe to hand and am sorry to find your want of salt, Money, and Barrels is so great. you can have your supplies salt pork Flemington and Pittstown, and in a very few days hope to have it in my power to furnish you with a sufficient sum of money to Carry on your Business there is a Gentleman at Burlington who has been recommended by the Governor & Council his name is Carlilse he will have it in his power to procure large Quantities—You Mention your going out with the Militia to serve your tour of duty, this you are to be Recommended for but sure I am you can render ten fold more service to your Country by paying proper attention to the fisherys in your Neighborhood and you must Decline your tour of duty for this Season, at least till the fishing is over. need not give yourself any concern about the Corn we have a plentifull supply, all the tight Barrells in Camp shall be sent you. and you must have Coopers to Repair them, shall be glad to hear from you and Know what Success you had in purchasing Wheat and

Flour, let no Opportunity be lost to procure all the fish you can and be very particular in salting them, hope you have it in your power to purchase a number of tight Casks in your Neighborhood am Sir with much Esteem—Your Most Obed^t. & Very Hble serv^t
Frame 1245.

Blaine to Langstone Carlisle

Sir,   Pawlings Ford 9th. April 1778
    The Governor and Council of this State have Recommended you to the Honourable the Congress as a proper person to Superintend and have Charge of the fisherys on Delaware beg you may Immediately prepare and being to that Salutary Business—your own Judgement must direct you in engaging hands & Materials—Col^o. Joseph Hugg will furnish you with Money & Salt, the appearance of the want of Beef in the Army and the scarcity of that article make it the duty of every friend to his Country, engaged in the fisheries to double their diligence and adopt every Method to engage Large Quantities which I made not the least doubt you will do shall be glad to hear from you and am Sir Your Most Hble Servt.
Frame 1246.

Carlisle was at Burlington, N.J.

Blaine to Joseph Hugg

Sir   April 9th. 1778
    The Honourable the Congress have pressed me to use every Exertion in procuring Shad fish for the Army, and have Recommended a Mr Carlisle of Burlington as a proper person to Assist in that Business. I have wrote him on that Subject, wish you to call upon him and fix matters so that every method May be adopted to procure all we possibly can, let a sufficient number of Men be employed, You must furnish the undertakers with salt and all the empty Barrels you possibly can—suppose the Issuing Commissaries had a great number of old Barrels the must be collected and Repaired for that purpose—have sent you all the Certificates I am possessed of which is Sixteen Thousand Dollars money I have money nor can I draw till my Acc^{ts}. are Settled up to the first of March beg you to have your Acc^{ts}. and Vouchers prepared as soon as possible and bring

them Over in order for settlement; have wrote M^r. Morris Youll please inform your Brother, (pray omit none) those you cannot discharge give them promissing Note payable on Demand. I am Determined As soon as my Acc^{ts}. are settled to Demand a sufficient sum to pay of all my Assistants shall be glad to here from you by M^r [S]h[or]t & am Sir Yours & &
Frame 1246.

Blaine, Circular Letter to His Assistants

Sir, Commissaries Office April 10, 1778
 I have been frequently called upon the Board of War and the Commissary General to settle my Acconts, and have pledged my honour to Accomplish it by the 30 of this Month. Must therefore request your immediate attention to this business and hope to see you here in a few days with all your Vouchers and Monthly purchases up to the first of March. Let each Months account of purchases be seperate and distinct from each other—The total of which must be carried to one General account of purchases Accompanied by the expences occur'd to each Month concluding the Whole with your own wages Giving Credit for the Monies received—As the Auditors of Accounts are determined not to adjust any but such as produce a proper Vouchers for all stores purchased—You will state an Acc^t. of Goods purchased and delivered chargeing it with all Stores purchased and Crediting the same by the delivery of stores & to whome the Ballance will show what remains on hand—This Accomplished I must request of you to attend here with the same on or before the 25th. Instant—In case of neglect you will have to attend at York Town for settlement where I purpose to retire to settle my Acc^{ts}. hope not to be prevented by deliquents which should it be the case shall be under the disagreeable necessity of reporting them to Congress— Justice to those who comply particularly such as are in advance require such as it will be out of my power to Receive Cash until a Settlement is made I am Sir Yours &
Frame 1247.

Blaine to William Buchanan

Sir,   Camp Valley Forge 10th April 78

    Since My arrival at camp nothing Extrodiny has happened, We are little more than Able to Keep the troops Regularly supplied with Provisions, there is a Considerable Quantity arriv'd at Head of Elk and Charles Town chiefly all in Bad order. have sent a Man down to repack and have put it into good Casks and Pickled. which hope in Some measure will preserve the greatest part thereof, the State law which calls out by the teams by Rotation Monthly is by no means calculated to Answer the Army, as the Waggon Masters greatest part of them Studys to put in their Month upon the easiest terms, and when the greatest demand for Waggons their time is up and they will not Detain in Service one Moment, am exceedingly Distress not one of my Assistants yet appeared with their Acc^{ts}., though I have made several applications for this two Months past. have now advertised those who neglect coming in & Settling by the 30th. of this Instant Must Repair to your Town where I mean to retire for a General Settlement, the excuse numbers make is the want Money to Obtain their Vouchers and Receipts my people are now in the greatest extremity & Hourly pestured for Cash. beg You may forward me a very large sum and without the least delay, the Country farmers who have sold their wheat and Flour are very Impatient and will not do without their Cash. as soon as a Number of Waggons can be ordered down to Elk & Charles Town mean to go there and examine the Stores and have them removed up in the Country—

A Detachment of the british Army have been over in Jersey and Destroyed part of the Town of Hattonfield and done Considerable Damage they are daily down the river Forraging and have Collected a considerable number of farmers posts and Rails suppose to inclose the Meadows about the City, hope to see you about the Close of this Month pray forward the cash with all Dispatch, shall be glad to hear from you and am with much esteem D^r. Sir Your Most Obt and Very Hble $Serv^t$.
Frame 1247.

Blaine to Azariah Dunham

Dr Sir,   Camp Valley Forge 11th. April 1778

    Your favour of the 9th. Instant have received, and am glad to hear you are well, am exceedingly sorry to find beef Cattle is getting Scarce

with you—we are pretty well supplied for the present but Shall want Considerable Assistance from you in the Month of May and Request you to make the necessary preparation to render us every Aid in your power— am Sorry to inform you that its not in my power to Send you Money or Certificates, but hope to have it in my power by the latter end of next Week, at which time shall expect you with your Monthly Acc^{ts}. and Vouchers regularly made out by the first of March, am press'd exceedingly for settlement there is new Regulations respecting our Department and a Commissary General talk'd off, will be very sorry Should they displace our Master though he has confin'd himself to much with Congress & extended his Idea of reducing the extravagance of the times to far, this is all he is to blame in, but he was Confident he could effect it without any injury to the Army which he in some measure has done and an honester man cannot be met with on the Continent—Am collecting all the poor Cattle to Send by your Brother have advised him to try to leave a number at the different Mills which are making Flour and let them be fed with Offals plentifully. however will leave the matter to your judgement—wish you wou'd buy me a Neat Horse, for the Saddle about Six Years old a Bay or Jet Black is my favourite Colour you are a judge therefore will leave the Choice to yourself. woud Wish you to bring him down with you provided you can purchase, M^{rss} Blaine is in the greatest distress for Girls, not one to be had in our Country, if in your travels you can meet with a good Negro house wench you will do me a particular favor in buying one I am Sir Yours & &
Frame 1248.

Blaine to Robert Lettis Hooper

Sir,   Camp Valley Forge 24th. April 1778
     The number of waggons daily from your County and the large quantities of chop'd Wheat which comes down from you to the Forage Masters, alarms me not a little your sundry appointments as Superintendant of purchases & Forage Master for Northampton County, points out a Mode of Economy for Manufactoring Wheat which will be serving the publick and an advantage to the Commissary and Forage Master Generals this beg you may comply with I now call upon you to order every Miller in your employ to take near One ten [*sic*] of Flour from every eighty odd Bushell of Merchantable Wheat, which hope will be done—your appointment as Quarter Master entitles me to call upon you

for a portion of all Waggons raised in your County which Request may be Loaded down with Flour. your Compliance will oblige Sir Your Most Hble Servt.
Frame 1249.

Blaine to Mr. Dunham

Sir,   Commissaries Office 29th. 1778

The publick will want a great Quantity of pasture Land for feeding beef and poor Cattle youl please to procure sufficient number of Lots for that purpose upon the most Reasonable terms you can, those who are not satisfied with a Moderate price, have the pastures valued by sworn Appraisers Request you will procure all the Wheat Flour, Pork, & beef cattle you can upon the most Reasonable terms, shou'd you meet with any Rum or Brandy buy giving not more than 55 for best Westindia 3£ for Jamaica spirits 50/ Brandy. the Regulating price in Jersey may put it in your power to purchase lower, use every exertion to procure and forward a Drove of Beef Cattle. we shall be in great want towards the last of May favor me with a line by every Opportunity and am Dear Sir. Your Most Hble Servt.
Frame 1249.

Blaine to Sebastian Graff

Sir,   Camp Valley Forge 30th. April 1778

The Regulating law taking place in the Middle States will greatly reduce the price of spirits and the Sutlers for they army being kept to a very low and Reasonable price by retail. those circumstances I hope will give me the Command of the Market of Whiskey request you to purchase every Gallon you possibly can and store it in some safe place in or near Lancaster not to exceed 15/ and as much under as you can purchase for. beg you to use every exertion in the Prosecution of this business hope to set out in the Course of a Week from this date for York Town and hope you will have your Acc^{ts}. ready for Settlement the 15th. May, am Sir Your Most Obt Servt
Frame 1249.

Blaine to Unidentified

Sir, Camp Valley Forge 30th. April 1778
We are Once more reduced to necessity for want of Beef, hope you will still have it in your power to purchase a small drove, also, every bushell of Wheat Barrel of Flour & Gallon of Whiskey you possibly can not to exceed 15/p Gallon of proof Whiskey and as much under as you can purchase for, the Regulating prices taking place in the Middle States and His Excellency General Washington fixing a Retail price in Camp will give me the preference of purchasing that Article the Forage Masters are Destroying the Wheat all Over the Country in getting it chop'd for feed to Horses, beg you to procure all the Wheat Flour and Whiskey that is by any means in your reach and forward us by every Opportunity of Waggons all you can The fifteenth of May is the time fix'd for settlement at York Town at which time hope you will have had your Acc^{ts} ready pray what Success have you had in procuring Shad hope pretty Considerable let me hear from you by the Bearer and am Sir Your Most Obt Servt
Frame 1250.

Blaine to Thomas Edwards

Sir, Camp Valley Forge 30th. April 1778
Hope by this time you have purchased very Considerable Quantities of Flour wheat and Whiskey sufficient to make a tolerable Magazine, beg that you may use every exertion to purchase as large Parcels as in your power and take every Opportunity of procuring Waggons to forward the same to Camp. the Destruction of the Article Wheat in Horse feed and the want of Economy in the Forage Masters obliges me to call upon you to double your diligence in securing every bushell of Wheat and Barrel of Flour, you can the Regulating price taking place in the Middle States and His Excellency General Washington obliging the Sutlers to retail at a very low price to the Soldiery will put it in my power to have the Command of the purchase of Whiskey for the Army therefore try you to purchase every Gallon in your District not to exceed 15/p Gallon and as much under as in your power and have it Collected to some safe store House. hope you will have it in your power to procure another Drove of Cattle & forward them to Camp without Delay. the fifteenth day of May is the time fixed for settlement at York

Town beg you may have your Acc^{ts} ready by that time. shall be glad to hear from you be the Bearer & am Sir Your Most Hble Servt.
Frame 1251.

Blaine to Henry Echart

Sir, Camp Valley Forge 30th. April 1778
your being an Assistant to Col^o. Patton and appointed one of the Commissioners of purchases for the County of Bucks, has put it in your power to procure all the Flour Wheat and Whiskey for sale in your District. beg you to procure every bushell of Wheat Barrel of Flour and Gallon of Whiskey you can, in the first place supply the post at Reading Lebanon with a sufficiency and let the Residue be forwarded by every opportunity to Camp; favour me with a Return by the bearer what Stores you have on hand what Quantity I have reason to expect form you, and how soon am Sir Your Most Hble Servt.
Frame 1251.

Blaine to John Patton

Sir, Camp Valley Forge 30th. April 1778
There is hourly complaints from Reading and Bethlehem Respecting the supplies of provisions at those places am exceedingly sorry on your Acc^t. and my own that you have not paid more attention to those post so long as you had any to do with Victualling the Army, beg upon Receipt of this that you fall upon some imme [sic[plan to throw in a sufficiency of provisions at those places to put a stop to the Complaints of those people, want a Return of what Stores you have on hand, and beg you may have all you Acc^{ts} ready for settlement by the 15th. March [sic] we have not a Single Barrell of Flour from you in the Course of this Month favour me with a line am Sir Your Most Obed^t Servt.
Frame 1251.

Blaine to Henry Hollingsworth

Sir,   Camp 1st May 1778
       The receipt of your sundry letters I now acknowledge and wou'd have answered you long eer but the Multiplicity of Business and my being absent from Camp, deprived me that pleasure, the bearer M^r. Howell will deliver you this and at the same time request your immediately forwarding all the flour you can to camp as we are much in want prudence will direct you in the removal of such parcels as are most Exposed to danger first. request you to make me a Return of all the Stores you have on hand that I may dispose of it accordingly—the first waggons under your Direction ought to more the Flour from those places most exposed to Danger, hope to have it in my power to forward a number of Waggons shou'd be exceedingly sorry that any purchasers under my directions should through any Difficulty in your way respecting your Department or intefer with any of your purchases as it is my desire that peace and Harmony shou'd Subsist and an Eye to the publick good, the Rum Rice Mollasses Barley and Pease are wanted for the Army. youll please to forward them by first Waggons to Col^o. Jones Commissary of Issues. for which shall Acc^t. with you, mean to sett off for Elk in the Course of three or four days at which time shall have the pleasure of seeing you and am Sir Your Most Hble Servt
Frame 1252.

Blaine to Francis Wade

Dear Sir,   Camp Valley Forge 1st May 1778
       there are large Quantities of Flour and Wheat in the Neighbourhood of Middleton N[ax]ington and Cantwells Bridge in New Castle C^o, youll greatly oblige me by granting M^r. Howell the Necessary Waggons to remove said Stores to places of safety it gives me particular pleasure to here of your being appointed Deputy Quarter Master General for the Delaware State and give you great Joy. from you hope to receive great advantage in Regard of timely and Regular Supplies of Waggons, for the use of the Commissary Department, (2) and if in your power to procure a Guard from General Smallwood when M^r. Howell is prepared to remove them, will be doing the public a particular service, and greatly oblige me. M^r. Howell Apprehends there will be danger in taking a number

of waggons to load them without a Guard shall wish to hold up a Correspondent with you and render you any Service and am D^r. Sir Your Most Obed^t Servt.
Frame 1253.

Wade was a Deputy Quartermaster General in Delaware.

Chaloner to Nicholas Patterson

Sir,   Commissaries Office May 1st. 1778
     Agreeable to promise when you was here I now Inclose you Copy of the Minutes of Council of this State respecting Waggoners enlisted in the service for the space of six Months or a longer time: as this will effectually remove the difficulty you complain'd of I flatter myself that you will in the course of a very few days raise and send to Head Quarters Two Brigades of Teams Loaded with Herrings Shad and Butter—The first which must be sent on immediately hope is overhall'd and properly secured as also the Pork lying at Sherrards—Pray exert yourself in the Fisheries and providing Teams to forward all the Stores in your Neighbourhood to Camp all which are immediately wanted here—Your compliance will essentially serve your Country and Particularly oblige Sir Your Most Hle Servt.
Frame 1253.

Blaine to Jonathan Potts

Sir,   Camp Valley Forge May 2^d. 1778
     Your favour of the 27th. April have received & am exceeding sorry I cannot Comply with your order respecting meat. Beef cattle are so scarce that it is almost out of my power to support the Army from day to day nor is it any part of my duty to furnish the Hospitals; tho I have often done it and has never refused when provisions were plenty: or to spare in the neighbourhood of Camp: You have many persons engaged to furnish the necessary provisions, wanting for your Department, which, if they paid proper attention to might accomplish; and the applications of your people to me is when they cannot procure it from those you have appointed for that purpose Lancaster County can produce good Veal and Mutton, with some young Cattle, sufficient to supply an Hospital of 2,500 Men, this two

Months. If you expect any Assistance from me (which cannot be before the Month of June in meat kind) You will dismiss all those persons who you have appointed to purchase, and on which Acc^t. the price of provisions have been raised Ten p[er] Cent and call upon me for what provision you want for the Hospital. or any article I can purchase in the Middle Department. which shall be supplied regular according to your Demand, or so far as I can procure it—Inclosed you have an order to Major Edwards at Grubs works who will furnish you with Flour for Leditzs, Ephrata and Sheffers Town Hospitals and Mathias Slough of Lancaster will Afford you Flour for that place and what small Beer he can procure. when the Commissary General returns to Camp, and I have the opportunity of seeing you, will adopt some Method of your being regularly supplied—Shall be at Lancaster and York Town next Week, where I hope to see you & have some further Conversation on that Subject—Am with esteem Sir Your Most Obt Servt.
Frame 1254.

Dr. Potts was Deputy Director of Hospitals in the Middle Department.

Blaine to Unidentified

Sir, Camp Valley Forge 4th. May 1778
    Being informed you had procured large Quantities of Pork & the late Commis^y. General having Assured me he had wrote you in the most pressing terms to forward the same by every conveyance. this gave me great hopes of relief as the Army has been from hand to Mouth this three Months past and I am likely to be greatly distress'd for want of Meat to supply them. am much at a loss to know what has delayed the coming forward of your provisions. only one Craft yet arrived and that in very bad Order a considerable Quantity of the Pork hardly fit for use, indeed doubt the Recovery of it thought proper persons has been appointed to examine sort & repack the same. Our stall'd fed Beef is Consumed no grass fed Beef fit for use & scarcely any salt provisions, therefore must intreat you to use every exertion in forwarding to Charles Town at the Head of Chesapeck Bay to the Care of Patrick Hamilton every ounce you have on hand. Continue to buy all the Bacon you can hear off, there will be very large Army to feed in one Months time & Indeed I almost despair of being able to accomplish it without very great & immediate supplys from your & the Eastern departments, should wish to Correspond with you by every

opportunity & give you a State of supplies of our department & also to receive such advises of the Assistance, I have reason to expect from you which will be a great satisfaction, The Governor & Council of your State has appointed a M^r. Hawkins a person of good Character for the purchase of Live Stock, from whom I hope to have considerable supplies. Pray dont that Gen^{tm}. interfere with your District or if it with your approbation he is appointed our sistem of purchase is upon a new plan—Col^o. Wadsworth a Gentleman from the Eastern States is appointed Com^{sy}. Genl. the purchasing Business is on Commission the Commissary General has half P[er] C^t. upon all Disbursements the Deputy Commissary General half P[er] C^t. on the purchasers of his district the Assistant purchasers two P[er] C^t. no allowance of clerk or expences. forage & Shoeing horses allow'd and Rations when upon Business at Camp or any post when they are to be had. I shall have Waggons ready at a Moments Warning to remove Stores when they arrive—We have great News in Camp the Court of France have acknowledg'd the independence of the United States & are about to form an alliance upon Friendly principles with us Spain has recided to the same & France has guaranteed all Claims of the Continent to the United States. a large Convoy of French Ships of War are coming over with French Merch^t. Vessels, loaded with Cloathing & Military Stores for our Army, Genl Howe recall'd Amherst to take the Command indeed a little time will make them very uneasy & I hope leave them in a very bad way. wish to God our General may be immediately reinforced with a Sufficient Number of Men to risk a General Action and either Defeat How and his army or have him a second Burgoyne which may God Grant is the sincere wish of Sir Your Most Ob^t Servt.
Frames 1255-56.

Blaine to Joseph Hugg

D^r. Sir,   Camp Valley Forge 7th. 78
     Yours of the 2^d. Instant have received and Am sorry you have such trouble respecting those Cargoes of Rum and Mollasses you have seized pay little regard to what M^r. Foster and those others say, them who are not satisfied with the state prices cannot do better than give us the preference of their Cargoes, I agreed with Mr Sacolus for his salt to be delivered Convenient to some good Store or ware House, write M^r. Furman pittstown who is Quarter Master General for your state make not

the least doubt be will Afford you the Necessary Waggons for the immediate removal of all the stores you have taken—M^r. Buchanan being out of Office and the Board of War pressing him for a Settlement of his Acc^{ts}. those Circumstances Obliges him to call upon all the Deputy Commissarys of purchases for an Immediate Settlement and this Month is fixed Request your Immediate attention to that Business next to Securing the Stores, which I hope will not delay you many days—

I have sent you by the Bearer Nineteen thousand five Hundred dollars and ten thousand five Hundred Certificates which hope will inable you M^r. Morris and your Brother to settle their Actt^s cou'd not your Brother attend to the Removal of the Stores and let you and M^r. Morris prepare your Acc^{ts}. I have wrote Capt. Patterson who will attend to the weighing and Invoicing the Butter, have nothing worth notice to communicate only new Regulations in our Department, am D^r. Sir Your Most Hble Servt.
Frame 1256.

Blaine to Unidentified

Dear Sir,   Camp Valley Forge 8th. May 1778

I had not seen Mr Fosters Acc^t. till after I wrote you am astonished at that Gent^{ms}. behaviour, upon Receipt of this Request you to Seize every Gallon of Rum he has got it he refuses taking the state price I settled with him in full for his Rum and salt & advanced him Twelve Hundred pounds towards the payment of his Sugar, therefore beg you may refer him to me for payment of the Old Acc^t. as well as the new, hope you will lose not time in securing the Stores and preparing you Acc^{ts}. for Settlement. pray purchase me the negroes and send them by first safe Opportunity am in haste Dr Sir. Your Most Hble Servt.
Frame 1256.

Blaine to Unidentified

Sir,   Head Quarters 8th. 1778

Yours of the 5th. Instant have received and observe the Contents, am much obliged to you for the Rum you have sent but the price is exceeding high have refused good Westindia rum Delivered in your Town

at Three pounds 2/6 p[er] Gallon. which is the highest I mean to give, common french or Country Rum thirty Seven shillings and Sixpence or 40/ the regulating Law being put in force in Jersey the price of every article is greatly fallen and it is my full Determination to reduce the extravagant Demands of the people by every Opportunity. all the Rum you can purchase at the above mentioned price beg you may do it, am sorry its not in my power to furnish with cash youll please render me your Acc^{ts}. the Quantity of provisions purchas'd the sum of Money you have received from the board of war the ballance of which will pay you—being deprived of going to Elk have sent Mr Chaloner to get a return of the Stores youll please to furnish him with one exact Return and such Instructions as you have Received from the Board of War, and in what places you have Deposited the provisions having not yet entered upon the Business of the new Commissary Genl nor will I before Return for York Town where I mean to go in a few days therefore cannot advise for the present beg your attention to this Business in forwarding all the flour you can to Camp favour me with a line am D^r. Sir Your Od^t. Servt
Frame 1257.

Blaine to James Caldwell

Sir,   Camp Valley Forge 10th. May 1778
    Will agree to pay you the under Mentioned prices for your rum and Salt if you accept of those prices apply to M^r. Thomas Donnela issuing Commissary who will receive them from you and give Receipts for the sundry Articles Delivered—
    Good Jamaica Spirits three pound fifteen shillings p[er] Gallon good West India Rum two pound Seventeen shillings and Sixpence, and Imported salt five pounds fifteen shillings p[er] bushell the Casks given in, upon producing M^r. Donnells Rec^t. will pay you the cash am Sir Your Most Obed^t Servt
Frame 1258.

Blaine to John Patton

Sir,   Camp Valley Forge 11th. May 78
    Shall leave Camp in two or three days for York Town, and will expect to see you there prepared for Settlement about the 24th. Instant pray have all your Vouchers regular else we shall have great trouble in setling the Complaints has been made regularly every two Weeks the wants of provisions must be best known to you & the issuing Commissaries make not the least doubt every thing in your power will be done to render the Necessary supplies at these posts but am astonished you have only Mentioned four Hundred lbls flour when you ought to have returned two thousand at least I have it not in my power to appoint Any person as yet, nor Will till I Return from York Town, but if in my power to render M^r. Echert any Service will do it with pleasure, and am Sir Your Most Hble Servt.
Frame 1259.

Blaine to Robert McGermont

Sir,   Camp Valley Forge 12 May
    I hope to leave Camp in a few Days for York Town & shall expect to see you there about the twenty fourth Instant with all your Acc^{ts}. and beg you may not omitt one Voucher as the Auditor of Acc^{ts}. will be very particular in settling, if in your power to purchase any Vinegar beg you may do it or contract with people who will undertake make—
    The Bearer M^r. Drain should you continue will come under your direction therefore you will have leave to advance him Cash as he may stand in need of at his post Lewis Town with Esteem Your Most Hble Servt.
Frame 1259.

Blaine to William Evans

Sir,   May 14th. 1778
    By the Return you made Col^o. Jones on Saturday last, there appears to be at the Cross Roads 50 lbls flour, and by Waggoners just now returned from there they report that there is not more than four Load left there—The Bearer M^r. Phillips waits on you for an exact return of all

the flour by you purchased and where deposited—For this purpose you must immediately proceed with him to each and every Mill or Other place you have flour, and take an Accurate Acc^t. of the same, Rapporting the distance from the Valley forge—This accomplished; M^r. Phillips will retire to the Cross Roads there to receive any Stores that may be sent to him you will inform him of all that is in that neighbourhood & with whom— No time must be lost in the execution of this business, at it Materially concerns your Reputation, and more particularly the Chief of the purchasing Department in the Middle district—relying on your immediately engaging in this business with the necessary dispatch and accuracy I conclude Sir

NB you must embrace every Opp^o. of reinf^g. from time to time your transactions in this matter otherwise we shall soon be at a loss to know where to send for flour
Frame 1260.

Chaloner to Henry Hollingsworth and Thomas Huggins

Sir

In consequence of His Excellencys orders to me of this date—It is expedient that Large Quantities of Flour Bread Salted Meat Livestock and Spirituous Liquor be immediately forwarded to the Jersey,—for the support of the Troops who it is expected will march into that State very shortly—You may be Assured the Enemy are leaving Phila^a. and purpose going to New York should our army be there before them it will be of great importance and is the desire of his Excellency—This I trust will suffice to influence You to exert every nerve to forward of each and every article above mentioned you have in Custody—we shall afford such assistance in Waggons as in your [sic] power but you must put no Dependance thereon this but procure every team You can possibly collect in your own Country & its Neighbourhood I am persuaded your people will have Virtue sufficient to turn out on this Occasion & enable you to send on the necessary supplies relying on your speedy exertions I am Genl^m. Yours & &
Frame 1261.

Chaloner to George Washington

May it please your Excellency
 I have this moment recd Your orders respecting the laying in of provisions between this and the North River your Excellency may be Assured of my immediately using my utmost endeavours to comply with the same I am Your Excel^s. most Obt Hble Servt.
Frame 1261.

Chaloner to Blaine

D^r. Sir
 By the Inclosed Letter you will readily discover the difficulty of my situation without The least Assistance—I have in consequence of the Inclosed Letter wrote to Col^o. Wadsworth Champion & Dunham for a sufficient supply for thirty thousand Men daily I readily see less will not to Huggins & Hollingsworth I have wrote for flour and Hugg for rum. I would fain hope shall be supplied in every However Your Authority and presence will be wanting unless Col^o. Wadsworth attends pray back my orders to each Department and I remain in hopes of a happy meeting with you and Jemmy in Philadelphia am Sir Your Very Hble Servt
Col^o. Blaine
Frame 1261.

Chaloner to Jeremiah Wadsworth

Sir, [May 17, 1778]
 Col^o. Blaine being absent I take the liberty of Inclosing you Copy of a letter received this day from His—[sic] The Contents will doubtless point out to you the necessity and propriety of ordering immediately to Jersey Quantity of provision sufficient to feed 30,000 Men daily I have taken the necessary Steps for forwarding the Flour but must Depend on your Deputies to the Eastward for Meat—which if provided I flatter myself the troops will not be retarded on their march by the Commissary Department which I know will afford you great satisfaction but on the other hand a disappointment will to His Excellency be exceedingly mortifying as also to Yourself to avoid which be assured of my utmost endeavours & in the meantime I remain Sir Your Most Obt Servt.
Frame 1262.

Congress had appointed Wadsworth Commissary General of Purchases on April 9, 1778. He replaced William Buchanan in the position and was far more effective. Chaloner was writing to him at Hartford, Ct.

Chaloner to Henry Champion

Sir

By orders from His Excellency this day I find it necessary that a sufficient Quantity of Meat Should be immediately thrown into Jersey to feed Thirty thousand Men p[er] day You are in consequence of which hereby ordered to forward immediately Cattle sufficient for this purpose to the care of Mr Azariah Dunham AC of Purchases at Morristown & there to receive his Instructions respecting their destination I am Sir Your Most Ob Servt.
Frame 1262.

Chaloner to Azariah Dunham

Sir

I have ordered from M^r. Champion to your Care a large Quantity of Cattle you will continue to forward them by way of Sherrads ferry untill further orders pray exert Yourself to Afford an immediate Supply for the Army in your State that will consume Thirty thousand W^t. of meat p[er] day it will be wanted and must be procured write Col^o. Stewart at his home what flour you have on Milstone Creek & where I am Dr Sir Yours & & &
Frame 1262.

Chaloner to Peter Aston

Sir   Commissaries Office May 18, 78
You must immediately on rect of this proceed to Bucks and forward immediately to Coryells Ferry Five Hundred Barrels of flour loose not a moment in Executing this business much depends upon it—See that a sufficiency of salt for 100,000 Rations be there proceed to trentown to forward all the Rum in M^r. Paxtons care to George Simpson AC of I at that place I am Sir Yours & &
Frame 1263.

Chaloner to John Mitchell

D^r. Sir   May 18th. 1778

Yours I rec^d. this Moment thank you for you Readiness to Assist our department—I Yesterday acquainted M^r. Pettit of my request to you who intirely approved of it this Morning He told me you had not many Necessary articles to send from Pottsgrove in Consequence If which might expect my order nearly compleated I must now inform you that we have not a single Barrel of salt provision in Camp and that lying at Wagners is the nearest—I must beg of you to send forward of them as many as possible. I am sir Yours & &
Frame 1263.

Mitchell was a Deputy Quarter Master General at Pottsgrove.

Chaloner to Unidentified

D^r. Sir,
    Having Shewn you the Complaint of Col^o. Moylan to His Excellency, I doubt not but everything in you power will be done to remedy the grievance Complainted Of as I am apprehensive that the Complaint is not well founded shall be glad you can procure of M^r. Paxon his Acc^t. of Provisions supplied them as also copy of his Letters To our Department demanding supplies & informing—You have also seen a Letter from His Excellency time of that 17th. Instant Requesting that provision Be immediately made to supply the Army in case they shoud move in New Jersey—You must therefore Forward immediately to Coryells Ferry Twenty hhds rum and Ten to Bound Brook in Brunswick—You must keep a carefull look out and guard against being surprized By the Enemy shou'd they attempt a march thro Jersey To New York or Amboy—The troops you may be Assured will march soon and without a sufficiency of Rum to supply We shall not give that satisfaction to his Excellency I coud wish for—Relying on your speedy endeavours to comply I remain Sir Yours & &
Frame 1264.

Chaloner to Joseph Carson

Sir,
    Yours to Col^o Blaine I this moment recd and notwithstanding the army is by no means in want of the Salt I should have advised the purchase of it had your price been any ways reasonable but on the Contrary I have directed Col^o. Hugg to have nothing to do with it unless otherwise instructed by Col^o. Blaine at his last interview with him—Should you think of disposing the salt at a reasonable price Col^o. Blaine will have no objection to furnish you will the Flour you require—The Rice is an article wanted for the Sick and I should be glad you would offer it to Col^o. Hugg on such terms as he would be Justifiable in purchasing of it Three pounds p[er] Cwt is certainly its value at this Juncture when all things are falling rapidly at Baltimore Rum and Salt are sent into our stores by the proprietors leaving the price to ourselves I am Sir Your Hble Servt
Frame 1264.

Chaloner to Joseph Hugg

Sir,
    I have this moment rec^d. a letter from J Carson informing me that he has a Cargo of salt & Rice Just arrived the—first he offers at £7.10 with sundry charges & the other between 4 & 5 P bushel—I could wish those Gentleman at this juncture to be left to make a Market for themselves the Q^{ty}. on hand and the present prospect I am sure will justify the measure as to the article of salt The Rice I could wish to be secured for the use of the sick but at a price more reasonable than they demand—If the publick create a markett for private adventurers when all others fail we may never expect to have the produce of other Counties at a Reasonable Rate—However notwithstanding this advice you must implicitly follow the instructions You recd from Col^o. Blaine when last at York Town unless other Cargoes arrive before you strike with the Gentlemen or receive this as in that case I am sure and other Conduct would by no means be Justifiable—It is be come a matter of certainty that the Enemy are about the leave the City and force a March thro Jersey to York. You will therefore Avail yourself of this advise and remove from all the Roads leading thereto any publick Stores that may be deposited there in executing that business no time must be lost—If you have not

199

forwarded the rum to Bound Brook—I cou'd wish is all sent to Coreylls or on the Road leading from thence to Bound Brook—Flemmington or at the head of the North Branch at Rarington might answer Genl. Maxwell with his Brigade marches for Your state to day You will therefore provide accordingly and must subsist them without drawing any of the supplies intended for this Army whose numbers are already so great that it is with great difficulty we can supply them we are frequently from hand to Mouth, and at a loss to know where to look for more—Maxwells Brigade, exclusive of those now with you will draw upwards of 600 Rations daily Should any other troops be orders over we shall endeavour to Afford you some supplies but do you utmost to support them in mean time I remain Sir—Yours &. &.
Frame 1265.

Chaloner to John Ladd Howell

Sir,
    Yours to Col^{o}. Blaine and myself of the 24th rec'd this day I shall see the Q M G and do all I can with him to promote a speedy removal of the Stores from Elk Charlestown &c I have wrote C H to remove the most valuable first thank you for your attention to this business continue pressing them to furnish you with teams and I shall back your applicaton to the Q.M.G. here our joint Exertions may produce some good—The Beef laid in for the Navy, should be sent on for the Army, if fit for use I wish to have the Stores in your Neighbourhood collected and not to remain in their present scattered condition I am D^{r}. Sir Your Very Hble serv^{t}.
Frames 1265-66.

Chaloner to Henry Hollingsworth

Sir
    Your several Letters of the 20th. and 24th. Instant arrived this day the Waggon M^{r}. Returns you must Load him with Stores &c. of the Most Value without regard of whom purchased. I expect Col^{o} Blaine will write You respecting the delivery of Stores to him or his Assistant purchased by you

I must still urge your using every exertion in the Line of the Q.M G Department to have the Stores removed from Elk Charlestown & the Cross Roads The Army will in a few days remove further from them and the difficulty of transportation be increased—besides all this the expence of paying and suporting the Militia now call'd out to guard them loudly calls for their removal our necessities require them and You must procure teams for this purpose Your letters shall be laid before Col^o. Blaine and those from the Board of war Sent to you p next Oppo in the mean time I remain Sir Your Most h Servt

NB M^r. May has his teams employed in haling the Publick Wheat I must request of you not to prevent or retard them in this necessary business
Frame 1266.

Chaloner to Jeremiah Wadsworth

Sir,
    I wrote you the 17th. Instant inclosing his Excel^{ys} Letter of the same date since which the army has been at the point of suffering for want of Beef and at this very moment are threatened with the like disaster there no being one live Bullock or barrel of salt provision in Camp So great is the difficulty and uncertainty of salt provisions coming from the Southward that a fortnight has elapsed without receiving from thence one Single Barrel this owing to the precarious navigation up the Bay of Chesapeck—and if necessity obliges us to put our whole dependance on the Eastern States for Beef our Army now consumes more than twenty six thousand Rations and will in a very short time increase the consumption to thirty thou^d—Col^o. Blaine being absent I must request of you to give the necessary instructions for an immediate supply equivelent to the above and remain with respect D^r. Sir Your Most Hble Servt.
Frame 1267.

Chaloner to Henry Hollingsworth

Sir,   May 29th 1778
    Inclosed I send you Col^o. Biddles order to Load three Brigades of Forage teams with provision On Rec^t of this you will Load such salt provisions if Beef or Pork as may be in your Custody and if you are

without any in that case must request of you to apply to Mr Huggins or Howell to Load them should they have none on hand You will please to order them immediately to Charles Town to Load with salt Provision only—desire M^r. Hamilton or whoever loads them to use all possible dispatch as the army is immediately in want and in great danger of suffering I have only to ad that your speedy attention to this matter will render Service to the Stores & particularly oblige Sir yours & &
Frame 1268.

Chaloner to Thomas Huggins or John Ladd Howell

Gent, May 29 1778
So great is our distress for want of salt provision that I have obtained a special order from Col^o. Biddle to Col^o. Hollingsworth to order 3 Brigades of Teams Loaded at Elk Charlestown or elsewhere as I shall direct the order is conveyed to him by this Oppo and in the first Instance I have directed him to load what Beef and Pork he may have in his own Custody and then subject the teams to go to Charlestown or take any that you may have in Custody—Must beg your attention to dispatching this business with the utmost alacrity taking care to forward none that is in the least degree doubtfull whilst better remains—Our wants are great and on your exertions do we depend for relief which I flatter myself will on this particular occasion be equal to the urgent necessity that demands them I am Gentm Yours & &
Frame 1268.

Chaloner to Unidentified

Sir
His Excellency has just made known to me that it is his desire that no stores be left at Trenton Princeton Brunswick or Bound Brook you will therefore take every necessary measure to remove the Stores at the former—Col^o. Stewart writes me that you was Offended at his sending M^r. Dunham into Your district to forward Stores and purchase such things as the Army might require—had you reflected that Col^o Stewart knew of your absence also the pressing and immediate necessity for making the provision You would have considered it as an Act of friendship to you in

no other light was it intended you will immediately do your utmost to remove all Stores of every kind in our department now Eastward of Trenton and leave in that place very little such as will by no means be worth the attention of the Enemy—

The removal of all the salt provision and Spiritous Liquor from Egg harbour requires your particular attention—must again Caution you to take the necessary steps to prevent teams coming from thence falling into the hands of the Enemy as they march thru Jersey to amboy & New York—Col⁰. Stewart I expect will write You respecting the deposits of the Spirtuous Liquor & salt provision which must request You will Endeavor to comply with as also any thing else he may require of You in our Line—I must repeat it again take care of the Roads leading to Amboy & York Allot the Stages so as they cannot be benighted or have occasion to stop near them I am Sir Yours & &
Frame 1269.

Chaloner to Unidentified

Sir

Yours of the [writer's blank] p M^r. Kitts came to hand since which I have informed His Excellency what Expectations we had of supporting the troops on the march—I shewed him your first Letter informed him that the flour and Bread would be deposited agreeable to the place there laid down as also I was under much doubt respecting meal but could not speak with Certainty thereon having no advise from Champion or Wadsworth since I wrote him—His Excellency disaproves of any Stores being left in Trenton or sent for Bound Brook at the latter not more than would feed 1 or 2,000 Men one day therewith you will receive a rout of the Road Stages and delay from which You will be able to fix on proper places for deposits I have wrote Hugg immediately to Remove all the Stores out of his District, and to comply with your orders respecting their destination or any other matters You may require of him as the troops march so far up the country any spirit sent to Bound Brook of Brunswick must be Removed Hugg had orders to send a small Q^{ty} there his Excell^y. desires that no Stores be left at Trenton Princetown or Brunswick to the first I have wrote Hugg & must request you if necessary to look to the others have one effort more to make in our favour to procure salt provisions in which should I fail the troops will not be supplied that is to

procure from Gen.¹ Green orders to Henry Hollingsworth to appropriate all Teams that are now or may within Six days be sent to Elk to bring up salt provision from Elk Charlestown If this is complied with I shall be able to do some good shall enforce the Requisition By His Excell^{ys} Letter wherein he informs that he has wrote the QMG to provide Waggons sufficient—I wrote Dod also to purchase all he can and deposit according to your Directions Inclosed you have Letter for Col°. Broderick which if you approved of send on by express or the Bearer as is most convenient Nehemiah and Azariah Dunham I know will be directed by you I have wrote Champion to send to the latter all his Cattle and the drovers to take his directions respecting the rout You will advise him as you See fit respecting this matter—On the whole I do not like the tour of March it is Carrying the troops thro a Hiley Country that they are not well prepared for—I think it would be well for you to Write Gray for to provide for the Army I am Sir Yours & &
Frame 1270-71.

Chaloner to Robert Dodd

Sir,   May 29 1778

As the will in all probability march thro Your district I must request of you to purchase every species of provisions you can possibly lay your hands on to assist us in supporting the troops though your Country—You can certainly purchase a number of Sheep and a quantity of Bacon they will be much wanted—Col°. Stewart will direct you to advise him what you can procure I am Sir Yours & &
Frame 1271.

Chaloner to Anthony Broderick

Sir,   May 30 1778

You must immediately on Rect of this Collect a number of Beef Cattle sufficient to Issue Four days provision for 15,000 men and have them ready or near to your own house to answer the orders of Col°. Stewart or Jones they will be immediately wanted and we must not be disappointed I am Sir, Yours & &
Frame 1271.

Chaloner to Blaine

Dear Sir, May 30th. 1778
   Yours of the 27th. p Geo. Morrison with Forty thousand Dollars came safe to hand, I now send him back to inform you that our Necessities for want of provision are still as great as ever and increases with the increase of the Soldiery. Notwithstanding Your Letters for augmenting the supplies and mine in your absence, Champion has rather diminished than added thereto. I have wrote him twice since your absence, as also to Col^o. Wadsworth—but as yet rec^d. no answer, nor any thing in Consequence thereof. Reduced at present to nothing I am in expectation of being hourly call'd on to receive the severe reprimand of His Excellency for the wants of the army: which to me is the more mortifying; as I know the fault lies not at my door. Sure I am, the negligent has not wanted for advices, and that to the more pressing in your absence, both now and at all times—But it is now my Lott preseverance and patience is my only remedys I expect and I hope not in vain, Your Brigades with Bacon will give us some relief this day—
Yesterday we were joined by Genl. Smallwood and a large number of Recruits Which will augment the Consumption three thousand rations— this at the present juncture is truly distressing to our departm^t. and will I fear be attended with fatal Consequences to the Army—
Inclosed I send you Copy of a Letter rec'd from Col^o. Wadsworth, and must observe thereon that it afford no prospect of redress
   Col^o. Stewart is in the Jersey forwarding flour &c to the different posts to support the troops in their tour thro that State; In the article of flour and Spirits I flatter myself we shall be tolerably well provided: but what we shall do for Meat god only knows
Your charge of providing a house in Phil^a I have given to M^{rs}. Thompson I doubt not but will do it to your fancy, and it will be out of my power together, unless M^r. Flint Col^o. Wadsworths assistant should arrive before our Departure from thence: I sincerely wish he may for I am fully tried of bearing the burden & important charge of feeding so large a Number of Men or at least being answerable for the neglect of those who are the cause of our wants. When he arrives I shall be glad to discharge myself of all publick business; and intend laying our for that purpose
   The Gent^m. Concerned thank you for the intelligence of the fate of their Lottery ticketts. I would also, had you laid me under the obligation.

Might just set in & no relief around. I have sent Geo. Kitts for a part of the poor cattle at Pottsgrove. This my last shift betwixt us & Death. The first Division marches in the morning without An ounce of Beef, or any kind of meat. I wish to be enabled to write to you better tidings. God send me an opportunity soon—Adieu I am Sir Yours & &^{ca}.
Frame 1272.

Document Chronology

Blaine to William Buchanan, August 16, 1777.
Blaine to Mr. Dunham, August 20, 1777.
Blaine to Mr. Murdock, August 20, 1777.
Blaine to William Buchanan, August 21, 1777.
Blaine to William Buchanan, August 22, 1777.
Blaine to Nehemiah Dunham, August 22, 1777.
Blaine to Zebulon Hollingsworth, August 30, 1777.
Blaine to Thomas Richardson, August 31, 1777.
Blaine to Ludwig Karcher, September 9, 1777.
Blaine to Peter Aston, September 9, 1777.
Blaine to Ludwig Karcher, September 9, 1777.
Blaine to John Patton, September 13, 1777.
Blaine to William Buchanan, September 13, 1777.
Blaine to John Chaloner, September 17, 1777.
Chaloner to Aaron Levering, September 19, 1777.
Blaine to William Buchanan, September 24, 1777.
Chaloner to Mr. Swaine, October 2, 1777.
Chaloner to Blaine, October 2, 1777.
Chaloner to Blaine, October 2, 1777.
Chaloner to Blaine, October 3, 1777.
Chaloner to William Buchanan, October 11, 1777.
Chaloner to Blaine, October 14, 1777.
Blaine to Thomas Huggins, October 15, 1777.
Blaine to Robert McGermont, Undated.
Blaine to Joseph Hugg, October 18, 1777.
Blaine to James White, October 23, 1777.
Blaine to Joseph Hugg, October 24, 1777.
Blaine to John Chaloner and Thomas Jones, October 28, 1777.
Blaine to John Patton, October 28, 1777.
Blaine to William Buchanan, October 28, 1777.
Blaine to Robert McGermont, November 1, 1777.
Blaine to Horatio Gates, November 2, 1777.
Blaine to John Patton, November 3, 1777.
Blaine to Mr. Gartes, November 3, 1777.
Blaine to William Buchanan, November 3, 1777.
Blaine to Unidentified, November 3, 1777.
Chaloner to Mr. Buff, November 5, 1777.

Chaloner to Mr. G., November 5, 1777.
Chaloner to Jacob Shallus and George Echleberger, November 5, 1777.
Chaloner to William Buchanan, November 5, 1777.
Chaloner to Joseph Hugg, November 5, 1777.
Chaloner to William Buchanan, November 7, 1777.
Chaloner to John Patton, November 9, 1777.
Blaine to Robert McGermont, November 11, 1777.
Blaine to William Buchanan, November 12, 1777.
Blaine to Joseph Hugg, November 12, 1777.
Chaloner to Mr. Dunham, November 14, 1777.
Blaine to William Crispin, Undated.
Chaloner to John Jennings, November 16, 1777.
Chaloner to Thomas Huggins, November 18, 1777.
Blaine to Peter Colt, November 18, 1777.
Blaine to Anthony Broderick, November 20, 1777.
Blaine to Joseph Hugg, November 20, 1777.
Chaloner to Casper Graff, November 22, 1777.
Chaloner to William Buchanan, November 24, 1777.
Chaloner to Unidentified, November 28, 1777.
Blaine to Mr. Forman, November 29, 1777.
Chaloner to Blaine, November 30, 1777.
Chaloner to James Paxton, November 30, 1777.
Chaloner to Anthony Broderick, November 30, 1777.
Chaloner to Unidentified, December 1, 1777.
Blaine to Anthony Broderick, December 2, 1777.
Chaloner to Joseph Hugg, December 3, 1777.
Unidentified to Unidentified, (partial letter), December 4, 1777.
Chaloner to Blaine, Undated.
Blaine to Unidentified, Undated.
Blaine to John Wilson, December 8, 1777.
Blaine to Henry Schenk, December 8, 1777.
Blaine to Unidentified, December 9, 1777.
Blaine to Unidentified, Undated.
Blaine to Unidentified, Undated.
Blaine to Azariah Dunham, December 10, 1777.
Blaine to Joseph Hugg or Israel Morris, December 10, 1777.
Blaine to Unidentified, December 11, 1777.
Blaine to Unidentified, December 12, 1777.
Chaloner to Unidentified, Undated.

Blaine to Chaloner, December 13, 1777.
Blaine to Sebastian Graff, December 15, 1777.
Blaine to Unidentified, December 15, 1777.
Chaloner to Unidentified, December 16, 1777.
Chaloner to Peter Aston, December 17, 1777.
Blaine to Chaloner, December 20, 1777.
Chaloner to Peter Colt, December 21, 1777.
Chaloner to Henry Miller, Undated.
Chaloner to Unidentified, Undated.
Chaloner to John Campfield, December 21, 1777.
Chaloner to Blaine, December 21 and 22, 1777.
Chaloner to William Buchanan, December 22, 1777.
Chaloner to Unidentified, December 23, 1777.
Chaloner to John Patton, December 23, 1777.
Chaloner to Unidentified, Undated.
Chaloner to Thomas Wharton Jr. and the Supreme Executive Council, December 24, 1777.
Chaloner to John Magee, December 24, 1777.
Chaloner to George Ross, December 24, 1777.
Chaloner to George Kitts, Undated.
Blaine to Chaloner, December 26, 1777.
Chaloner to William Buchanan, December 28, 1777.
Chaloner to Unidentified, Undated.
Chaloner to Thomas Huggins, December 29, 1777.
Chaloner to James White, December 30, 1777.
Chaloner to James White, December 30, 1777.
Chaloner to Robert Dodd, December 30, 1777.
Blaine to Unidentified, January 1, 1778.
Chaloner to Unidentified, January 3, 1778.
Chaloner to Unidentified, January 3, 1778.
Chaloner to James White, Robert Dodd, or Gustavus Risberg, January 4, 1778.
Chaloner to Thomas Huggins, January 4, 1778.
Chaloner to Robert McGermont, January 4, 1778.
Chaloner to Henry Fuller, January 4, 1778.
Chaloner to George Washington, January 4, 1778.
Chaloner to William Buchanan, Undated.
Blaine to Chaloner, January 4, 1778.
Chaloner to Unidentified, Undated.

Chaloner to Azariah Dunham, January 7, 1778.
Chaloner to Blaine, Undated.
Chaloner to Blaine, Undated.
Blaine to Chaloner, January 11, 1778.
Chaloner to Thomas Huggins, January 12, 1778.
Chaloner to John Ladd Howell, January 12, 1778.
Chaloner to John Ladd Howell, January 12, 1778.
Chaloner to Unidentified, Undated.
Blaine to Mr. Dunham, January 12, 1778.
Blaine to Joseph Hugg, January 16, 1778.
Blaine to Mr. Dunham, January 16, 1778.
Blaine to Anthony Broderick, January 16, 1778.
Blaine to Robert McGermont, January 16, 1778.
Blaine to William Evans, January 16, 1778.
Blaine to Nehemiah Dunham, January 16, 1778.
Blaine to Robert Dodd, January 16, 1778.
Blaine to Robert Hanson Harrison, January 18, 1778.
Blaine to Unidentified, January 19, 1778.
Blaine to Mathias Slough, January 20, 1778.
Blaine to James Smith, January 20, 1778.
Blaine to George Washington, January 20, 1778.
Blaine to William Buchanan, January 20, 1778.
Chaloner to Blaine, January 26, 1778.
Blaine to Unidentified, January 27, 1778.
Chaloner to Blaine, January 29, 1778.
Chaloner to Unidentified, January 31, 1778.
Francis Dana to Chaloner, January 31, 1777.
George Washington to Chaloner, January 31, 1777.
Chaloner to Unidentified, February 1, 1778.
Chaloner to Mr. Roberts, February 1, 1778.
Chaloner to John Patton, February 1, 1778.
Chaloner to James White and Robert Dodd, February 1, 1778.
Chaloner to Thomas Huggins, February 1, 1778.
Chaloner to Sebastian Graff, February 1, 1778.
Chaloner to Robert McGermont, February 2, 1778.
Chaloner to George Echelberger, February 2, 1778.
Blaine to James Smith, February 3, 1778.
Blaine to Mr. Cox, February 3, 1778.

Blaine to Thomas Edwards, February 3, 1778.
Blaine to Alexander Blaine, February 3, 1778.
Blaine to John Patton, February 3, 1778.
Blaine, Account of Cattle Expected, February 3, 1778.
Chaloner to William Buchanan, February 3, 1778.
Blaine to George Washington and the Committee of Congress, February 4, 1778.
Blaine to Anthony Broderick, Feb 5, 1778.
Blaine to Stephen Porter, February 5, 1778.
Blaine to David Frazer, February 5, 1778.
Blaine to Henry Fuller February 5, 1778.
Blaine to William Buchanan, February 5, 1778.
Blaine to Joseph Hugg, February 5, 1778.
Blaine to Henry E. Lutterloh, February 7, 1778.
Blaine to Joseph Hugg, February 7, 1778.
Blaine to Nehemiah Dunham, February 7, 1778.
Blaine to Henry Schenk, February 7, 1778.
Blaine to Henry Champion, February 7, 1778.
Blaine to Peter Colt, February 7, 1778.
Blaine to George Kitts, February 8, 1778.
Blaine to Azariah Dunham, February 9, 1778.
Chaloner to Azariah Dunham, February 9, 1778.
Blaine to Thomas Huggins, February 10, 1778.
Blaine to Robert McGermont, February 10, 1778.
Blaine to Alexander Hamilton, February 12, 1778.
Blaine to William Evans, February 12, 1778.
Blaine to Thomas Wharton Jr., February 12, 1778.
Blaine to Mathias Slough, February 12, 1778.
Blaine to Peter Aston, February 13, 1778.
Blaine to Francis Murray, February 13, 1778.
An Estimate of Provisions in the Middle Department, February 14, 1778.
Blaine to Thomas Huggins, February 15, 1778.
Blaine to Joseph Hugg and Israel Morris, February 15, 1778.
Blaine to Henry Hollingsworth, February 15, 1778.
Blaine to James Young, February 17, 1778.
Blaine to John Patton February 17, 1778.
Blaine to Robert McGermont, February 18, 1778.
Blaine to Joseph Hugg, February 18, 1778.

Blaine to William Buchanan, February 18, 1778.
Blaine to Henry E. Lutterloh, February 18, 1778.
Blaine to Major Armstrong, February 19, 1778.
Chaloner to Mr. Rush, February 19, 1778.
Blaine to George Ross, February 20, 1778.
Blaine to Unidentified, February 20, 1778.
Blaine to Francis Dana, February 20, 1778.
Blaine to John Cox, February 20, 1778.
Blaine to Peter Aston, February 21, 1778.
Blaine to Jacob Anderson, February 21, 1778.
Blaine to James Young, February 23, 1778.
Chaloner to Joseph Hugg, February 24, 1778.
Chaloner to Henry Fuller, February 25, 1778.
Chaloner to John Coryell, Mr. Robinson and John Sherrard, February 27, 1778.
Chaloner to James White and Robert Dodd, February 27, 1778.
Chaloner to John Lacey Jr., February 27, 1778.
Chaloner to Azariah Dunham, February 27, 1778.
Chaloner to William Buchanan, February 27, 1778.
Chaloner to William Buchanan, February 1778.
Chaloner to Unidentified, Undated.
Chaloner to Robert McGermont, February 28, 1778.
Chaloner to Anthony Broderick, February 28, 1778.
Chaloner to Mark Bird, March 1, 1778
Chaloner to Henry E. Lutterloh, March 1, 1778.
Chaloner to Henry Champion, March 1, 1778.
Blaine to Chaloner, March 1, 1778.
Blaine to Robert McGermont, March 1, 1778.
Chaloner to James Young, March 2, 1778.
Chaloner to Henry Fuller, March 3, 1778.
Chaloner to Robert Dodd, Undated.
Chaloner to David Desher, March 3, 1778.
Chaloner to Robert Wilson, Undated.
Chaloner to Jacob Anderson, March 4, 1778.
Chaloner to Alexander McCaskey, March 4, 1778.
Chaloner to John Lesher, March 4, 1778.
Chaloner to Henry E. Lutterloh, March 4, 1778.
Chaloner to William Evans, March 4, 1778.

Chaloner to Alexander Hamilton, March 4, 1778.
Chaloner to Thomas Smith, March 6, 1778.
Chaloner to Henry Echart, March 8, 1778.
Chaloner to Henry E. Lutterloh, Undated.
Chaloner to Blaine, Undated.
Chaloner to Henry Champion, March 9, 1778.
Chaloner to John Ladd Howell, March 9, 1778.
Chaloner to Henry Hollingsworth, March 9, 1778.
Chaloner to Blaine, Undated.
Chaloner to Joseph Hugg, March 15, 1778.
Chaloner to John Lesher, March 1[7], 1778.
Chaloner to Henry Champion, March 17, 1778.
Chaloner to Unidentified, March 19, 1778.
Chaloner to Thomas Huggins, March 19, 1778.
Chaloner to Andrew Boyd, March 20, 1778.
Chaloner to Azariah Dunham, March 20, 1778.
Chaloner to Henry E. Lutterloh, March 20, 1778.
Chaloner to James Young, March 20, 1778.
Chaloner to George Washington, March 21, 1778.
Chaloner to Nicholas Patterson, March 21, 1778.
Chaloner to Henry Hollingsworth, March 2[2], 1778.
Chaloner to George Morrison, March 2[3], 1778.
Chaloner to Henry Hollingsworth, March 24, 1778.
Chaloner to John Ladd Howell, March 24, 1778.
Chaloner to Tench Tilghman, March 24, 1778.
Chaloner to Lachlan McIntosh, March 25, 1778.
Chaloner to Thomas Huggins and Robert McGermont, March 27, 1778.
Chalonerc to Mr. Harnett, March 30, 1778.
Chaloner to Azariah Dunham, March 30, 1778.
Chaloner to John Phillips, March 30, 1778.
Chaloner to Nicholas Patterson?, March 30, 1778.
Chaloner to the Committee of Congress at Camp, Undated.
Chaloner to Patrick Hamilton, March 31, 1778.
Blaine to Unidentified, March 31, 1778.
Chaloner to Henry Champion, April 2, 1778.
Chaloner to Azariah Dunham, April 2, 1778.
Chaloner to Thomas Richardson, April 4, 1778.
Chaloner to Joseph Hugg, April 4, 1778.

Chaloner to William Livingston, April 4, 1778.
Chaloner to William Buchanan, April 5, 1778.
Blaine to Joseph Hugg, April 6, 1778.
Blaine to Israel Morris, April 6, 1778.
Blaine to Unidentified, April 6, 1778.
Blaine to Robert McGermont, April 8, 1778.
Blaine to Undentified, April 8, 1778.
Blaine to Langstone Carlisle, April 9, 1778.
Blaine to Colonel Joseph Hugg, April 9, 1778.
Blaine, Circular Letter to His Assistants, April 10, 1778.
Blaine to William Buchanan, April 10, 1778.
Blaine to Azariah Dunham, April 11, 1778.
Blaine to Robert Lettis Hooper, April 24, 1778.
Blaine to Mr. Dunham, April 29, 1778.
Blaine to Sebastian Graff, April 30, 1778.
Blaine to Unidentified, April 30, 1778.
Blaine to Thomas Edwards, April 30, 1778.
Blaine to Henry Echart, April 30, 1778.
Blaine to John Patton, April 30, 1778.
Blaine to Henry Hollingsworth, May 1, 1778.
Blaine to Francis Wade, May 1, 1778.
Blaine to Nicholas Patterson, May 1, 1778.
Blaine to Jonathan Potts, May 2, 1778.
Blaine to Unidentified, May 4, 1778.
Blaine to Joseph Hugg, May 7, 1778.
Blaine to Unidentified, May 8, 1778.
Blaine to Unidentified, May 8, 1778.
Blaine to James Caldwell, May 10, 1778.
Blaine to John Patton, May 11, 1778.
Blaine to Robert McGermont, May 12, 1778.
Blaine to William Evans, May 14, 1778.
Chaloner to Henry Hollingsworth and Thomas Huggins, Undated.
Chaloner to George Washington, Undated.
Chaloner to Blaine, Undated.
Chaloner to Jeremiah Wadsworth, May 17, 1778
Chaloner to Henry Champion, Undated.
Chaloner to Azariah Dunham, Undated.
Chaloner to Peter Aston, May 18, 1778.

Chaloner to John Mitchell, May 18, 1778.
Chaloner to Unidentified, Undated.
Chaloner to Joseph Carson, Undated.
Chaloner to Joseph Hugg, Undated.
Chaloner to John Ladd Howell, May 25, 1778.
Chaloner to Henry Hollingsworth, Undated.
Chaloner to Jeremiah Wadsworth, Undated.
Chaloner to Henry Hollingsworth, May 29, 1778.
Chaloner to Thomas Huggins or John Ladd Howell, May 29, 1778.
Chaloner to Unidentified, Undated.
Chaloner to Unidentified, Undated.
Chaloner to Robert Dodd, May 29, 1778.
Chaloner to Anthony Broderick, May 30, 1778.
Chaloner to Blaine, May 30, 1778.

INDEX

References to the most common types of foodstuffs such as beef, cattle, pork, bread, wheat, and flour have not been indexed. Nor have the names of Ephraim Blaine and John Chaloner, as they are common in the text. Money, cash, and similar references have not been indexed, with the exception of the prices for commodities.

Alexander, William, 74; division of, 1
Amboy, N.J., 197, 202
Amherst, Jeffrey, 190
Anderson, Jacob, 150; letters to, 136, 149
Andrew, John, 82
Appoquinimink Creek, Del., 145
Armstrong, John, 9
Armstrong, Major, 133, 136
Army, British, 7, 10, 50, 51, 63, 87, 91, 139, 141, 143, 165, 170, 182, 190, 194, 197, 198, 202
Army, Continental; arrival of recruits, 171, 204; different rations in, 42; draws 40,000 rations a day, 33; expected to move to New Jersey, 194, 195, 196, 202; on verge of mutiny, 131; rations of, 96, 109, 117, 195, 200; recruits arriving, 159; reinforcement for, 13, 11, 41; reinforcments arriving, 32; reinforcments expected, 29; will dissolve without food, 76
Aston, Peter, 9, 19, 46, 49, 69, 125, 132, 136, 150, 158, 159; letters to, 7, 56, 124, 135, 196
Aylett, William, 172
Bacon, 38, 189, 203, 204
for the Generals, 157
Bakers, 8, 111, 115
Baltimore, Md., 16, 22, 32, 37, 121, 126, 130, 131, 176, 198
Barrels, 8, 16, 17, 18, 24, 37, 45, 52, 55, 80, 122, 129, 146, 149, 164, 169, 172, 174, 179, 180; poor quality of, 97, 116

Beans, 50
Beasle, John, 65
Bedford County, Pa., 82
Beer, 143, 189
Berks County, Pa., 36, 70, 80, 118, 125, 158
Berry, Sidney, 98
Bethlehem, Pa., 12, 77, 186
Biddle, Clement, 5, 122, 128, 143, 149, 150, 162, 200, 201
Billingsport, N.J., 3
Bird, Mark, 95, 107; letter to, 143
Black Horse, N.J., 79
Black, Captain, 53
Blackles Mill, 27
Blacks, purchase of, 90, 146, 178, 183, 191
Blaine, Alexander, 21; letter to, 106
Blaine, Mrs., 183
Blair, William, 82
Board of War, 73, 84, 89, 90, 93, 97, 98, 99, 105, 110, 111, 114, 115, 131, 149, 155, 165, 176, 177, 178, 181, 191, 192, 200
Boats, 150
Boats, Reading, 107, 128
Bombacks, Pa., 77
Booryhell, Mr., 135
Bordentown, N.J., 17
Boston, Ma., 79
Boundbrook, N.J., 197, 199, 201, 202
Boyd, Andrew, letter to, 161
Bradford, William, 28, 29
Brandy, 94, 184
Brandywine River, 59
Brannon, Thomas, 82
Bristol, Pa., 13

Broderick, Anthony, 41, 43, 77, 84, 107, 117, 118, 119, 154, 203; letters to, 39, 44, 91, 110, 143, 203
Brunswick, N.J., 197, 201, 202
Buchanan, Mr., 57
Buchanan, William, 3, 5, 13, 19, 25, 26, 27, 29, 43, 44, 48, 56, 57, 58, 67, 68, 69, 73, 84, 98, 100, 102, 155, 172, 191; letters to, 1, 3, 4, 8, 10, 25, 28, 29, 32, 41, 63, 68, 78, 96, 108, 112, 131, 140, 141, 175, 182
Bucklystown, 65
Bucks County, Pa., 68, 81, 86, 87, 121, 123, 125, 132, 136
Buff, Mr., letter to, 26
Burlington, N.J., 17, 90, 179, 180
Burner, Mr., 52
Butchers, 1, 12; some of the worst of mankind, 1
Butter, 173, 174, 175, 188, 191
Byard, Mrs., 52
Byers, John, 89, 91, 93
Calaghan, Mr., 132
Caldwell, James, letter to, 192
Campbell, Mr., 37, 52, 53
Campfield, John, 61; letter to, 60
Candles, 8, 13, 14, 22; lack of, 1, 11, 13, 80, 85, 141; poor quality of, 141
Cantwells Bridge, Del., 145, 187
Cape May, N.J., 89, 109, 115, 173, 177
Carlisle, Langstone, 179, 180; letter to, 180
Carlisle, Pa., 34, 49, 53, 67, 81, 106, 108, 135, 157
Carnarvon, Pa., 95
Carson, Joseph, 105, 198; letter to, 198
Cecil County, Md., 55
Champion, Ephaphoditus, 23
Champion, Henry, 2, 20, 154, 195, 196, 202, 203, 204; letters to, 116, 144, 156, 159, 171, 196

Chandler, Colonel, 132
Charlestown, Md., 145, 146, 182, 189, 199, 200, 201, 203
Cheney, Mr., 54
Chesapeake Bay, 118, 146, 189, 200
Chester County, Pa., 80, 81, 125, 140, 146
Chester, Md., 146
Chester, Pa., 61, 89
Civilians; cattle and salt to be seized from, 47; food and spirits to be seized from, 111; food seized from, 5, 16, 18, 22, 65, 69, 79, 81, 134, 145; food sold to detachments, 45; food to be seized from, 15, 26, 37, 40, 49, 50, 53, 59, 62, 69, 74, 75, 87, 88, 90, 91, 92, 99, 105, 110, 112, 119, 124, 125, 129, 130, 132; ignore price regulations, 109; liquor seized from, 19, 190, 191; liquor to be seized from, 17; property to be seized from, 74; rum to be seized from, 77; salt seized from, 16, 33, 47; salt to be seized from, 16, 17; ship's cargo to be seized, 173; uncooperative attitude of, 30, 57, 80, 86, 109, 142; wagons seized from, 123; wagons to be seized from, 60, 67, 121, 126, 127, 146; whiskey seized from, 33, 111; whiskey to be seized from, 112
Clements Bridge, N.J., 18
Clinton, George, 160, 162
Coles Mills, 145
Colt, Peter, 20, 25, 41, 60, 61, 69, 78, 97, 100, 108, 113, 116, 144, 154; letters to, 38, 58, 117
Concord, Pa., 78
Conroo, Mr., 19
Continental Congress, 3, 6, 15, 16, 17, 18, 20, 21, 23, 27, 33, 34, 39, 42, 43, 44, 45, 48, 53, 57, 62, 70, 74, 79, 89, 90, 99, 120, 129, 133, 134, 136, 141, 148, 149, 158, 171, 174, 177, 179, 180, 181, 183;

Committee at Camp, 100, 102, 103, 104, 108, 109, 114, 120, 131, 134, 159; letter to, 170; extends martial law, 21
Cook, Mr., 46
Coopers, 8, 16, 17, 39, 45, 80, 172, 179; exempt from military service, 52, 55
Coryell, John, letter to, 138
Coryells Ferry, N.J./Pa., 4, 17, 74, 77, 95, 101, 111, 112, 137, 140, 196, 197, 199
Cox, John, letter to, 135
Cox, Mr., letter to, 105
Crispin, William, 130, 155; letter to, 36
Cross Roads, Pa., 1, 3, 4, 193, 194
Crouse, Michael, 165
Cultbertson, Robert, 82
Cumberland County, Pa., 26, 82, 125
Cuyler, Jacob, 78
Dana, Francis, letter to, 134
Delaware, 47, 77, 116, 155
Delaware River, 17, 29, 38, 74, 87, 111, 112, 172, 174, 180
Denny, Mr., 16, 18
Dermon, Mr., 14
Desher, David, letter to, 148
Deshlar, David, 82
Dill, James, 82
Dodd, Robert, 65, 72, 156, 203; letters to, 73, 75, 93, 102, 147, 203
Donellan, Thomas, 192
Dover, Del., 107, 114, 125, 126, 144, 145, 146
Downingtown, Pa., 7, 14, 59, 69, 92, 161; suitable for a magazine, 165
Drain, John, 193
Drovers, 1, 2, 38, 61, 85, 101, 118, 153, 154, 156, 167, 172, 203
Dunham, Aron, 35
Dunham, Azariah, 41, 43, 76, 77, 98, 101, 117, 118, 120, 155, 160, 168, 196, 203; letters to, 119, 120, 139, 152, 162, 169, 172, 182, 196

Dunham, Mazeniah, 38
Dunham, Mr., 3, 4, 12, 14, 18, 25, 96, 107, 141, 195, 201; letters to, 2, 35, 89, 90, 184
Dunham, Nehemiah, 41, 76, 77, 107, 203; letters to, 4, 93, 115
Dunham, Samuel, 154
Easton, Pa., 49, 70, 77, 128, 143, 172
Echart, Henry, letters to, 152, 186
Echelberger, George, 97, 113, 131; 27, 104
Echert, Mr., 193
Edwards, Thomas, 82, 107, 128, 137, 189; letters to, 106, 185
Egg Harbor, N.J., 16, 17, 18, 20, 21, 22, 28, 33, 45, 49, 53, 109, 115, 130, 173, 175, 177, 202
Elkton, Md., see Head of Elk
Emory, Mr., 112, 142, 146
Ephrata, Pa., 189
Evans, Peter, 81
Evans, William, 54, 59, 61, 69, 137, 140, 155; letters to, 92, 123, 151, 193
Ewing, George, 29
Fatland Ford, Pa., 9, 57
Finey, Mr., 129
Finn, Mr., 39
Fish, 54, 79, 125, 126, 164, 172, 173, 179, 180, 188; herrings, 188; shad, 164, 169, 172, 173, 174, 180, 185, 188
Fisher, Harry, 22
Fishkill, N.Y., 25, 48, 144
Flemington, N.J., 65, 79, 179, 199
Flint, Royal, 204
Food, seizure of, 5, 16, 18, 22, 26, 53, 59, 64, 65, 69, 75, 80, 81, 86, 88, 90, 99, 119, 124, 134, 145; ship's cargo to be seized for the army, 173; to be seized, 15, 37, 40, 62, 74, 75, 87, 91, 92, 99, 105, 110, 111, 112, 125, 127, 129, 130, 132, 134

Forage, 58, 95, 117, 122, 134, 136, 149, 150, 163, 165, 172, 185, 190, 200
Foragemasters, 53, 69, 92, 134, 136, 149, 165, 178, 183, 185
Forman, David, 43
Forman, Mr., 89, 115, letter to, 42
Fort Mercer, N.J., see Red Bank
Fort Mifflin, Pa., 36
Fort Pitt, Pa., 10, 21
Foster, Mr., 166, 177, 190, 191
Frat, Mr., 124
Frazer, David, 77, 111, 112
Frazer, David, letter to, 111
Frederick County, Md., 3
French Alliance, 190; hopes for, 118
French Creek Bridge, Pa., 165, 166
Fuller, Henry, 111, 128
Fuller, Henry, letters to, 77, 112, 138, 147
Funk, Mr., 57
Furman, Moore, 190
Gammons, for Washington and his Generals, 148
Gardiner, Captain, 161
Gartes, Mr., 24
Garts, Mr., 16, 25, 32, 33, 37
Gast, Mr., 3, 9, 10
Gates, Horatio, 25, 35
Germans, 86; make good whiskey, 19
Germantown, Pa., 169
Gibbs, Caleb, 46
Gordon, Mr., 77
Graff, Sebastian, 8, 30, 95, 98, 135; letters to, 55, 103
Gray, Samuel, 13, 38, 39, 203
Gray, William, 82
Great Valley, Pa., 37, 52, 92
Greene, Nathanael, 40, 154, 203; division of, 1
Gulph, Pa., 56
Guyer, Mr., 113
Hackett, Mr., 46
Hackettstown, N.J., 48, 144, 162
Haddonfield, N.J., 182
Ham, for the generals, 157

Hamilton, Alexander, letters to, 122, 152
Hamilton, Mr., 148
Hamilton, Patrick, 145, 146, 189, 201; letter to, 170
Harnett, Mr., letter to, 168
Harrison, Robert Hanson, letter to, 93
Hartford, Conn., 38
Harvey, Michael, 114
Haslip, Thomas, 82
Hawkins, John, 190
Hay, 16, 39, 118, 143, 145
Head of Elk, Md., 5, 42, 70, 78, 91, 92, 103, 107, 110, 114, 122, 125, 126, 127, 129, 131, 132, 134, 140, 144, 145, 146, 162, 163, 165, 166, 182, 187, 192, 199, 200, 201, 203
Heath, William, 30
Henry, Colonel, 166
Hessians; assault on Red Bank, 18
Hides, 1, 3, 29, 36
Hollingsworth, Henry, 103, 166, 195, 201, 203; letters to, 127, 157, 164, 166, 187, 194, 199, 200
Hollingsworth, Zebulon, letter to, 5
Hooper, Robert Lettis, 47, 98, 134, 149, 155; letter to, 183
Hospitals, food for, 88, 91, 117, 188, 189
Howe, William, 12, 39, 51, 190
Howell, John Ladd, 98, 121, 122, 145, 166, 187, 201; letters to, 87, 157, 166, 199, 201
Hudson River, 116
Huff, Conrad, 49, 60
Hugg, Captain, 113
Hugg, Joseph, 1, 3, 10, 11, 12, 14, 22, 33, 41, 43, 63, 69, 75, 77, 78, 100, 107, 119, 147, 154, 155, 175, 178, 179, 180, 195, 198, 202; letters to, 18, 28, 34, 40, 45, 51, 89, 113, 114, 127, 130, 137, 158, 173, 177, 180, 190, 198

219

Huggins, Thomas, 16, 22, 63, 70, 77, 79, 103, 107, 129, 130, 146, 195, 201; letters to, 15, 37, 71, 76, 86, 103, 121, 126, 160, 167, 194, 201
Indian meal, 122, 125, 126, 132, 143, 145, 147, 170; for the hospital, 91, 98; needed for smallpox inoculation, 88, 121, 130, 139, 142, 167, 168
Ink powder, shortage of, 148
Irvine, James, 51
Irwin, John, 21
Jennings, John, letter to, 36
Johnson, Thomas, 166, 172
Johnston, Mr., 27
Johnston, William, 89
Johnstone, Mr., 129
Johnston's Ferry, 144
Jones, John, 93, 94
Jones, Thomas, 11, 46, 49, 52, 53, 58, 62, 64, 68, 81, 86, 112, 132, 145, 151, 153, 176, 187, 193, 203; letter to, 19
Juniata River, Pa., 55
Karcher, Ludwig, 11, 12; letters to, 6, 7
Kenedy, Mr., 80
Kennedy, Mr., 141, 155, 176
Kingwood, N.J., 14
Kitts, George, 18, 49, 61, 98, 107, 168, 202, 205; letters to, 67, 118
Kuher, Mr., 10
Lacey, John Jr., 132, 133, 138, 139, 167; letter to, 139
Lancaster County, Pa., 11, 36, 68, 70, 82, 118, 123, 125, 188
Lancaster, Pa., 8, 13, 20, 21, 27, 30, 32, 40, 42, 49, 52, 54, 55, 57, 61, 65, 66, 67, 70, 71, 78, 81, 84, 86, 95, 98, 108, 124, 135, 137, 146, 153, 155, 184, 189
Laurens, John, 98
Leaming, Mr., 174
Lebanon, Pa., 8, 186
Lee, Henry Jr., 129, 145, 146, 154

Lesher, John, 150; letters to, 150, 158
Levering, Aaron, letter to, 9
Lewes, Del., 22
Lewis Town, 193
Lincoln, Benjamin, division of, 1
Liquor, 24, 74, 194, 202;
  Jamaica spirits, 184, 192;
  rum, 10, 14, 17, 77, 94, 105, 125, 126, 176, 184, 187, 192, 195, 196, 197, 198, 199; price of, 17, 32, 184, 191, 192; seizure of, 177, 190; shortage of 197; to be seized, 17, 75, 191;
  spirits, 17, 39, 53, 122; to be seized, 75, 111;
  West India spirits, 17;
  whiskey, 8, 11, 13, 15, 23, 26, 27, 30, 31, 32, 41, 49, 54, 67, 73, 77, 81, 85, 88, 97, 99, 105, 106, 109, 112, 123, 125, 126, 184, 185, 186; price of, 25, 26, 33, 35, 38, 53, 55, 82, 99, 132, 185; ration of, 96; seized from the sutlers, 23; seizure of, 86; shortage of, 8, 12, 14, 19, 21, 23, 28, 31, 41, 46, 57, 95, 106; to be seized, 19, 46, 74, 81, 111, 112, 135
Lititz, Pa., 189
Little, John, 82
Livingston, William, 173, 174, 179; letter to, 174
Lottery, 204
Lowry, Thomas, 93
Ludwick, Christopher, 62
Lutterloh, Henry E., 135, 146, 153; letters to, 114, 132, 143, 151, 162
Magee, John, 40, 41; letter to, 66
Magill, Mr., 111
Marcus Hook, Pa., 3, 74
Maryland, 8, 25, 77, 85, 138, 146, 159, 162, 163, 166
Maxwell, William, 199
May, Mr., 200
McCaskey, Alexander, 149, 150; letter to, 150

220

McDermont, Mr., 20
McDormont, Mr., 11
McGermont, Robert, 10, 15, 63, 77, 79, 112, 113, 121, 145; letters to, 15, 21, 31, 76, 91, 104, 122, 129, 142, 145, 167, 179, 193
McIntosh, Lachlan, 167; letter to, 167
McLean, Captain, 130
McPherson, Robert, 99
Means, William, 111
Meers, Mr., 81
Middlebrook, N.J., 172
Middletown, Del., 145, 163, 166, 187
Middletown, Pa., 55, 135
Mifflin, Jonathan, 61
Militia, 17, 20, 43, 47, 70, 132, 164, 179; Maryland, 200; New Jersey, 14, 25, 90; Pennsylvania, 87, 132, 133, 136, 139, 167
Miller, Henry, 59, 60; letter to, 59
Miller, William, 173
Mitchell, John, letter to, 197
Moland, Captain, 151
Molasses, 187, 190
Moore Hall, Pa., 100, 101
Moore, John, 81
Moore, Mr., 44
Moreland, Mr., 153
Morgan, Daniel, 32, 40
Morgan, George, 21
Morgan, Mr., 21
Morris, Israel, 1, 3, 34, 35, 40, 82, 83, 113, 115, 130, 181, 191; letters to, 51, 127, 178
Morris, Joseph, 51
Morrison, George, 204; letter to, 165
Morristown, N.J., 14, 28, 38, 43, 117, 118, 160, 162, 168, 196
Moulder, John, 74
Mount Holly, N.J., 41
Mount Hope Ironworks, N.J., 144
Moylan, Stephen, 197
Mullen, Mr., 157
Murdock, Mr., letter to, 3

Murray, Francis, 124, 135
Murray, Mr., 136
Murray, Mrs., 125
Mutton, for the sick, 188
New Castle County, Del., 187
New Hanover, Pa., 10
New Windsor, N.Y., 44, 48, 58, 84
Newtown Square, Pa., 75
Newtown, Pa., 124
Nixon, John, 52
North Wales, Pa., 13, 19, 20
Northampton County, Pa., 36, 70, 80, 82, 112, 118, 125, 158, 183
Northeast, Md., 145
Northumberland County, Pa., 82
Nottingham, Md., 16
Oakley, Mr., 77
Oaths of Allegiance, 4, 6, 35, 89, 90, 105
Ohl, Mr., 158, 159
Oley, Pa., 67, 78, 136, 150
Orange County, N.Y., 48
Ottenhamer, Mr., 102
Paoli, engagement at, 10
Parr, Captain, 125
Patterson, Nicholas, 111, 112, 172, 174, 191; letters to, 164, 169, 188
Patton, John, 8, 9, 12, 13, 14, 28, 36, 98, 100, 101, 111, 112, 137, 138, 147, 186; letters to, 8, 19, 23, 31, 64, 102, 107, 128, 186, 193
Pawlings Ford, Pa., 57, 114, 122, 125, 126, 127, 132, 135, 178, 179, 180
Pawlings Mill, 165
Pawlings Neck, Pa., 52
Paxton, James, 196, 197; letter to, 43
Pay, as assistant purchaser, 5, 53; for purchasers, 55; in Commissary Department, 171; inadequate for purchasing commissaries, 90; of commissaries, 190
Payne, William, 64, 71
Pearson, John, 80
Peas, 50, 125, 126, 129, 142, 187
Perkiomen Creek, Pa., 19

Pettit, Charles, 197
Philadelphia County, Pa., 81, 125
Philadelphia, Pa., 2, 3, 4, 6, 9, 11, 14, 16, 18, 38, 50, 87, 89, 146, 165, 194, 195, 198, 204
Philips, Mr., 193
Phillips, John, letter to, 169
Phillips, Mr., 194
Pierce, Cromwell, 74
Pittstown, N.J., 16, 58, 72, 73, 89, 179, 190
Pollard, Mr., 30, 94
Pollard, William, 22
Polloch, Mr., 26
Pollock, James, 124
Pollock, Mr., 10, 19, 48, 68
Porter, Stephen, letter to, 110
Potatoes, 130, 173
Potomac River, 81, 85, 105
Potter, James, 87
Potts, Jonathan, letter to, 188
Potts, Mr., 130
Pottsgrove, Pa., 10, 14, 15, 19, 28, 30, 50, 67, 69, 134, 136, 149, 150, 165, 167, 197
Prices, exorbitant for food, 20, 30; extravagant, 110; extravagant for food and whiskey, 35; fixed in Pennsylvania, 38, 81, 86; high for rum and salt, 32; of barrels, 8, 39, 50, 80; of beef, 2, 3, 6, 7, 15, 18, 36, 38, 53, 55, 57, 73, 78, 82, 87, 88, 92, 99, 132, 147; of Brandy, 184; of corn, 82, 88; of fish, 169; of flour, 34, 36, 52, 53, 82, 87, 88, 92, 111, 112, 132, 146; of hay, 39; of Indian corn, 38; of Jamaica spirits, 184, 192; of oats or spelts, 88; of pork, 18, 37, 38, 39, 49, 50, 53, 55, 57, 73, 82, 87, 88, 92, 99, 113, 130, 132, 147, 155; of rice, 198; of rum, 17, 184, 192; of rye, 38, 82, 88; of salt, 33, 40, 99, 130, 192, 198; of spirits, 17, 184; of West India spirits, 17; of wheat, 36, 53, 55, 70, 82, 87, 88, 92, 99,

132; of whiskey, 26, 30, 38, 53, 55, 99, 132, 184, 185
Princeton, N.J., 201, 202
Prisoners of War, 78, 117; proposed exchange of, 169
Providence, R.I., 79
Purdy, Robert, 137
Putnam, Israel, 25, 118, 144
Quakers, 79
Quartermaster Department, 123
Quartermaster General, 71, 154, 199, 203
Quartermasters, 17, 21, 32, 42, 53, 54, 55, 57, 65, 66, 67, 70, 71, 93, 95, 105, 114, 123, 130, 134, 178, 183, 187, 190
Quills, shortage of, 151
Ramapo, N.J., 144
Ramsay, Mr., 3
Reading, Pa., 8, 13, 14, 69, 95, 98, 101, 137, 155, 186
Red Bank (Fort Mercer), N.J., 25, 28, 29, 35, 36, 37; reported evacuated, 40; Hessian assault on, 18
Redstone, 81
Reed, Morris, 82
Reed, Mr., 61
Reedy Island, Delaware River, 94
Reese, Captain, 94
Reynolds, Mr., 100
Rice, 187, 198; needed for the sick, 98, 198
Richardson, Thomas, letters to, 5, 172
Risberg, Gustavus, 4, 102; letter to, 75
Road, Horseshoe, 147
Roads, poor condition of, 71, 106, 107, 116, 118, 119, 122, 123, 143, 145, 150, 151, 153, 164
Roberts, Mr., letter to, 101
Robinson, Colonel, 144
Robinson, Mr., letter to, 138
Robinsons Ferry, N.J./Pa., 139
Rock Run, Md., 129, 130

Rodman, J., 98
Ross, George, 103, 153; letters to, 66, 133
Rudolph, Captain, 11
Ruse, William, 75
Rush, Mr., 132, 135, letter to, 133
Sacolus, Mr., 190
Salem County, N.J., 115
Salen, Captain, 67
Salt, 6, 13, 18, 22, 24, 32, 33, 34, 39, 45, 47, 53, 55, 75, 94, 97, 99, 109, 111, 115, 130, 138, 164, 169, 170, 178, 179, 180, 190, 191, 192, 196, 198; being brought from Boston, 79; from New England, 19, 21, 27, 32, 38, 44, 48, 84, 89, 116, 154; from New Jersey, 20, 49, 53; high price of, 32; made in New Jersey, 11; needed by the Army, 4, 10, 11, 13, 17; reported in Maryland, 8; seizure of, 22, 33, 47, 176, 177; shortage in the Middle States, 118; shortage of, 32, 33, 38, 40, 47, 83, 98, 147, 148, 154, 158, 174; to be seized, 16, 17, 32, 37, 81
Saunders, Mr., 161
Schenck, P., 97
Schenk, Henry, 48; letters to, 48, 116
Schenk, Mr., 100
Schuylkill River, 95, 102, 107, 162
Scott, William, 82
Semple, Mr., 34
Shaefferstown, Pa., 189
Shallus, Jacob, 8, 40; letter to, 27
Sheep, 40, 90, 203
Sherrard, John, letter to, 138
Sherrards Ferry, N.J./Pa., 139, 144, 148, 162, 167, 174, 175, 188, 196
Shigar, Mr., 107
Shrewsbury, N.J., 115
Shrolls Tavern, Pa., 139, 141, 165
Simpson, George, 137, 196
Sinapuxent, Md., 16, 20, 22
Slough, Mathias, 9, 98, 189; letters to, 94, 124

Smallpox, cases in the Army, 98; Indian meal needed to treat, 121; inoculation against, 130, 139, 142, 168; smallpox inoculation, Indian meal needed for, 88
Smallwood, William, 10, 121, 187, 204; division of, 126
Smith, James, 107, 137; letters to, 95, 105
Smith, John, 75
Smith, Major, 9
Smith, Mr., 21, 61, 63, 68, 85, 98, 113, 119
Smith, Thomas, 155; letter to, 152
Soap, 8, 11, 13, 14, 22, 141; lack of, 1, 11, 13, 80, 141, 176; to be issued, 85
Spear, Mr., 105
Spears, Mr., 95
Springfield, Pa., 63
Sproul, Mr., 32
Sprowl, Mr., 41, 43
Stadlers Tavern, Pa., 67
Stansbury, Mr., 31
Steel, Alexander, 90, 113, 166
Stephen, Adam, division of, 1
Stephens Ferry, Md., 145
Stevenson, Robert, 176
Stewart, Charles, 4, 11, 13, 14, 34, 42, 61, 62, 68, 69, 70, 84, 149, 164, 196, 201, 202, 203, 204
Stewart, Colonel, 115
Stewart, Walter, 87, 88
Stirling, Lord, see Alexander, William
Stores, Lemuel, 144
Succasunna Plains, N.J., 144
Sugar, 166, 167, 169, 191; seizure of, 177
Sullivan, John, division of, 44
Susquehanna River, 9, 55, 69, 99, 129
Sussex Court House, N.J., 58, 144
Sussex, N.J., 84, 117, 118
Sutlers, 23, 26, 33, 184, 185; all allow to be a nuisance, 46; banned

from camp, 24, 25, 28; whiskey to
  be seized from, 46
Swain, Mr., 11, 49
Swaine, Mr., letter to, 11
Swedes Ford, Pa., 9
Tallow, 1, 3, 8, 11, 36, 141, 142,
  153, 176
Talmans, N.J., 79
Tenant, Mr., 168
Thompson, Mrs., 204
Thorn, Joseph, 82
Thornton, Mr., 135
Tilghman, Tench, 142, 160, 167;
  letter to, 167
Todd, Mr., 127
Tongue, 173, for Washington's staff,
  174
Torrence, Mr., 61
Trappe, Pa., 15, 24, 28, 30, 50, 143
Trenton Ferry, N.J./Pa., 50
Trenton, N.J., 14, 17, 42, 79, 169,
  196, 201, 202
Trumbull, Jonathan, 144
Trumbull, Joseph, 1, 4, 25, 118
Ulster County, N.Y., 4, 14, 20, 25,
  35, 48
Union Ironworks, N.J., 144
Valley Forge, Pa., 9, 57, 144
Vancamp, Mr., 111, 112
Vanhorn, Mr., 25
Vanhorn, Phil, 172
Veal, for the sick, 188
Virginia, 25, 34, 38, 109, 114, 133,
  162
Wade, Francis, letter to, 187
Wadsworth, Jeremiah, 190, 195,
  202, 204; letters to, 195, 200
Waggoner, B., 165
Wagoners, 24, 28, 75, 140, 188, 193;
  abandon their loads, 146; abuses
  by, 94, 153; should be men of
  integrity, 164
Wagonmaster General, 128, 143,
  144, 151, 157
Wagonmasters, 57, 65, 135, 139,
  151, 163, 164, 170, 182, 199

Wagons, 10, 14, 16, 17, 18, 27, 47,
  57, 66, 67, 74, 94, 99, 105, 107,
  114, 122, 123, 129, 130, 131, 132,
  133, 134, 137, 145, 146, 157, 161,
  162, 165, 168, 171, 175, 184, 185,
  187, 188, 190, 203; from Easton,
  Pa., 183; from Maryland, 172;
  number needed to supply the
  army, 126; seizure of, 123; sent to
  New York, 38, 48; shortage of, 32,
  65, 70, 79, 104, 122, 123, 127,
  128, 144, 151, 153, 154, 157, 158,
  162, 163, 175, 177, 182, 194; 30;
  to be seized, 27, 30, 53, 54, 60,
  66, 67, 71, 121, 126, 127, 146; to
  be sent to Maryland, 103; to be
  sent to New Jersey, 45; to be sent
  to New York, 44; to go to New
  England, 19, 21; with four horse
  teams, 164
Wallkill, N.Y., 4
Warren Tavern, Pa., 74
Washington, George, 1, 9, 10, 28,
  30, 39, 56, 59, 62, 65, 69, 72, 76,
  77, 83, 84, 88, 94, 97, 98, 102,
  103, 104, 108, 110, 115, 116, 118,
  119, 126, 138, 144, 152, 158, 159,
  162, 165, 166, 167, 168, 172, 185,
  194, 195, 196, 197, 200, 201, 202,
  204; concerns on food shortage,
  69, 70, 72, 82, 85, 118, 125;
  gammons for, 148; needs
  reinforcement, 190; orders to
  secure ships cargo, 173, 175;
  orders wagons seized, 127; seizes
  food from civilians, 64; slurs
  against, 94; swears, 69; the most
  unhappy man in the world, 131;
  urges forwarding of food, 103;
  urges procuring a large amount of
  shad, 169; wants army in the field
  early, 171; wants the men
  inoculated for smallpox, 98; letter
  from, 101; letters to, 77, 96, 109,
  163, 195
Washington, Lud, 173

Washington, Martha, 148
Watson, David, 82
Wayne, Anthony, 10, 142, 154
Weather, 19, 28, 31, 46
Weaver, Mr., 95
Weed, Elijah, 54
Wells, Ephraim, 4
Wells, Mr., 156
Westmoreland County, Pa., 82
Wharton, Thomas Jr., letters to, 65, 123
White, James, 1, 2, 6, 11, 13, 17, 79, 98, 100, 107, 156; letters to, 17, 72, 75, 102
White, Mr., 43
Whitemarsh, Pa., 51, 140
Whittle, Mr., 35
Wilmington, Del., 5, 6, 7, 14, 53, 74, 79, 142, 144, 168
Wilson, John, 48; letter to, 47
Wilson, Mr., 100
Wilson, N., 162
Wilson, Robert, 98, 155; letter to, 148
Windsor Forge, Pa., 93
Wine, 29, Claret, 173; Madeira, 169
Wints Tavern, 165
Woodford, William, brigade of, 122
Wright, John, 44
Wrights Ferry, Pa., 65, 71
Yellow Springs, Pa., 137
York County, Pa., 26, 82, 125
York, Pa., 8, 13, 16, 19, 20, 21, 25, 27, 30, 32, 34, 42, 46, 48, 49, 51, 52, 53, 61, 62, 65, 67, 68, 70, 73, 81, 99, 104, 105, 129, 131, 135, 137, 140, 161, 162, 171, 176, 177, 181, 184, 185, 186, 189, 192, 193, 198
Young, James, 128, 143, 161; letters to, 128, 137, 146, 163

Heritage Books by Joseph Lee Boyle

"My Last Shift Betwixt Us & Death": The Ephraim Blaine Letterbook, 1777–1778

"Their Distress is Almost Intolerable": The Elias Boudinot Letterbook, 1777–1778

From Redcoat to Rebel: The Thomas Sullivan Journal

"this grand supply": The Samuel Hodgdon Letterbooks, 1778–1784
Volume 1: July 19, 1778–March 31, 1781
Volume 2: April 3, 1781–May 24, 1784

Writings from the Valley Forge Encampment of the Continental Army:
December 19, 1777–June 19, 1778
Volume 1

Writings from the Valley Forge Encampment of the Continental Army:
December 19, 1777–June 19, 1778
Volume 2, "Winter in this starved Country"

Writings from the Valley Forge Encampment of the Continental Army:
December 19, 1777–June 19, 1778
Volume 3, "it is a general Calamity"

Writings from the Valley Forge Encampment of the Continental Army:
December 19, 1777–June 19, 1778
Volume 4, "The Hardships of the Camp"

Writings from the Valley Forge Encampment of the Continental Army:
December 19, 1777–June 19, 1778
Volume 5, "a very Different Spirit in the Army"

Writings from the Valley Forge Encampment of the Continental Army:
December 19, 1777–June 19, 1778
Volume 6, "my Constitution got quite shatter'd"

Writings from the Valley Forge Encampment of the Continental Army:
December 19, 1777–June 19, 1778
Volume 7, "I could not Refrain from tears"

www.ingramcontent.com/pod-product-compliance
Lightning Source LLC
Chambersburg PA
CBHW071913160426
43198CB00011B/1278